This book examines the history of white-collar crime in England from the Victorian period to the early twentieth century.

In the period between the 1840s and the 1920s the British economy was transformed from small-scale capitalism dominated by individual traders and partnerships to a complex financial structure dominated by large, joint-stock companies. The tremendous growth of big business and the complexity of the corporate form created a world of new opportunities for criminal exploitation. The promotion and management of public companies and the trading of commercial securities proved vulnerable to the white-collar crimes of fraud and embezzlement on the part of those directors, managers and stockbrokers who were entrusted with investors' money. Problems of financial fraud were exacerbated by a climate of *laissez-faire* which championed the most permissive commercial legislation in the world, and which undermined efforts at greater state regulation of business. White-collar crime wreaked havoc on the modern British economy, robbing the public of millions of pounds, undermining trust in commercial integrity and depressing the level of investment in new industries.

WHITE-COLLAR CRIME IN MODERN ENGLAND

WHITE-COLLAR CRIME IN MODERN ENGLAND

Financial fraud and business morality, 1845–1929

GEORGE ROBB

Assistant Professor of History, St. Bonaventure University

CAMBRIDGE
UNIVERSITY PRESS

Published by the Press Syndicate of the University of Cambridge
The Pitt Building, Trumpington Street, Cambridge CB2 1RP
40 West 20th Street, New York, NY 10011-4211, USA
10 Stamford Road, Oakleigh, Victoria 3166, Australia

First published 1992

Printed in Great Britain by Bell and Bain Ltd., Glasgow

A catalogue record for this book is available from the British Library

Library of Congress cataloguing in publication data

Robb, George.
White-collar crime in modern England: financial fraud and business morality, 1845–1929 /
George Robb.
p.   cm.
Includes bibliographical references.
ISBN 0 521 41234 X
1. Commercial crimes – Great Britain – History – 19th century.
2. Commercial crimes – Great Britain – History – 20th century.
3. Securities fraud – Great Britain – History – 19th century.
4. Securities fraud – Great Britain – History – 20th century.
HV6771.GBR63 1992
364.1'68'0941 – dc20   91-46847   CIP

ISBN 0 521 41234 X hardback

WV

For Ann

Contents

Tables

Acknowledgments

With great appreciation I wish to acknowledge the United States–United Kingdom Fulbright Commission which funded most of the initial research for this book. St. Bonaventure University also generously provided a research grant that enabled me to complete revisions. I could never have written this book without the enormous generosity of my colleagues and friends. My greatest thanks go to Standish Meacham whose superb teaching first stimulated my interest in Victorian England and to Harold Perkin who supervised this project at its inception and whose brilliant critical insights benefited it at every stage. T.W. Heyck's advice also helped me immensely in narrowing my focus and Joel Mokyr's criticisms were a godsend to one "innocent of economics." All of these scholars were an endless source of encouragement and good humor, and I am fortunate to have worked with them. Harold and Joan Perkin were also frequently a source of food and shelter and my debt to them is unpayable. The readers appointed by Cambridge University Press additionally offered a number of helpful and constructive criticisms from which this book has benefited. Lastly I would like to thank three friends and colleagues, Patricia Cleary, Antoinette Burton and Marilyn Oliva, for helping me maintain my sanity throughout graduate school and during my first year of teaching and for helping me believe that there is a place in our profession for people who do not wear tweed or sensible shoes.

Acknowledgements

White-collar crime and the criminal "upperworld"

Fraud has been characterized as the growth industry of our times.[1] After all, one can scarcely open a newspaper these days without reading about some new financial scandal on Wall Street or in the City of London. The recent collapse of the Bank of Credit and Commerce International, the break-up of the late Robert Maxwell's media empire and the continuing saga of the American Savings and Loan crisis have all given rise to numerous charges of fraud. This has been the era of Ivan Boesky, the Wall Street financier who in his heyday proclaimed "greed is good!" though was sentenced to three years' imprisonment for insider trading in 1987. Boesky's downfall was followed shortly by the indictment and trial in England of Guinness Chairman Ernest Saunders for the secret purchase of his company's own shares and in America of "junk bond" king Michael Milken for fraudulent trading. In September 1990 Saunders and three other Guinness board members were found guilty of numerous breaches of commercial law and received prison sentences ranging from twelve months to five years. In December Milken was sentenced to ten years for securities fraud.

In these days of money laundering through Swiss bank accounts and of dummy corporations registered in Panama or Liechtenstein, we are apt to imagine that white-collar crime is a recent phenomenon – the product of Reagan's America or Thatcher's Britain. The real origins of white-collar crime, however, lie almost two hundred years in the past, in the tremendous financial growth which accompanied the British Industrial Revolution.

The Industrial Revolution called into being a complex economy increasingly dependent on finance and investment. This new economy was characterized by a vast banking network, a burgeoning commercial nexus of insurance, stocks and credit, and an

increasingly complicated legal system. These phenomena as well as
the concomitant increase of lawyers, brokers and financiers greatly
expanded the potential for white-collar crime.

White-collar crime is a topic of great significance for British
history. This type of crime, especially business fraud, embezzlement and financial chicanery of various kinds, has affected large
amounts of property and threatened the savings or even ruined the
lives of many thousands of individual investors. To take but one
example, the collapse in 1892 of the Liberator Building Society,
brought on by the malfeasance of its directors, consumed over a
million pounds, the loss of which was borne by thousands of small
investors many of whom were reduced to penury. Frauds of this
sort permeated the Victorian consciousness, causing many to question the very integrity of the business world.

In 1860, Charles Dickens recorded a series of bizarre
coincidences concerning financial fraud. It seems that William
Robson, a City clerk who had certified the Great Northern Railway's deed of settlement, went on to commit frauds upon the
Crystal Palace Company to the extent of £30,000. The Railway
that Robson had symbolically launched was later defrauded by
its Registrar, Leopold Redpath, of a quarter of a million pounds.
Redpath channeled his ill-gotten gains into the Union Bank of
London, from which cashier W.G. Pullinger later embezzled as
much money as Redpath had deposited – £250,000. By yet
another coincidence, John Chapman, a director of the Union
Bank and auditor of the Great Northern Railway, failed to detect
Redpath's frauds at the railway, Pullinger's at the bank, or the
frauds of yet another clerk who embezzled some £30,000 from
Chapman's own firm.[2] Was all this merely a coincidence?
Dickens thought not. To him these "very singular things in the
City" were symptomatic of dishonesty which pervaded the
financial community. Nor was Dickens alone in his pessimism. In
1866 the journal *Temple Bar* lamented: "Go where you will, in
business parts, or meet who you like of business men, it is – and
has been for the last three years – the same story and the same
lament. Dishonesty, untruth, and what may, in plain English, be
termed mercantile swindling within the limits of the law, exists
on all sides and on every quarter."[3] Thirty years later, at the
century's end, an article in the *National Review* struck a similar
chord:

In the domain of finance – which, whether local or cosmopolitan, is fast becoming the world's tyrant – the primeval "forest-burn rapacity" of the human species may be seen in full and almost unfettered operation . . . At any rate, as regards the fraternity of promoters, both individuals and corporate, their morals may be best described in the words of Gabriel Borkman, the financier in Ibsen's latest drama, as "the morals of the higher rascality." The sootiest sheep of the financial flock may hope to find absolution if he only sin on a large enough scale.[4]

The Victorians had few illusions regarding the world of finance. The stereotypical image of the virtuous and respectable Victorian businessman is almost wholly the creation of twentieth-century sentimentalists and conservative ideologues.[5] The Victorians themselves were plagued by white-collar crime as no other people before or since.

The most significant aspect of the new financial structure and that most vulnerable to fraud, was the rise and proliferation of the joint-stock company, an organization formed through the issuance of capital shares to a number of investors. Purchasers of shares were joint owners of the business and entitled to a portion of the profits commensurate with their investment. The great advantage of joint-stock companies was that, unlike individually owned businesses or partnerships, there was virtually no limit to the amount of wealth they could draw upon. At the same time, companies provided an investment outlet for the growing national wealth created by industrialization. By the late Victorian period, middle and upper-class England truly had become a nation of shareholders. As a measure of the public's passion for company investment, Sir John Clapham recorded that by 1914 the seven largest industrial companies alone had an aggregate of almost 400,000 shareholders. In addition, by 1927, there were some 300,000 distinct bank shareholdings and 900,000 railway shareholdings. Total joint-stock assets represented hundreds of millions of pounds.[6]

Company organization transformed the opportunities for financial dishonesty. The rising scale of organization increased the distance between the nominal owners, the shareholders and the active directors, and heightened the impersonality of this relationship. Thus the directors and their allies, the company floatation experts, were more open to the temptation to subject the investments of the faceless thousands to a wide variety of manipulations.

Discussions of business frauds filled the newspapers and journals of Victorian and Edwardian England. There were rogues enough among company directors to attract the attention of novelists like Dickens and Trollope and dramatists like W.S. Gilbert and Granville Barker. Fraudulent company promoters such as Albert Grant, Ernest T. Hooley and Horatio Bottomley became notorious villains of the Victorian era. At lower levels of infamy, absconding bankers, dishonest stockbrokers and embezzling clerks had a place in economic demonology. These less celebrated criminals threatened not only the rich and comfortable but also the widow and orphan, the genteel poor and the small investor generally. As Harold Perkin writes in *Origins of Modern English Society*: "From the 'railway mania' of 1846–47 onwards the investing public was compulsorily educated in a whole new world and vocabulary of ingenious crime, which could only be perpetrated by business men, and by large, prominent, wealthy or at least credit-worthy business men at that."[7]

The term "white-collar crime" was first used by the sociologist Edwin Sutherland in the 1940s. Sutherland defined it "as a crime committed by a person of respectability and high social status in the course of his occupation."[8] Thus, according to Sutherland, non-occupational crimes committed by members of polite society, such as murder or rape, would not be considered white-collar crimes. Likewise, work-related crimes such as larceny by domestic servants or the theft of building materials by construction workers cannot be categorized as white-collar crimes because they were carried out by lower-class persons. Typical white-collar crimes include acts as varied as embezzlement by bankers or trustees, graft among public officials, stock fraud, false advertising and falsified accounts. Since modern business and professional relationships are largely based on trust, white-collar crime can be further defined as breaches of trust within business and professional communities or between those communities and the general public. Trust is that evanescent quality without which the operations of modern business would be impossible. Trust enables people to turn over their hard-earned savings to banks or stockbrokers rather than burying it in basements or stuffing it in mattresses. Trust enables the directors of large corporations to rely on the honesty of their employees rather than tallying every penny themselves.[9] By widening our definition of white-collar crime to include breaches of trust, we therefore include behavior widely held to be unethical and immoral as well as that which violates the letter of the law.

While white-collar occupations encompass a wide range of financial, mercantile and professional activities, this study will concentrate on the world of finance and big business. Commercial and mercantile frauds such as false weights and measures, the adulteration of foodstuffs, false advertising and trademark, patent and copyright infringements are not germane to this study, though commercial abuses of credit and false accountancy are.[10] Professional malfeasance by groups such as doctors and lawyers is not included, but misdeeds by those professionals intimately connected with finance, such as accountants and stockbrokers, will be studied. Lastly, political corruption will be examined only where it intersects with the financial world, as in using privileged information to make profits on the Stock Exchange.[11] These other types of white-collar crime are deserving of separate treatment, and it is to be hoped that this study of financial fraud will stimulate such work.

The scope of our study extends from the first period of major company speculation, the "Railway Mania" of the mid-1840s down to the collapse of the international financial market in 1929 and places particular emphasis on the structures and institutions of investment, finance and credit, especially the joint-stock company and the unfolding possibilities it afforded for cheating the system. We will explore the characteristics of company organization, banking and the stock market which allowed or even encouraged disreputable activity. Popular attitudes toward white-collar crime will also be scrutinized along with the various ways in which society attempted to deal with such crime, including the state's endeavors to master the problem through Parliamentary legislation, as well as the development of business ethics, the professionalization of management and improvements in auditing. Lastly, this study will gauge the significance of white-collar crime by examining the effects of fraud on both individual investors and the economy as a whole.

This study of white-collar crime hopes to redress an imbalance in both business and criminal history. Although a number of economic historians have made notable contributions to our understanding of modern business, the history of the City is still virtually unexplored. Pioneering work by J.H. Clapham, B.C. Hunt and H.A. Shannon in the 1930s has been followed up only recently, and most work in this area rarely touches upon questions of fraud and deceit.[12] One exception to this rule is Edward Smithies' *The Black Economy in England Since 1914*, though Smithies' work is principally devoted to the history of the black market, tax fraud, smuggling and pilfering – topics outside this study's scope.[13] A number of fruitful contemporary researches into English business history have originated at the London School of Economics' Business History Unit. Most recently the Business History Unit has published a multi-volumed *Dictionary of Business Biography* which goes a long way toward increasing our knowledge of nineteenth and twentieth-century entrepreneurship and includes a number of entries on business frauds.[14] Another new biographical collection, *Speculators and Patriots*, brings out some of the seamier aspects of modern finance as does Philip Cottrell's excellent study, *Industrial Finance, 1830–1914* and William P. Kennedy's provocative *Industrial Structures, Capital Markets and the Origins of British Economic Decline*.[15] Although the best work in business history is increasingly sensitive to the criminal aspects of its subject matter, the story of white-collar crime has yet to be told.

In the realm of criminal history, the situation is even more lop-sided. While there has been much interest in recent years in the history of crime and punishment, those who have written about criminality in industrial England have dwelt almost exclusively on lower-class crime and criminals – the so-called "criminal under-world."[16] The assumption that crime was the province of the masses has been embraced by historians of all stripes, from those who analyse the institutions of law and authority to those who study popular culture. Even historians of the left, rather than challenging the notion that crime was primarily a working-class phenomenon, have instead elevated it to a form of social protest or class conflict.[17] Studies of the criminal underworld must be counterbalanced by an examination of "upperworld" crime.[18]

The historiography of white-collar crime is slight. The serious study of elite misconduct only began in 1949 with the publication of Edwin Sutherland's pathbreaking investigation of corporate fraud in America, *White Collar Crime*.[19] Although Sutherland's work raised many questions for further research, little else was heard on the subject for the next twenty years. The seventies and eighties have witnessed an explosion of interest in white-collar crime, with dozens of books and scores of articles written on the topic.[20]

Renewed scholarly interest in white-collar crime is almost certainly linked to a resurgence of financial fraud, as hardly a day goes by without new scandals coming to light concerning insider trading, money laundering or leveraged buy-outs. This current work, however, has been overwhelmingly sociological, criminological and contemporary. With the exception of a few popular accounts of sensational cases, white-collar crime has been ignored in the field of history.[21]

Rob Sindall's article on "Middle-Class Crime in Nineteenth-Century England" was thus a welcome addition to criminal history.[22] Sindall studied the calendars of prisoners appearing before the Quarter Sessions and Assize Courts of London, Birmingham and Manchester during certain years in the last century and concluded that the middle class displayed a greater criminality than the lower classes and that middle-class crimes represented a much larger financial loss.[23] Sindall's conclusions may well be correct, but they are not generally substantiated by the official statistics on which he relies. For example, in comparing the criminal "takings" of the different classes, Sindall gives average receipts for fraud cases as follows:

	middle class	other social classes
Surrey 1855–65	£9	£1
Surrey 1878–88	£15	£6
Birmingham 1880–1900	£62	£7

These figures are most unimpressive in both absolute and comparative terms and fail to support Sindall's claim that the middle class misappropriated "far greater" amounts than the lower classes.[24] Sir Leon Radzinowicz has commented that Sindall's sampling of the criminal record was too small and that more work must be done.[25] Here Radzinowicz seems to have missed the point, for the problem with Sindall's study is not an inadequate data base, but the assumption that the history of white-collar crime can be written from criminal statistics.

Any study of crime must confront the problem of the official criminal record. Among criminologists the debate centers around the theory of "positivism."[26] Positivists view criminal statistics as both an accurate measure of what crimes are most prevalent in a given society and as a reasonable approximation of any particular crime's extent. The counter-approach, usually labeled "interactionist," defines crime in terms of cultural relativity and views criminal statistics as highly subjective, unreliable data. Interactionists believe that the official criminal record primarily reflects bureaucratic determination to emphasize certain crimes and the police's resolve or ability to pursue such crimes.

Historians, while generally acknowledging the fragmentary nature of criminal statistics, exhibit great reluctance to abandon a statistical approach. Thus, positivist assumptions remain implicit in most criminal history. V.A.C. Gatrell has presented the most thorough defense of the English criminal record, arguing that national figures when taken over an expanded period will eliminate regional peculiarities and give a good picture of the pattern, though admittedly not the extent, of crime.[27] The counter-argument has been most forcefully made by J.J. Tobias in *Crime and Industrial Society*, where he concluded that "criminal statistics have little to tell us about crime and criminals in the nineteenth century."[28]

Both sides in the argument have probably overstated their cases. The criminal record *does* tell us which crimes were most vigorously pursued and prosecuted by private citizens and officialdom in modern England.[29] Although this information cannot be equated absolutely with criminal reality, it does provide keen cultural insights and useful details about particular crimes. Yet with forms of delinquency about which society was ignorant, indifferent or impotent, the criminal record tells us very little indeed.

The hidden nature of most white-collar crime ensures its absence from official statistics. Unlike murder or robbery, which left tangible evidence, many white-collar crimes merely involved the manipulation of paper assets, while the impersonality of the financial structure increased the distance between criminal capitalists and their victims. The attentions of the police were largely directed against lower-class criminals who were clearly more visible and believed to pose an immediate threat to the social order. It was also far easier and less expensive to go to law against prostitutes and pickpockets than directors of large corporations. As Philip Jenkins put it, "to find one's way into the crime statistics virtually requires that an offender be relatively poor, probably inept and lacking in powerful friends."[30]

Statistics for white-collar crime are generally comprised of the most trivial offenses. Sindall's figures for embezzlement in London and Birmingham are typical. In Surrey, for example, between 1855 and 1865 the criminal record reveals that £412 was embezzled by some sixty-four middle-class persons. This averages to only £6 8s per crime. Again in Surrey, statistics for the ten years between 1878 and 1888 show that only £1,153 was embezzled by the middle classes, while in Birmingham during the twenty year period 1880 to 1900 a mere £1,981 was appropriated by white-collar criminals – *as recorded in the official record.*[31] These figures chiefly represent clerical embezzlement, but even this most petty of white-collar crimes is not accurately portrayed in the statistics since many cases would go unreported to avoid bad publicity.

A statistically insignificant number of powerful businessmen could steal millions. During the 1850s, for example, Leopold Redpath, Registrar of the Great Northern Railway, embezzled some £240,000 through fraudulently created stock and forged share transfers. When the banking house of Strahan, Paul and Bates collapsed in 1855, it was discovered that the directors had illegally disposed of some £100,000 of customers' assets with a further loss to shareholders and depositors of £650,000. Even these most notorious of white-collar criminals probably represent but a small fraction of all such malefactors. Many others simply escaped detection or prosecution. George Hudson, for example, misappropriated securities worth thousands of pounds from the railways he managed during the 1840s, but was never prosecuted. This study does not reject the criminal record, it merely regards it as the tip of the iceberg.

A non-statistical approach is more profitable in researching the history of white-collar crime. Other forms of evidence such as Parliamentary investigations of financial crises, the Board of Trade's annual reports on bankruptcy, and reports from shareholders' committees of investigation throw light upon financial misconduct that never saw the inside of a courtroom. Expert opinion as expounded in City journals like *The Economist*, the *Accountant* and the *Bankers' Magazine*, or in testimony before Select Committees on Company Law Reform points out both specific crimes and general types of criminal activity that have not found their way into official statistics.

Literary evidence is another fruitful source for criminal history, though one that is not without its drawbacks.[32] J.A. Sharpe has discussed various pitfalls to a literary approach, including the fact that many popular writings about crime romanticized the criminal or else dealt only in stock figures and stereotypical situations.[33] Fictionalized accounts of crime were often more concerned with exciting or titillating the reader than with espousing social realism. In *The Novelist and Mammon*, Norman Russell discounted the accuracy of literary depictions of Victorian business fraud, arguing that such characterizations were colored by a general disdain for financial activity and that conventions of fiction led to exaggeration and distortion for dramatic effect.[34] These criticisms should be borne in mind, but they are not prohibitive. Literary accounts of financial fraud were widespread in modern England and point to genuine concerns regarding white-collar crime. Obviously novels, plays and other popular forms of expression furnish an imperfect view of crime, yet historians ignore these sources at their peril. As Philip Jenkins pointed out in a recent review article: "no scholar should write the history of Victorian crime based on the portrayal of Bill Sikes . . . it would be equally unsound to attempt such a history without at least referring to characters like Merdle, the epic fraudsman of *Little Dorrit*, or a hundred such characters from fiction whose crimes do not generally emerge in courts."[35]

The transgressions of these great criminal capitalists were of such magnitude that the receipts of burglars and shoplifters pale in comparison. White-collar crimes affected not only individuals but the entire economy, contributing to commercial malaise and a breakdown of trust. Such crimes were a telling indictment of the doctrines of *laissez-faire* and *caveat emptor* that tolerated high levels of fraud and offered investors little or no protection. White-collar crime also challenges traditional images of middle-class respectability and Victorian business probity.

Toward the end of *Little Dorrit*, Dickens described the hero's walk through the City of London – the financial heart of England, indeed, of the world:

As he went along, upon a dreary night, the dim streets by which he went, seemed all depositories of oppressive secrets. The deserted counting-houses, with their secrets of books and papers locked up in chests and safes; the banking-houses, with their secrets of strong rooms and wells, the keys of which were in a very few secret pockets and a very few secret breasts; the secrets of all the dispersed grinders in the vast mill, among whom there were doubtless plunderers, forgers, and trust-betrayers of many sorts, whom the light of any day that dawned might reveal; he could have fancied that these things, in hiding, imparted a heaviness to the air.[36]

It is this study's intention to cast light into these dark areas of the commercial past.

CHAPTER I

The new economy: transformation of finance and opportunities for crime

The extensive white-collar crimes of the nineteenth and twentieth centuries were born of the financial revolution that radically altered English finance during the early eighteenth century. The growth of a securities market and experiments in company organization fashioned a world of new possibilities for dishonest businessmen. The Industrial Revolution greatly accelerated developments in banking, credit and company formation, culminating in a second, and more profound, financial revolution in the mid-nineteenth century. The company explosion initiated by the Railway Mania of 1845, the Limited Liability Act of 1855 and the Companies Acts of 1856 and 1862 created tremendous opportunities for fraud. Big business and business crime have never been the same since.

Financial crime is as old as capitalism itself. In the fifty years following the Glorious Revolution of 1688, England experienced a profound "revolution" in public borrowing which transformed the economy and opened many doors for the resourceful swindler.[1] The Bank of England was created in 1694 to finance the national debt, and the government securities issued by the bank, and traded on the Stock Exchange, soon became an important source of investment for the wealthier classes. These securities, or funds, were also the source of some of the earliest white-collar crime. Sir Henry Furnese, a seventeenth-century director of the Bank, participated in a number of schemes for artificially lowering the price of the funds and then purchasing as much as possible at the reduced price.[2] Such transactions had a demoralizing effect on the entire Exchange. In 1697, Parliament found that numerous stockbrokers "unlawfully Combined and Confederated themselves together, to raise or fall from time to time the Value of such Talleys, Bank Stock, and Bank Bills, as may be most Convenient for their own private Interest and Advantage."[3]

New instruments of credit facilitated trade, but also proved vulnerable to abuse. The first fraud in Exchequer Bills, for example, occurred within a year of their creation. These bills were issued by the Treasury as a form of government borrowing in advance of yearly revenues and circulated among the public as paper currency. In 1697, three high-ranking revenue officials fraudulently endorsed some of these securities and then collected large amounts of interest from them.[4] Other innovations in credit, such as bills of exchange and bank drafts, were frequently subject to misuse.[5]

In days of unreliable news, false rumors could greatly affect the value of government securities, and this type of fraud was commonly resorted to in the eighteenth century. In 1711 rumors that Queen Anne was dead caused a sharp fall in the funds, allowing some to make a handy profit at panic prices.[6] Certain brokers in 1715 spread false rumors about the Old Pretender's capture to raise the value of the funds.[7] Reports issued in 1803 that the British and French had concluded a peace treaty caused a rise in securities, though in this case the bargains were declared void and a reward was offered to discover the perpetrators of the hoax. In 1814 Charles de Berenger, masquerading as a French colonel, spread rumors of French defeat and Napoleon's death by strewing pamphlets to that effect from his carriage during a procession through the City. Government funds rose quickly and de Berenger and his accomplices, including a Member of Parliament, sold out for a profit of £10,000.[8]

During the eighteenth century, brokers conducted most of their business in the coffee houses of Change Alley. There were few regulations regarding dealings in company shares or government stock and the general tone of financial morality was low. The wickedness of speculation was the theme of righteous anger, with especially harsh criticism leveled against brokers. In 1719 Defoe wrote *The Anatomy of Exchange Alley; or A System of Stock Jobbing*, "proving that scandalous trade, as it is now carried on, to be knavish in its private practice and treason in its public."[9] Samuel Johnson's dictionary defined stock-jobber as "a low wretch who makes money by buying and selling shares in the funds."[10] In 1767 a pickpocket who was apprehended on the Exchange boldly asserted that he was only stealing what the brokers had stolen from others.[11] By the 1790s increasing fraud led many traders to lobby for a closed market. Reputable dealers, desirous of excluding adventurers, established the modern Stock Exchange at Capel Court in 1801.[12]

Securities frauds in the eighteenth century had usually involved government stock, for joint-stock companies were still in their infancy. Most businesses were either privately owned or run as partnerships. Only large trading concerns like the East India or Hudson's Bay Companies tended to rely on the joint-stock principle since such companies could raise much larger capital sums than private enterprise and their shares were readily transferable. Shareholders in a joint-stock company had the additional advantage of limited liability, whereby they were only responsible for the company's debts to the extent of their own shareholdings. The benefits of incorporation, however, were also subject to abuse by unscrupulous traders. The South Sea Bubble of 1720 made manifest the fraudulent possibilities of company organization.

The South Sea Company was chartered in 1711 to supply New Spain with slaves and to carry on other trade with the Spanish colonies.[13] The Company did a lackluster business until 1718, when war with Spain halted its trading altogether. As an antidote to this lull in commerce, the directors of the Company devised a scheme for converting part of the government's funded debt into South Sea stock. This procedure would allow the government to reduce its debt while increasing the Company's capital and, incidentally, its prestige.[14] To facilitate their plan, directors bribed Members of Parliament and Court officials and also bought-up blocks of South Sea shares to boost the price.[15] At the time of the conversion, in 1720, South Sea stock rose precipitously, inspiring a mania for new companies.

A multitude of joint-stock promotions mushroomed around the South Sea Company, hoping to emulate its success.[16] Most of these companies were hopelessly ill-conceived and many others swindles, pure and simple. One pathetic example purportedly advertised "to carry on an undertaking of great advantage, but nobody to know what it is." The projector opened his office and closed it on the same day, decamping with £3,000 in deposits.[17] Such obvious frauds alarmed a number of prudent businessmen and politicians. The South Sea Company, however, was more worried about competition from this new issue market, and thus lobbied its allies in the government to pass the so-called Bubble Act of 1720 – forbidding further company formation without Royal Charter or

Parliamentary sanction.[18] Yet by this time the damage had been done.

Shares in the South Sea Company and its host of imitators were desperately oversubscribed with no real chance of repaying the initial investment. Furthermore, the total capital involved was far too great ever to have been raised. Many speculators had purchased shares on borrowed money, paying small deposits in hope of reselling before the next payment was due. As demands for payment mounted, people had to sell shares in order to meet obligations or repay loans. Prices fell and in turn more shares were thrown upon the market. Thus the bubble burst in the autumn of 1720.

The inevitable crash brought ruin to thousands of humble investors as well as a number of prominent merchants and tradesmen. Criminal allegations were leveled against the South Sea Company, and many of its directors fled abroad. Sir Robert Walpole became a power in the state by his deft screening of the Crown and other members of the Court involved in the Company.[19] The South Sea catastrophe exercised a psychological restraint on joint-stock organization for over a century. The Bubble Act rendered incorporation impossible without the trouble and expense of a private bill in Parliament. Fortunately the requirements of eighteenth-century commerce were not so complicated as to demand incorporation. Most business could be accommodated by private firms or partnerships.

The Industrial Revolution quickened the pace of earlier financial developments. Industry required new refinements in banking and credit, and enterprises such as canals, docks, gas-works and railways could only be financed through the floatation of public companies. The proliferation of joint-stock companies during the nineteenth century constitutes a second financial revolution which in size, numbers of people involved and real operation was more profound than earlier financial developments. Company shares came to compete with government securities, and, in 1811, industrial shares were quoted on the Stock Exchange for the first time, making them as accessible as Treasury stock.

By the 1820s the strictures of the Bubble Act flew in the face of an expanding economy. In 1824 the numbers of bills for granting corporate status had grown so large that Parliament could hardly cope with them. By April of 1825, 250 bills were before the Commons seeking the privileges of joint-stock organization, and in June the Bubble Act was repealed as a hindrance to company formation. Parliamentary sanction was no longer a prerequisite to incorporation, but limited liability, traditionally inseparable from the joint-stock company form, was henceforth a privilege only doled out by private Act or Royal Charter to a small number of companies.[20]

The stimulus for the 1825 boom, like that of the South Sea Bubble a century earlier, was the fabled wealth of Spanish America. In 1824 and 1825 the British public raised £17.5 million in loans for the newly independent South American republics, and this was soon followed by a tremendous investment in South American mining companies.[21] As with any bubble period there were ample opportunities for fraud. John Francis related: "Among the companies which sprung up daily, was one to make gold; and success was declared to be undoubted. The shares were all greedily taken; and it was then advertised that, as the expense of producing one ounce of gold would cost double the value of the produce, the company would be dissolved, and the deposits kept to pay expenses."[22] This was the classic type of fraudulent promotion – advertising a new company only to bilk investors of their share deposits.

The 1825 boom went the way of all speculative manias. Company shares were outrageously overvalued and often purchased on borrowed money. The drain of bullion for foreign loans or overseas mining companies led the Bank of England to restrict credit and, with this restriction, the whole speculative structure collapsed. Of the 624 companies floated in two years, only 127 still existed in 1827. The surviving companies had a nominal value of £103 million though only £15 million had been paid-up. Another 118 companies had issued shares and taken in some £2 million but were abandoned within a few months of formation – a category which smacked strongly of fraud.[23]

Forming joint-stock companies with limited liability under the registration process laid down by the Companies Acts only became the norm after the middle of the nineteenth century. The two decades from 1825 to 1844 were a nebulous period for public companies. Even with the repeal of the Bubble Act in 1825, the legal position of joint-stock companies remained unclear. There were no special laws regulating company formation, which was left to the inadequate provisions of the common law.[24] Anyone could promote a company for any purpose. Directors were under no obligation to report to shareholders, to publish accounts, or even to audit the company's books. In this atmosphere of confusion fraud flourished. As the *Edinburgh Review* complained in 1836:

If [companies'] power of doing good, when rightly applied and conducted, be great, their power of doing mischief, when in the hands of craft and perverted to improper purposes, is ten times greater. They then become the most prolific sources of bankruptcy and ruin; enriching a select coterie of knaves and jobbers, while they involve thousands, who were led to believe that they would add prodigiously to their wealth, in irremediable poverty and beggary.[25]

This complaint was far from academic, for the 1830s witnessed a growing number of frauds, especially among life insurance companies.

The most notorious fraud of the thirties involved the Independent West Middlesex Life and Fire Assurance Company. This grandly titled firm, pretending to have been incorporated in 1696, first opened its doors in 1837 with a falsely advertised capital of one million pounds. Advertisements also claimed the Bank of England as the company's banker and included as directors a "Drummond" and "Perkins" whom simple people assumed to be the famous banker and brewer of those names. The company attracted a mass of business by insuring lives on small premiums and granting annuities for meager sums. Other insurance companies knew the Independent West Middlesex to be thoroughly fraudulent, but felt powerless to interfere. In 1839, however, a crusading journalist, Peter Mackenzie, launched a campaign against the company in the *Scotch Reformers' Gazette*. At first the company fought back vigorously but, ultimately fearing detection, its directors fled the country in 1840 having secured from an unsuspecting public £250,000.[26]

This sort of crime had become so common as to provide novelists a subject for burlesque. Thackeray satirized the Independent West Middlesex in his 1841 novel *The Great Hoggarty Diamond* where it appeared as the West Diddlesex Assurance Company. In Dickens' 1844 novel *Martin Chuzzlewit*, the petty swindler Tigg Montague forms the Anglo-Bengalee Disinterested Loan and Life Assurance Company as an easy way of making a dishonest fortune. As Montague explained to his partner in crime, Jonas Chuzzlewit:

"We grant annuities on the very best and most advantageous terms known in the money market; and the old ladies and gentlemen down in the country buy 'em. Ha, ha, ha! And we pay 'em too – perhaps. Ha, ha, ha! . . . Then there are the Life Assurances without loans: the common policies. Very profitable, very comfortable. Money down, you know; repeated every year; capital fun!"

"But when they begin to fall in," observed Jonas. "It's all very well, while the office is young, but when the policies begin to die; that's what I'm thinking of."

Such a trifling matter as paying out claims did not worry Tigg Montague:

"Whenever they should chance to fall in heavily, as you very justly observe they may, one of these days then; – " he finished the sentence in so low a whisper, that only one disconnected word was audible, and that imperfectly. But it sounded like "Bolt."[27]

Real frauds of this sort alerted Parliament to the need for company regulation, and in 1841 a Select Committee was appointed "to inquire into the state of the law respecting joint-stock companies with a view to the prevention of fraud."[28] The first sittings dealt primarily with life insurance frauds, but in 1843 the Committee was reconstituted under the chairmanship of Gladstone, then President of the Board of Trade, and the focus was broadened to include the possible regulation of all joint-stock enterprise. The Committee solicited testimony from businessmen and lawyers with expertise in company matters, and the picture which emerged was far from reassuring. In its Report of 1844, the Committee listed a number of unsavory practices whereby dishonest promoters deceived the public. Companies, for example, would often use, without permission, the names of famous people in their advertisements. Promoters would further "puff" their concerns by falsely advertising the amount of capital subscribed or else getting reports of pretended meetings inserted into papers. Companies might try to project a facade of respectability by opening accounts at the Bank of England or selecting "offices in respectable situations, and fitted up in a respectable manner." To bring in more money directors sometimes published fraudulent accounts or else paid unearned dividends out of capital. Directors could ward off inquiries by creating fictitious votes or proxies to outvote *bona fide* shareholders, and if directors conducted their business at a distance, through agents, or under assumed names, inquiries would be doubly difficult.[29]

The Committee was rather optimistic about its ability to combat company fraud, arguing in its Report that "publication of the Directors, of the Shareholders, of the amount of capital, and whether subscribed or not subscribed, nominal or real, would baffle every case of fraud which has come under the notice of your Committee."[30] Publicity was to be the antidote to fraud, and in 1844 the Committee's recommendations were embodied in "An Act for the Registration, Incorporation and Regulation of Joint Stock Companies."[31] The Act provided for a Registry Office to coordinate company affairs. Henceforth, before any new company could advertise to the public, it had to inform the Registrar of its name and purpose, and the names and addresses of its promoters. At this point the company was *provisionally* registered. It had thereafter to inform the Registrar of its place of business, the names of its directors and the names of all shareholders. Provisionally registered companies could only require a 5% deposit on shares. Furthermore, new companies were required to file with the Registry Office copies of every prospectus or advertisement issued.[32]

To achieve complete registration, a new company had within a year to present the Registrar with its Deed of Settlement, specifying the amount of nominal capital, the total number of shares, the names and addresses of shareholders, the number of shares held by each member and the deposits paid on those shares. The Deed had to be signed by at least one fourth of the shareholders holding at least one fourth of the total shares. Once a company was fully incorporated it had still to meet certain requirements of the Act. Half-yearly returns of members had to be sent to the Company Registry Office. All companies had to draw up a yearly balance sheet of assets and liabilities which was to be signed by the company auditor and at least three directors, presented at a yearly meeting of shareholders, and then filed with the Registrar. To insure full publicity, the documents of any company were open to inspection at the Registry Office for the fee of one shilling.[33]

The new act did not govern banking companies, which were provided for in separate legislation. For banks, like other businesses, were also developing along the joint-stock principle during the 1820s and 1830s, and unfortunately they were also experiencing high levels of fraud. Before the Industrial Revolution England had possessed a meager banking structure. In 1750, there were only about a dozen banks outside of London; by 1810 the number had skyrocketed to almost 800.[34] At the apex of the banking system were the old and established London banks, which numbered sixty-two in 1832. Their principal business was discounting bills of exchange and acting as agents for banks in the provinces. The country banks were primarily note-issuing bodies created to meet the increasing need for currency by trade and industry.[35]

Before 1826 all banks had been privately owned, each with a legal maximum of six partners, since the Bank of England had secured a national monopoly of joint-stock banking in 1708.[36] With trade expanding, the burdens placed on the private banks, especially small country banks, became too great for their limited resources. As J.H. Clapham has noted: "Some of the lessor country bankers were not well educated or wise and not all were honest. Their failures were astonishingly frequent, even apart from times of special crisis. There was never a year from 1815 to 1830 in which at least three banks did not break, and the total of bankers' bankruptcies for the fifteen years was 206."[37] During the financial crisis of 1825, no fewer than sixty-one English banks stopped payment.[38]

The instability of the English banking system was underscored by widespread fraud, perhaps the most remarkable example being the embezzlements of Henry Fauntleroy in the 1820s. Fauntleroy, managing director of the London bank Marsh, Stracey and Company, appropriated trust monies and securities of bank customers to support the insolvent firm. By forging powers of attorney, Fauntleroy was able to sell out Consols and other government stock to the tune of several thousand pounds before he was discovered in 1824.[39] Among the banking failures of 1825 were a number of firms that had been carrying on business for a number of years in a state of insolvency. According to one observer, "so desperate were the shifts resorted to in order to maintain the credit of the bank, that the acting principals had not hesitated to lay themselves open to criminal proceedings, had creditors thought proper to institute them."[40]

The banking failures and frauds of the 1820s delivered a severe blow to the nation's confidence in private banks. Critics delighted in contrasting the English banks with their Scottish counterparts which had long been organized along the joint-stock principle and which weathered the 1825 crisis without a hitch. As Lord Liverpool complained to Parliament in 1826: "Any grocer or cheesemonger, any petty tradesman, however destitute of property, might set up a bank in any place; whilst a joint-stock company, however large their capital, or a number of individuals exceeding six, however respectable and wealthy they might be, were precluded from doing so."[41] In lieu of such considerations, an Act was passed in 1826 permitting joint-stock banks to be formed outside a sixty-five mile radius of London.[42] The restriction was in deference to the Bank of England's monopoly, but even this last bit of favoritism was eliminated in 1833 with the renewal of the Bank's Charter.[43]

Joint-stock banks experienced a boom in the 1830s, increasing from 32 in 1833 to 79 in 1836 to 115 in 1841.[44] Between 1825 and 1843, ninety-three private banks were absorbed by joint-stock concerns, while many other private banks reorganized themselves along joint-stock lines.[45] Private banks thus fell from 436 in 1831 to 321 in 1841, causing *Blackwood's* to observe that private bankers were a vanishing species, and "if perchance a specimen is preserved in the British Museum, he will be gazed on as we now look upon the Dodo."[46]

Joint-stock banks offered customers and creditors greater security than private banks through their ability to raise much larger capital funds. It was also believed that joint-stock banks were better protected against fraud and embezzlement. The smallness of most private banks was viewed as an inducement to fraud since the owner/manager had sole control of bank funds and was in practice accountable to no one. Thomas Joplin, one of joint-stock banking's great advocates, argued that the directors of joint-stock banks would act as checks on each other and on the manager. A further division of responsibilities between different departments and among numerous clerical staff in a large joint-stock concern would, Joplin reasoned, prevent an over-mighty banker from regarding his customers' money as his own.[47] Large banking establishments, however, were not immune to fraud, they were simply vulnerable in different ways.

The Banking Act of 1826 left joint-stock banks unregulated in all matters relating to management and accounts. In practice anyone could form a banking company, regardless of experience or financial resources or business probity. In 1836, the *Edinburgh Review* gave its readers an alarming example of the ease with which banks were sometimes incorporated. A forger of government stamps had been arrested in Manchester, and among his belongings were letters from a friend who desired to establish a joint-stock bank. The would-be banker borrowed a few pounds from the forger (knowing full well the source of the money) to pay for the printing of a prospectus and advertisements. And thus the bank was launched by a penniless adventurer on funds advanced by a forger.[48] A number of banks were founded to finance commercial enterprises through the issue of paper money, and many of these banks were insolvent almost from the beginning. Of the twenty-nine banks which failed between 1839 and 1843, seventeen had never paid dividends. A popular adage held that "free trade in banking is synonymous with free trade in swindling."[49]

Unsavory banking practice in the 1830s and a spate of failures during the commercial crisis of 1836 gave rise to Select Committees on Banking in 1836–38 and 1840–41.[50] Like Gladstone's simultaneous hearings on company law, the Banking Committees also found a need for more stringent regulations to counteract fraud, and in 1844 their recommendations were embodied in two different Bank Acts. The more celebrated Bank Notes Act restricted the issuance of paper currency by banks other than the Bank of England.[51] Yet, for purposes of fraud prevention, the more important statute was the Joint Stock Bank Act.[52] Under this Act future banks had to obtain a charter from the Board of Trade. To be eligible for incorporation, a bank needed a minimum capital of £100,000, and a deed of partnership had to be arranged with the holders of half the total shares. Share denominations could not be less than £100, and banks could only commence business once 50% of their capital was paid-up.

The middle years of the 1840s were thus a watershed in English financial history. The 1844 Banking Acts had profoundly changed the nation's banking system. Private banks were in decline and joint-stock banks on the ascendant. The Company Act of 1844 revolutionized business organization. At the time of the Act there were some 900 English joint-stock companies in existence. In the next ten years, another 900 were registered.[53] This figure does not include railway companies, which were outside the jurisdiction of the Company Acts and which also experienced a phenomenal boom in 1845. The Registrar of joint-stock companies reported that over a thousand railway companies had provisionally registered in 1845.[54] The mid-forties marked a "take-off" period for joint-stock promotions, as clearly discernible today as it was to contemporaries. As the financial journalist David Morier Evans wrote in 1859, "it is with the railway mania of 1845 that the modern form of speculation may be said to begin, and the world has not yet recovered from the excitement caused by the spectacle of sudden fortunes made without trouble, and obscure individuals converted, as if by magic, into *millionaires*."[55]

Not surprisingly the 1840s was also the take-off period for white-collar crime of all types, even despite the reforms of the same decade. The financing of companies and the speculation in company shares created innumerable new possibilities for graft and corruption among business people. In 1843 the *Illustrated London News* commented on the growth of commercial dishonesty:

A perusal of the public journals . . . would lead anyone to imagine that the agents of our trading and fiscal affairs live, move, and breathe, in a perfect atmosphere of fraud. If we progress at the same rate for half a generation longer, commercial dishonesty will become the rule, and integrity the exception. On every side of us we see perpetually – fraud, fraud, fraud . . . Can nothing be done to stem the torrent of corruption? or is it to sweep on unchecked, threatening to destroy the fabric of society, by shaking every confidence between man and man?[56]

A generation later, David Morier Evans struck a similar chord in his book *Speculative Notes*:

It is evident that the tone of financial morality has experienced considerable deterioration since the memorable railway mania of 1845. Indeed, it is a common subject of remark among parties who have watched the career of events, that the gambling encouraged through the fictitious value which shares attained has done much to aggravate the existing evil – the looseness of principle and the sacrifice of probity to secure the golden prize, having been only too freely sanctioned in circles where a higher sense of moral rectitude should have prevailed.[57]

White-collar crime cast a pall over the entire business community.

Innovations in finance were often viewed with suspicion. Fraud led some critics to condemn the whole speculative structure, as in *Blackwood's* 1849 exhortation against the "Monster of Finance":

Like the small reptile of the old Northumbrian legend, it has grown into a monstrous dragon, capable of swallowing up both herd and herdsman together. The wisest of our statesmen have tried to check its advance and failed; the worst of them have encouraged its growth, and almost declared it harmless; the most adroit have yielded to its power. Interest after interest has gone down in the vain struggle to oppose it, and yet its appetite still remains as keen and insatiable as ever.[58]

Many Englishmen reacted with similar horror and alarm at their nation's new and increasingly complex economy.

Most laymen were uninitiated into the mysteries of shares, discount, transfers, debentures, arbitrage and a hundred other hard names and figures. The investing public had to submit itself to the tender mercies of professional stockbrokers, bankers and company promoters who alone possessed the requisite "expertise" to operate in the inscrutable world of high finance. Only the fragile bonds of trust stood as a surety between the experts and the rest of society. It was a trust that was all too easily abused. Fraudulent businessmen could cloak their crimes in the esoteric language of their professions. How was the average shareholder to know whether his investment had been lost through malfeasance or economic forces beyond his understanding?

The proliferation of paper transactions and paper securities made white-collar crimes even more difficult to detect. Unlike shoplifters or burglars who appropriated tangible objects, white-collar criminals often altered account books, forged instruments of credit, or manipulated paper securities. Such crimes might easily be committed in the course of an otherwise legitimate business, and, if correct form were observed, would excite no suspicion. In the 1820s, for example, the banker Roland Stevenson concealed embezzlements of £200,000 by presenting investigators sealed packets labeled with depositors' names and numbers of Exchequer Bills. The investigators concluded that actual securities were enclosed and did not examine the envelopes further. They also saw on paper that the bank had £44,000 on account at the Bank of England. The actual balance at the Bank was £4,000 – artfully enlarged by the addition of a four.[59] The ease with which crimes of this sort could be effected impressed Dickens, who shrewdly remarked that "a 'pass-book' costs only a few shillings at any City stationers, or less than the price of a course and vulgar crowbar."[60]

The rising scale of organization, exemplified by the joint-stock company, rendered the role of trust far more problematic than it had been in pre-industrial society. In the eighteenth century, the aristocracy had often been cheated by their estate agents and business partners had defrauded one another. In these more intimate business relationships, however, ties of loyalty could be strengthened through friendship and inter-marriage. This was hardly possible in a large, impersonal company. Joint-stock organization was characterized by the divorce of ownership and control. The nominal owners of the company, the shareholders, had become mere purchasers of income and in practice could exert little influence over the company's affairs. Most shareholders did not attend company meetings; many could not because of residence or gender.[61] As one witness testified to Parliament in 1844: ". . . the proprietors are a mere rope of sand; there is the greatest difficulty in getting them to act in any way; there is a body of directors who have their friends, and then a large mass of proprietors who know nothing of business, who are always inclined to place great confidence in the directors; it is a most difficult thing for shareholders to work successfully against the directors."[62] Herbert Spencer echoed this sentiment ten years later in the *Edinburgh Review*: "Is it any wonder that the wide-spread, ill-informed, unorganized body of shareholders standing severally alone, and each pre-occupied with his daily affairs, should be continually out-generalled by the comparatively small but active, skillful, combined body opposed to them, whose very occupation is at stake in gaining the victory?"[63] Directors were by law the shareholders' trustees and had at all times to place shareholders' interests above their own; however, as we shall see, they were seldom as scrupulous as the law required.

Problems of financial impropriety were exacerbated by a growing atmosphere of *laissez-faire*. At the same time as classical economic thought was influencing policies of foreign trade, as in the much celebrated repeal of the Corn Laws in 1846, it was also busily at work in the realm of domestic commerce. The cautionary restrictions of the 1844 Company Act and the 1844 Joint Stock Bank Act were unpopular with free traders who whittled away at their provisions. In 1847 promoters were relieved of the "burdensome" task of registering prospectuses and advertisements.[64] Although the 1853 Select Committee on Assurance Associations found that most companies never filed annual balance sheets, Parliament refused to give the Registrar powers of enforcement.[65] Indeed, the government had no duty to prosecute violators of the 1844 Act, who could only be brought to justice by aggrieved shareholders or creditors.[66] The tradition of *caveat emptor* was well established in the common law and underscored the case for governmental non-interference in business matters. Even safeguards against fraud were regarded as undue restrictions of freedom. Fraud, or no fraud, the disciples of Adam Smith resented all state interference in the economy. The government could not, so the argument ran, make people honest by Act of Parliament.[67]

By the 1850s, limited liability was the one prize still sought by the advocates of *laissez-faire*. Since 1825 the shareholders in most public companies had been liable for their companies' debts to the entire extent of their fortunes.[68] Needless to say this principle of unlimited liability had deterred a number of prudent investors from buying company shares. In 1850 businessmen testified before the Select Committee on the Savings of the Middle and Working Classes that unlimited liability hindered British investment and that too much of the nation's capital was lying idle.[69] Other witnesses pointed out that limited liability prevailed in the United States, France, Prussia, the Netherlands and Belgium, and "it was said there to be of great utility in facilitating local enterprises and improvements, and affording local investments."[70] One witness believed that with unlimited liability only incautious people invested in companies and that directors were thus more likely to engage in fraud.[71] Again in 1851, witnesses before the Select Committee on the Law of Partnership overwhelmingly suggested the adoption of limited liability for shareholders.[72]

Conservative voices in the business community opposed limited liability on the grounds that it would encourage speculation and fraud. Professional opponents like the economist J.R. McCulloch reasoned:

If parties will every now and then be careless of their interests, and forget or decline to adopt the necessary precautions to guard against abuse and loss when everything that they have is staked on the result, their carelessness will be immeasurably increased if they may limit their liabilities at pleasure, and speculate or gamble without any fear of the consequences.[73]

To bolster his case McCulloch cited the Victorian ideal of individualism, arguing that "in the scheme laid down by Providence for the government of the world, there is no shifting or narrowing of responsibilities, every man being personally answerable to the utmost extent for all his actions."[74] Yet with the divorce of ownership and control in large companies, McCulloch's argument was increasingly irrelevant. Shareholders had ceased to be entrepreneurs in the usual sense of the word.

Advocates of limited liability admitted that the principle was likely to be abused, but as they pointed out, the 1844 Company Act did "not limit the liability of shareholders; and it is unfortunately well known that under those Acts many reckless schemes ruinous to shareholders and injurious to the public, have been carried on."[75] Given the high degree of company fraud, limitation of liability was seen as a necessary protection for shareholders. Thus, in 1855 an Act was passed allowing joint-stock companies to limit their members' liability so long as the deed of settlement stated clearly that the company was limited and the word "limited" always appeared at the end of the company's name.[76]

In 1856 the champions of free trade scored another victory with the total repeal of the 1844 Company Act and the institution of more permissive legislation. Under the 1856 Companies Act, to achieve incorporation a company need only submit a Memorandum of Association to the Registrar containing the name and object of the company, the type of liability – whether limited or unlimited, the amount of nominal capital and the total number of shares.[77] It was only necessary for seven people holding one share apiece to sign this document. Provisional registration was dropped as was the requirement for a minimum paid-up capital. Companies were still required to hold annual shareholders' meetings and to send the Registrar a yearly list of members and their holdings, but there was no longer a mandatory audit.[78] The liberal provisions of the 1856 Act were defended in the Commons by Robert Lowe. The science of political economy, Lowe argued, taught that: "to interfere with and abridge men's liberty, and to undertake to do for them what they can do for themselves, is really lulling their vigilance to sleep, and depriving them of that safeguard which Providence intended for them, and helping fraudulent men to mislead and delude them."[79] The principles of *laissez-faire* had triumphed in the realm of company finance. In 1857 the restrictive Joint Stock Bank Act of 1844 was also repealed, and in 1862 a consolidating Act was passed which essentially recapitulated the 1856 Act and extended its privileges to banks and insurance companies.[80]

The passage of the Limited Liability Acts brought a big increase in the number of companies. Between 1844 and 1856, 966 companies had been registered.[81] Thereafter the numbers increased at a remarkable rate. In the six years from 1856 to 1862, nearly 2,500 companies were registered. In another six years 4,000 more companies were incorporated. By the end of the nineteenth century, there were almost 5,000 registrations a year.[82]

The number of promotions was high, but so too was the number of failures. The business historian B.C. Hunt estimated that of 7,000 odd companies formed between 1844 and 1868 only some 2,900, or 42% were still doing business in 1868.[83] While this figure illustrates the uncertainty attendant on big business generally, it also conceals a high proportion of fraud. For many companies which proved abortive or failed in their early stages had been incorporated solely to enrich the promoter and his accomplices.[84] Unfortunately, when discussing business failures, the line between incompetence and fraud is difficult to draw.

Many Victorians made no distinction between misadventure and malfeasance. Nineteenth-century England was a society which worshipped success and vilified failure.[85] As Carlyle remarked in *Past and Present*, "what is it that the modern English soul does, in very truth, dread infinitely, and contemplate with entire despair? What is his Hell . . .? With hesitation, with astonishment, I pronounce it to be: The terror of 'Not succeeding.' "[86] In *Culture and Anarchy* Matthew Arnold gave a chilling example of this phenomenon from the business community:

The newspapers a short time ago contained an account of the suicide of a Mr. Smith, secretary to some insurance company, who it was said, "laboured under the apprehension that he would come to poverty and that he was eternally lost." And when I read these words, it occurred to me that the poor man who came to such a mournful end was, in truth, a kind of type, – by the selection of his two grand objects of concern, by their isolation from everything else, and their juxtaposition to one another, – of all the strongest, most respectable, and most representative part of our nation.[87]

In a culture where failure was anathema, but where failure in business was extremely common, businessmen were under extraordinary pressures to do well. In the nineteenth century, once companies started making losses they tended to hang on for long periods of time – hoping against hope that things might be made right again. Thus, when Victorian companies finally went into liquidation, they usually had enormous liabilities.[88] The dread of failure was so great that many businessmen would conceal losses from shareholders or resort to other crimes in desperate attempts to rescue their failing concerns.[89]

Alongside the entrepreneurial culture, with its pressures to succeed, was a culture of investment driven by the same necessity. Industrialism had created too much new wealth to be effectively

channeled into traditional avenues of investment such as landhold-
ings. The burgeoning middle class also required more modest
investments. Much of the public debt, however, was in the hands of
trustees and the turnover in Consols was always rather slow.[90]
Shareholdings in public companies thus became an important supplement and alternative to land and government securities for the
propertied classes.

Much of the wealth of industrialism found its way into joint-
stock companies. In 1843 it was estimated that almost £200 million
was invested in the 900 public companies then quoted on the
London Exchange.[91] The spectacular growth of joint-stock
organization following the Railway Mania, the limitation of
liability and the new Companies Acts greatly expanded investment
opportunities. By 1897 there were approximately 24,000 limited
companies with paid-up capital of almost £1,300,000,000. If one
added companies such as railways and banks that were not
registered under the 1862 Act, this would raise the total capital by
another billion pounds. Altogether about one fifth of the total
national wealth was invested in company shares by the century's
end.[92] This figure was more than double the amount of French and
German company investment combined, and it did not even
include money invested in colonial or foreign companies.[93] It has
been estimated that British overseas investment grew from around
£100 million in 1829 to £230 million in 1854 to a staggering £4
billion by 1914.[94]

The number of Victorian shareholders is more difficult to assess
as no figures exist for the nineteenth century. As a later measure of
investment, by 1927 there were alone some 900,000 distinct railway
shareholdings and some 300,000 distinct bank shareholdings.[95]
Clapham suggests that the number of shareholders may have been
close to the number of income-tax payers in 1914 – about
1,200,000.[96] Whatever the estimate, company investment was for
obvious reasons a phenomenon of the affluent classes.

The social backgrounds of late Victorian and Edwardian shareholders can be assessed from data recently collected by L.E. Davis
and R.A. Huttenback for their book *Mammon and the Pursuit of
Empire*.[97] Based on an impressive sample of some 80,000 shareholders from the years 1883 to 1907, the authors found that only
1% of shares were held by the working class. Conversely, the
gentry and aristocracy, a group that constituted only 1 or 2% of the

population, held between 25 and 30% of company shares. The bulk of shareholdings – some 50 to 60% – can be attributed to the middle classes.[98] These figures probably represent a slight broadening of the base of investment from an earlier period. During the 1840s the average share denominations had been between £50 and £100, thereby excluding nearly all but the wealthiest investors. In the 1860s £10 and £25 shares were more common, and by the 1880s and 1890s the £1 share had come into its own thus placing company investment within the grasp of the petite bourgeoisie.[99] The *fin de siècle* also saw the rise of institutional shareholdings. In Davis and Huttenback's sampling, some 10% of company shares were held by other public companies.[100]

By funneling their surplus wealth into the securities market, the rich often got richer. Fortunes could be made in the City of London, but they could also be lost or stolen. In this atmosphere of high risks, the very rich could afford a certain margin of error. Many others were more vulnerable to the vicissitudes of the market. Large numbers of the middle class and gentry depended on investments for their very survival. Widows, spinsters, clergymen, retired army officers and many elderly persons made up the ranks of the genteel poor – people who by birth or position were members of polite society, but whose incomes were so low that they were hard-pressed to maintain social standing. Often all that stood between these people and social disgrace was a small annuity or the yearly dividends from joint-stock investments.

The genteel poor were often tempted by risky and speculative promotions which promised them huge returns for their modest capitals. The plight of such investors was captured with feeling by an article in *Blackwood's* in 1876:

Take a mother who has been left a widow with £5,000 and a rising family. "Put the money safely away in the funds; it would be sheer insanity to do anything else with it," says one friend of the family when she asks for advice as to its disposal; and he steps complacently into his carriage and is driven smilingly away. Another gentleman, a shade less scrupulous, is disposed to admit of first-class railway debentures, although he takes care to dwell on possible fluctuations to the extent of two to three percent. Very good! The lady acts on the advice of one or the other. But she finds that with her £150 to £220, she is not only embarrassed as to providing food, clothing, and houseroom for her growing family, but that she is compromising their future beyond remedy, from better fortunes. She is falling out of the circle of family acquaintance where her boys would be likely to find helpful friends and her girls to make happy marriages. She is unable to give them the education indispensable to their taking advantage of future opportunities. If she is to persevere in pinching, she condemns them to sink to an inferior grade of life, unless something in the nature of a miracle comes to save them. So, sorely against the grain, and at first in mortal apprehension, she has recourse to some of those more highly priced stocks which are the refuge of the widow, the clergyman, and the reckless.[101]

Impecunious investors like this imaginary widow were easy prey for swindlers and frauds. As a London detective wrote in the 1870s, "it is a curious reflection that people who have the least money to spare are those from whom the professional swindler derives in many instances the largest revenue."[102]

It would be mistaken, however, to assume that white-collar criminals preyed solely on desperate people. The nets of frauds and embezzlers could accommodate fish of all sizes. Investors, from the wealthiest to the most humble, shared the desire to conjure up fortunes out of thin air. This was the stuff dreams were made of, and, as we shall see, this was the criminal capitalist's window of opportunity.

CHAPTER 2

The Railway Mania

Before the Railway Mania of 1845–46, large-scale financial fraud had been episodic, appearing dramatically in speculative disasters such as the South Sea Bubble of 1720 or the 1825 Commercial Crisis. With the coming of the railways, however, big business and business fraud were here to stay. Railways pioneered the joint-stock company form a half-century before it became general in most other fields. In the words of Harold Perkin, "big business on the scale we know it today began with the railways in the nineteenth century."[1] So too did white-collar crime.

Railways transformed English finance as surely as they changed the face of the English landscape. The *London Gazette*, which published all Parliamentary schemes for companies, had been, previous to 1845, a slender volume. Due to the enormous proliferation of railway companies in 1845, the *Gazette* swelled to over 4,000 pages. It would never be light weight again.[2] In 1845 Parliament sanctioned 2,816 miles of new railway line, an amount equal to all the miles sanctioned between 1821 and 1843. An additional 4,540 miles were sanctioned in 1846. At its peak in 1846–47, railway expenditure absorbed almost 7% of national income.[3]

Railways broadened the base of investment. For the first time the Stock Exchange dealt significantly with company shares instead of government bonds. The Mania of the mid-forties drew in the whole nation of investors. The aristocracy and gentry became heavily involved in railway shareholding since they were often given large blocks of shares to secure their goodwill for lines crossing their estates.[4] At mid-century, Thomas Tooke observed: "In every street of every town persons were to be found who were holders of Railway shares. Elderly men and women of small fortunes, tradesmen of every order, pensioners, public functionaries, professional men, merchants, country gentlemen – the mania had affected all."[5] All

31

propertied people, that is. Or in the words of J.H. Clapham, rail-way shares had become "a universal family investment for all families which had anything to invest."[6]

Perhaps no aspect of the Railway Mania fascinated con-temporaries so much as the creation of railway millionaires. Fortunes were made by enterprising new men such as the engineer George Stephenson or the contractor Samuel Morton Peto. The parvenu *par excellence*, however, was George Hudson, the "Railway King." A Yorkshire draper turned banker and railway promoter, Hudson parlayed his shrewd business sense into a railway fortune, a country estate and a Parliamentary seat. Hudson was chairman of several important lines, including the York and North Midland and the Eastern Counties. For a time, he appeared to have the Midas touch. The mere mention of Hudson's name in connection with a proposed railway would guarantee full subscription of its shares.[7]

Hudson was courted by Society and his financial advice eagerly sought by the highest in the land. Cartoons at the time depicted aristocrats prostrating themselves before the Railway King. At the opening of one of Hudson's lines in 1846, Sir Thomas Legard apostrophized:

> When railways and railway shares were dark as night,
> Men said that Hudson ruled, and all was right.[8]

Thomas Carlyle captured the mood of Hudson-worship in a par-ticularly sardonic passage:

The practical English mind contemplating its divine Hudson, says with what remainder of reverence is in it: "Yes, you are something like the Ideal of a Man; you are he I would give my right arm and leg, and accept a pot-belly, with gout, and an appetite for strong waters, to be like! You out of nothing can make a world, or huge fortune of gold. A divine intellect is in you, which Earth and Heaven, and Capel Court itself acknowledge; at the word of which are done miracles. You find a dying railway; you say to it, Live, blossom anew with scrip; – and it lives, and blossoms into umbrageous flowery scrip, to enrich with golden apples, surpassing those of the Hesperides, the hungry souls of men. Diviner miracle what god ever did? Hudson, – though I mumble about my 39 articles, and the service of *other* divinities, – Hudson is my god, and to him I will sacrifice this twenty-pound note: if perhaps he will be propitious to me?"[9]

Carlyle gives us the capitalist as false-Messiah. As such he espouses the intellectual view that businessmen were vulgar materialists – Philistines who worshipped the golden calf.

Literary depictions of railway tycoons were generally scathing. In Robert Bell's 1850 novel, *The Ladder of Gold*, the Hudson-like protagonist, Richard Rawlings, rises from provincial clerk to railway millionaire. Rawlings' success owes no small part to dishonorable business practices. He rides rough-shod over company meetings, going so far as to hire Irish thugs to silence dissident shareholders. In *Doctor Thorne* (1858), Anthony Trollope embodies the vulgarity of the *nouveaux riches* in the character Sir Roger Scatcherd, a brutish, drunken Barchester stonemason who becomes a wealthy railway contractor. Scatcherd is made a baronet for his railway building, enters Parliament, but is unseated for election bribery.[10]

The most popular Victorian satire of the Railway Mania was undoubtedly Thackeray's "Diary and Letters of C. Jeames de la Pluche" which appeared in *Punch* during 1845 and 1846. Jeames Plush is a London footman whose £20 speculation in railway shares escalates to half a million. Jeames becomes director of numerous railway companies and sets himself up as a gentleman – newly styled Jeames de la Pluche. Thackeray has Jeames describe his newfound eminence:

Railway Spec is going on phamously. You should see how polite they har at my bankers now! Sir Paul Pump Aldgate & Company. They bow me out of the back parlor as if I was a Nybobb. Everybody says I'm worth half a million. The number of lines they're putting me upon, is inkumseavable. I've put Fitzwarren, my man, upon several. Reginald Fitzwarren, Esquire, looks splendid in a perspectus; and the raskle owns that he has made two thousand.

How the ladies & men too, foller and flatter me! If I go into Lady Binsis hopra box, she makes room for me, whoever is there, and cries out, "O do make room for that dear creature!" And she complyments me on my taste in musick, or my new Broom-oss, or the phansy of my weskit, and always ends by asking for some shares.[11]

These literary accounts express the belief that railway promoters were vulgar upstarts, bereft of honor and integrity. Many were depicted as coming by their fortunes dishonestly. Clearly this view reflected both old, aristocratic prejudices against commerce as well as the newer attitudes of the professional middle class.[12] Professional types such as Trollope, Thackeray and Matthew Arnold, along with other writers, civil servants and academics, condemned much commercial and financial activity as "money grubbing" and

"Mammonism." Professionals stressed the ideals of service and intellectual merit over productivity and profit margins. Yet the fact that professional men had ideological axes to grind does not invalidate their critiques. For, as we shall see, condemnation of the Railway Mania and railway promoters was grounded in real miscreance.

As in all economic boom periods, the Railway Mania provided ample opportunities for enterprising white-collar criminals. Walter Bagehot analysed this phenomenon in *Lombard Street*: "The good times of too high price almost always engender much fraud. All people are most credulous when they are most happy; and when money has just been made, when some people are really making it, when most people think they are making it, there is a happy opportunity for ingenious mendacity."[13] The phenomenal growth of the Victorian railway network and its accompanying profusion of large corporations gave rise to numerous possibilities for fraud.

The very immensity of railway promotions was in itself overwhelming. As Robert Bell observed in his railway novel:

A colony of solicitors, engineers, and seedy accountants had settled in the purlieus of Threadneedle. Every town and parish in the kingdom blazed out in zinc plates on the door-ways. From the cellars to the roofs, every fragment of a room held its committee, busy over maps and surveys, allotments and scrip. The darkest cupboard on the stairs contained a secretary or clerk, shut up and palpitating in its mysterious organism, like the lady in the lobster.[14]

The Times saw the country "stifled in the froth of a thousand schemes."[15] Among the hundreds of proposed railway lines dangled before the English public, were many that were downright fraudulent. The nation, however, was ill-equipped to separate the sheep from the goats. Parliament could barely cope with the hundreds of railway bills before it in 1845 and 1846. Investors had little access to good financial advice or even to accurate financial data. Fraud thrived in this atmosphere of ignorance and confusion.

The ease with which railways could be promoted ensured an abundance of new companies. In 1846, the M.P. Thomas Duncombe complained to the Commons: "Any man might go and get any scheme, how absurd soever, provisionally registered on paying £5. In November and September last, every man who dreamed almost of a railway got it registered. It would generally be found that most of the parties who registered were only solicitors or surveyors."[16] Railway companies were a source of limitless fees for lawyers, engineers and surveyors. It was of little regard to these men whether or not the proposed lines were feasible or the resulting companies successful. Money was to be made simply in drawing up maps, prospectuses and articles of association. An abortive company was almost as valuable to lawyers as a successful one. In the general rush to make money discrimination was thrown to the winds.[17]

Landowners also fueled the Mania. The nobility and gentry could gain vast sums in compensation for lines crossing their estates, and they thus supported these lines regardless of their true merit. Great landowners in Parliament often used legislative influence to gain for themselves exorbitant compensation for lines running across their property. According to *Fraser's Magazine*, "hundreds of thousands have been paid in supposed compensation for injury, which could not as injury have been estimated at more than a few thousands. In some cases no injury whatever was incurred."[18] Even the Church was not above profiting from railways at extortionate rates. In one notorious case the Great North of England Railway purchased fifty acres from the Dean and Chapter of Durham Cathedral for £9,000, but, deciding not to build on it, resold the land to the Chapter for £1,300. Soon afterwards the Newcastle and Darlington Railway wished to buy the same land, and the Chapter now demanded £12,000, including £5,000 for "wayleave" and £3,000 for "damage by severance."[19]

Railway promotion took on a life of its own. People stopped asking whether a given line was viable or whether it met any real need. If money could be made, practical questions were ignored. In 1846, John Hawkshaw, Engineer of the Manchester and Leeds Railway, estimated that half of the lines projected that year were projected by mere speculators who had no intention of actually constructing railways.[20] These railways were proposed for the sole purpose of securing deposits from prospective shareholders. Provisional Committees would squander deposit money in fees to themselves and their cronies, leaving deceived subscribers in the lurch.[21]

All railway companies had to secure their own Parliamentary Acts before they were officially incorporated. Yet, while railway bills were being promoted before Parliament, the embryo company could collect deposits from prospective shareholders who would be issued "scrip" in the proposed railway. If a company's bill passed, scrip would be converted into shares. For fraudulently promoted companies, the success of their bill was a thing to be dreaded. According to *Fraser's Magazine*, "the experienced in these matters were often able to see a bill *skilfully lost*." In such cases, "a strange lassitude would creep over the concern. Witnesses when needed would be out of the way, counsel at the critical time would be busily engaged elsewhere, some capital fault would be suddenly dis- covered, and, after a sham fight and proper delay, the committee would decide against the proposed bill."[22] Form letters would then be sent out to scripholders regretfully informing them of the com- pany's demise and of the unfortunate loss of their deposits which had been absorbed in "Parliamentary expenses."

The courts had clearly ruled that if proposed railways, for whatever reason, were not incorporated, the provisional share- holders were entitled to a full return of their deposits. Most railway promoters and provisional committees, however, failed to do so, knowing full well that scripholders were not likely to risk the expense of a court battle, but would prefer to cut their losses. Individual deposits might not be great, but the aggregate of lost deposits on an abortive line could total thousands of pounds.[23]

In the spring of 1846, *Bradshaw's Railway Gazette* initiated a series entitled "Progress of Exposure" in which it detailed defalcations by provisional committees. The West End and Southern Counties Railway, for example, spent illegally all shareholders' deposits before its bill was rejected. The abortive Bristol and Liverpool Line and the Northampton, Bedford and Cambridge Railway were shown to have absorbed half of their depositors' money without authorization.[24]

Investors were especially vulnerable when dealing with embryonic companies. The only *bona fides* such companies pos- sessed was the integrity of their promoters. Many proposed railway lines advertised in newspapers and amassed deposits, but never bothered to submit bills to the legislature or to return deposits. In December of 1845 *The Times* discussed the case of a country gentle- man, Mr. Gregory, who, upon seeing a prospectus for the Birmingham, Oxford, Brighton Railway, applied for twenty shares, received a letter of allotment, and paid a deposit of £50. He never received his scrip, however, and journeyed to London three times before being told that the company had been dropped before its bill was introduced into Parliament and that deposits had all been expended. Mr. Gregory had little legal recourse, unless he suspected fraud, in which case he would have to sue the promoters in the Bankruptcy Court.[25] Yet, as numerous frustrated shareholders discovered, suspecting fraud and recovering one's money were very different things.

In the period between advertising a proposed railway line and its final incorporation, existed a nebulous business entity. There was no company or directors for aggrieved parties to sue, only promoters and provisional committees – the most evanescent financial entities. The murky legal atmosphere of railway incorporation afforded dishonest promoters great latitude in carrying out their schemes. At the height of the Mania, new railway lines had only to advertise in the papers to be flooded with applications for shares. Money did not always come so easily, however, and promoters resorted to numerous strategies of dubious legality or morality for attracting investments.[26]

Railway promoters tried to assemble provisional committees composed of well-known or distinguished persons such as peers of the realm, Members of Parliament and churchmen to act as "decoy ducks" for potential investors. Many of these persons had nothing to offer the company but their status, being altogether ignorant of railway matters or even elementary finance. According to *The Cornhill*, "probably not one in a hundred had the remotest idea of the cost of a line when they gave in their names as provisional directors, nor dreamt of any personal liability."[27] Such decoy directors were also known as "guinea pigs" since they supposedly received money (guineas) for merely attending board meetings.[28] Even engineers were not above playing this sordid game. Samuel Smiles noted in his biography of George Stephenson:

No scheme was so mad that it did not find an engineer, so called, ready to indorse it, and give it currency. Many of these, even men of distinction, sold the use of their names to the projectors. A thousand guineas was the price charged by one gentleman for the use of his name; and fortunate were the solicitors considered who succeeded in bagging an engineer of reputation for their prospectus.[29]

Investors naively believed that the presence of distinguished persons on a provisional committee guaranteed the integrity of a company. The public also assumed that these committeemen had material interests in the railway line and participated fully in potential liabilities of the company. This was seldom the case, however, as many railway promoters lured eminent figures by giving them free shares and shielding them from liability.

In 1846 the legislator T.S. Duncombe read out in Parliament a letter he had received from railway promoters, tempting him to join their committee:

Sir, I beg to forward to you a prospectus of the projected Portsmouth and Langston Railway and Dock Company, of which I respectfully solicit your perusal. The fact of the Lords of the Treasury having made a grant of the site for the proposed docks, coupled with the eminency of the engineers, Messrs. Coverdale and Lee, will, I trust, in your opinion, fully warrant my application to you to become one of the provisional committee for carrying out this great national undertaking; and in that case to sign and return the enclosed consent. Annexed is the Company's guarantee. I have the honour to be, Sir, your most obedient, humble servant,

J. Pole, Assistant Secretary

The guarantee was even more to the point:

Sir, On behalf of myself and the other projectors of the Portsmouth and Langston Railway and Dock Company, I hereby guarantee you, as a member of the provisional committee, against all costs, charges, and liabilities whatsoever in any wise relating to this undertaking.

George N. White, Secretary

As a Member of Parliament, Duncombe had received many such letters from different railways, some only requesting the use of his name.[30]

Guinea-pig directors were only one of many ways in which cunning promoters "puffed" a new company. Puffing railways – that is, publicizing them with exaggerated or distorted claims – became a fine art. To this end it was important for railway financiers to project an image of authority and affluence. In the words of *The Cornhill Magazine*: "The promoters of railways who visited the provinces baited the trap well; always travelling with four horses, liberal in their payment of hotel-keepers, post boys, waiters, etc., and ready to stand a champagne lunch on the slightest provocation."[31] The paraphernalia of respectability often concealed the most disreputable projects.

During the Mania, railway schemes were puffed incessantly in the press. Newspapers were not at all scrupulous about whom they took advertisements from, and promoters often had their own accounts of company meetings inserted into papers as regular news items. Railway advertisements made the most extravagant claims for companies, frequently overstating capital funds and quoting shares at higher values than they had ever achieved on the Stock Exchange. In 1846, the Great European Railway Company advertised its shares at premium in several newspapers, though, in fact, the company was not even listed on the Stock Index.[32] Newspaper editors would also puff certain lines in which they were interested parties. Even *The Times*, generally skeptical of railway schemes, shamelessly puffed the Direct London and Exeter Line for several months in 1845 because the paper's editor, William Delane, was a director of the company.[33]

If puffing failed to excite sufficient interest in a railway, directors secretly bought their own company's shares to drive up the price. In 1846, for example, the provisional directors of the Shropshire Mineral Railway used £21,000 of shareholders' deposits to buy their own shares.[34] Transactions of this kind were known as "rigging" the market. In conjunction with rigging, promoters would often hold back a substantial amount of company shares to enrich themselves at the public's expense. Once share prices had been artificially raised through rigging, promoters marketed their reserve shares at the higher price.[35]

Railway promoters were not the only persons attempting to manipulate the share market to their advantage. Many *bona fide* promoters were themselves victimized by unprincipled speculators who specialized in applying for shares which they never intended to keep, but only to sell at a profit. Speculative abuses in railway shares were facilitated by the practice of only requiring a small deposit on each share (usually 5%) and leaving the remainder to be "called-up" as needed. Anyone with a few pounds could thus become a gambler in shares.

The term "stag" was coined in the 1840s to describe those people who applied for railway shares only to sell them.[36] Stags dealt not only in shares but also in letters of allotment – letters which informed prospective shareholders how many shares had been assigned them as well as the deposit required to receive those shares. Letters of allotment were not valid securities and their sale was illegal, though stags traded in them extensively during the Mania.[37]

Many stags were penniless adventurers who could only secure letters of allotment or shares by using fictitious names and false addresses. Clerks at small salaries in banks or counting houses would write for shares as if they represented their employers. Domestic servants at fashionable addresses were especially favored, Thackeray's footman Jeames being a fictional example of a real phenomenon.[38] George Hudson discredited a rival line by delving into its share register and discovering a number of stags. A pensioner on ten shillings a week, for example, had obtained a large allotment by giving his rich brother's address. Altogether, Hudson demonstrated that shares worth £29,000 had been assigned to persons who could not be traced and £44,000 to persons possessing no property.[39]

Legitimate companies attempted to weed out frivolous applicants by drawing up black-lists of known stags.[40] It was a hopeless task. H.G. Ward, a railway director and M.P. for Sheffield, argued in Parliament that half the shares in railway lines were taken up by people with no interest or knowledge in those lines, but purely as a speculation. Directors were confronted with a mass of unsound applicants and forged references. According to Ward, not more than 40,000 out of 100,000 shares could be allotted with safety.[41]

It would be a mistake to attribute all problems of share speculation to a hoard of small-time confidence men. Many otherwise respectable persons entered the mêleé. In *A History of the English Railway*, John Francis noted:

Men who went to church as devoutly as their counting houses – men whose word had ever been as good as their bond – joined the pursuit. They entered the whirlpool, and were carried away by the vortex. They first cautiously wrote for shares in the names of their children, and sold the letters at a price which, while it consoled them for present turpitude, tempted them to fresh sin.[42]

This share-dealing spirit possessed all classes and changed the nature of railway enterprise. Speculation became the driving force behind railway promotion. In the words of Samuel Smiles "many people, utterly ignorant of railways, knowing and caring nothing about their general national uses, but hungering and thirsting after premiums, rushed eagerly into the vortex of speculation. They applied for allotments, and subscribed for shares in lines, of the engineering character or probable traffic of which they knew nothing. 'Shares! shares!' became the general cry."[43] Interestingly, both Smiles and Francis characterized the Mania as a "vortex," almost as if it were a force of nature over which mere mortals could exercise little control.

Parliamentary control over railway speculation was certainly ineffective, and the spirit of *laissez-faire* took the edge off many legislative attempts at regulation. Nonetheless, because of railways' public usefulness, state interference in railway matters was always greater than in business generally. Railways remained outside the province of the regular Companies Acts for, unlike other joint-stock enterprise, each railway company still required its own Act of Parliament.

In the late 1830s Parliament decreed that new railway companies must demonstrate their good faith by depositing 10% of their proposed capital with the Court of Chancery while their bills were under consideration.[44] Railways also had to prove that a genuine interest in their lines existed by providing a signed "subscription list" of investors holding at least half the proposed share capital.[45] These salutary provisions helped separate the wheat from the chaff, but unscrupulous promoters soon found ways of evading Parliamentary strictures.

Subscription lists were often swelled with fraudulent signatures. Railway secretaries recruited penniless people to sign for large blocks of shares, sometimes paying them to do so. The Deptford and Dover Line, for example, paid four shillings for signatures.[46] Among the subscribers to the London and York Railway, was a Charles Guernsey, the son of a charwoman and broker's clerk at 12 shillings a week, who was assigned £52,000 in shares. Guernsey was simply used by his employers, the brokers, who were promoters of the line.[47] Parliamentary deposits, also meant to demonstrate popular interest in a line, did not always consist of shareholders' money. The Parliamentary deposit was often put up by a wealthy promoter or raised through a loan. Promoters were not at risk in using their own money to prime the pump, since deposits were always returned whether a bill succeeded or failed.[48]

The Board of Trade had little power over either proposed or existing railways. In 1840 the Treasury created the Railway Department at the Board of Trade, but this was mainly to allay public fears over railway safety and to ensure transport of troops and the mails. The Railway Regulation Act enjoined the Department to inspect tracks and stations, though undue interference in company affairs was prohibited.[49]

In 1844, Gladstone unsuccessfully attempted to establish more effective government regulation and supervision of railways. He proposed a Bill giving Parliament authority to revise the tolls and to even purchase railway lines outright. The railway interest and advocates of *laissez-faire* neutralized Gladstone's Bill and the resulting legislation was innocuous and soon outdated. Under the Act, Parliament had the option of purchasing future railways (existing lines were exempt) only after twenty-one years. State control over tolls would likewise not be effective until twenty-one years had lapsed, and then, only if Parliament could permanently guarantee shareholders the enormous dividend of 10%.[50]

Gladstone did succeed in having the Railway Department temporarily transformed into a more prestigious, five-member Railway Board presided over by Lord Dalhousie. The Board was established in 1844 to guide Parliament through the vast series of railway bills, recommending some schemes and rejecting others. The Board, however, never gained support in the Commons, where members were increasingly reluctant to interfere with business matters, and was disbanded in 1845 under pressure from the railway lobby. Thus ended the only attempt at planned development of the English railway system.[51]

Other bodies were created to coordinate railway matters, though they dealt largely with questions of passenger safety. In 1846 Parliament established five Railway Commissioners.[52] In 1851 the Board of Trade absorbed the Commissioners into a new Railway Department.[53] These various governmental bodies inspected lines, investigated accidents, and arbitrated disputes between different railway companies. Conspicuously absent from their duties was the inspection of company accounts. The Board of Trade's powers did not include financial oversight.[54]

Previous to 1844 each railway company was governed solely by its own Act of Parliament with the result that different lines had vastly different requirements for accounting. In 1844 and 1845 general Acts were passed in an attempt to better regulate railway finance. The 1844 Regulation of Railways Act, however, only specified that "full and true accounts shall be kept."[55] The Company Clauses Consolidation Act of 1845 was rather more specific. This Act stipulated that shareholders were to elect auditors at half-yearly meetings, that directors were to draw up half-yearly balance sheets which the auditors would examine against the company's accounts, and that dividends were not to be paid out of capital.[56]

The Company Clauses Consolidation Act proved woefully

inadequate at curbing railway fraud, yet its accounting requirements were not strengthened until 1868. Although the Act mandated the keeping of financial records, it failed to specify the form which company accounts or balance sheets should take. With no standards of bookkeeping, railway accounts were often confusing jumbles of misinformation. In describing one company's accounts, *The Times* remarked: "The Caledonian Railway Company, the work neither of lawyers, nor of old women, nor spendthrifts, but of shrewd middle-aged mercantile men, is just such a tangle as one might dream of after supping on lobster salad and champagne."[57] The directors of the North Wales Railway kept some accounts in cipher to conceal illegal transactions from shareholders.[58] Balance sheets were not required to distinguish between a company's capital, which was only to be used in constructing the line, and its revenue, out of which salaries and dividends were to be paid. Thus, unscrupulous directors could easily pay dividends out of capital undetected – projecting a false image of profitability and enticing further investment in their lines.[59]

The audit of railway accounts was usually a farce. Auditors did not have to be accountants, or even possess bookkeeping skills. Although auditors were supposed to be the shareholders' watchdogs, they were more often the directors' cronies. At a company's first meeting, the directors' candidates for auditor were invariably approved by the shareholders.[60] Critics of this system proposed a government audit of railway accounts. In 1847 Edward Strutt, President of the Railway Commissioners, sponsored legislation that would give his office broad powers of entry and inspection of all railway books. George Hudson led railway directors in a successful campaign against the bill which was eventually withdrawn.[61]

The spirit of *laissez-faire* brooded heavily over Parliament, though political opposition to railway legislation had baser motives as well. The railway interest within both houses was tremendous. A large number of M.P.s were themselves directors of railway companies. Railway directors in the Commons grew from 80 in 1847 to 96 in 1857 to 157 in 1865 – the last number approaching a quarter of the House's some 650 members. Directors in the Lords were not as numerous, though by 1865 49 peers out of some 450 were railway directors.[62] Many legislators also held railway shares. An 1845 Parliamentary return revealed that 157 M.P.s had each subscribed over £2,000 in railway undertakings.[63] Presumably numerous others were shareholders for lessor sums. Conflict inevitably arose between Members' personal interest in railway promotion and their responsibility to legislate for the common good of the nation.

Minimal government interference in railway matters along with primitive auditing procedures created a situation in which there was no real check on the operations of directors. Shareholders were mostly ignorant of railway finance and, as long as respectable dividends were maintained, rarely if ever opposed directors. If shareholder opposition did materialize, directors could usually neutralize it by creating dummy voters and false proxies to guarantee themselves a majority. Hudson's biographer R.S. Lambert argued that "it was fatally easy to deceive the shareholders, who almost entered into a conspiracy to defraud themselves."[64] We have already seen the fraudulent possibilities of railway promotion. The management of actual railway lines continued to afford directors with ample opportunities for fraud.

Railway directors and their allies often used company funds for illegal purposes such as paying dividends out of capital. Dividends represented the stockholders' share of company profits. A high rate of dividend was a sign that a company was doing well and would usually boost the company's share value on the Stock Exchange. Directors were therefore under great pressure to declare substantial dividends. In new railway lines, however, there was a lag time between construction and the generation of revenue. To placate shareholders during the construction period, directors began paying "dividends" out of the shareholders' own capital. The practice soon spread to completed lines, the most notorious example being the Eastern Counties Railway under George Hudson. For years Hudson attempted to excite interest in the nearly bankrupt line by swelling dividends with money from the capital account. Table 1 illustrates Hudson's distortions.[65]

Other companies were more circumspect in supplementing dividends. The Grand Junction Railway, for example, paid dividends amounting to £73,144 in June 1845 when its half-year revenue was £68,514.[66] Yet whatever the extent of such chicanery, paying dividends out of capital created the false impression that a company was more profitable than it actually was.

Illegal borrowing was another serious problem among railway companies. Most railway acts allowed companies to borrow funds equal to one third of their share capitals. Many railways circum-

Table 1 *Eastern Counties Railway dividend distortions*

	Dividend paid	Dividend Earned (per £10 share)
Jan. 1846	*9s*	*4s 10d*
July 1846	*9s*	*3s 8d*
Jan. 1847	*10s*	*2s 1d*
July 1847	*10s*	*5s 10d*
Jan. 1848	*8s*	*4s 5d*
July 1848	*8s*	*2s 4d*
Jan. 1849	*4s 6d (proposed)*	*3s 4d*

vented the law by issuing "loan notes," a kind of pseudo-security on which they borrowed beyond their authorized limits. As of 1844, railways had borrowed several millions on loan notes. Those making the loans believed such notes to be valid security, but, in situations where railways exceeded their statutory borrowing limits, the lenders actually had no legal rights to demand repayment should directors prove unwilling to do so. To protect lenders, in 1844 Gladstone legalized loan notes still in circulation, but prohibited their further issuance.[67]

Railway directors frequently authorized the building of needless branch lines and extensions to enrich themselves and their friends at company expense. In *The Bubble of the Age*, Arthur Smith wrote:

In 1844 and 1845, the only thought amongst directors, was (to use their own term) how "to calve" – that was, how to propose branches that would appear plausible – the real object being the creation of new shares, in which the directors took great care of themselves by issuing largely to their nominees . . . These shares were puffed and rigged to large premiums, and immediately sold.[68]

Directors made enormous sums by overspending on branch lines to bring about a rise in share prices. When older railway companies were confronted with newer rivals, they often started building branch lines in an attempt to foil their competitors. Branch lines could also be a source of lucrative fees for lawyers and engineers friendly to the directors. "Calving" resulted in too many unnecessary, unprofitable lines. Herbert Spencer condemned the whole system of extensions in his essay "Railway Morals," arguing that this policy demonstrated "the essential viciousness of railway administration."[69]

Large railway companies often acquired smaller lines as part of the process of amalgamation. This practice lent itself to "insider trading." When the intended purchase of branch lines was made public, the share value of those lines would skyrocket. To those in on the secret, fortunes could be made. One of the earliest known cases of insider trading in railway shares was in 1843 when the York and North Midland purchased the Leeds and Selby Line. George Hudson, who was chairman of the York and North Midland, informed some of his friends of the intended purchase enabling them to buy up Leeds and Selby shares at a discount and later sell them to the York and North Midland for greatly enhanced prices.[70] The use of inside information to make money was considered immoral, yet there were no laws in the nineteenth century to combat this behavior. To compound the problem, insider trading was very difficult to prove as "information" is the most intangible evidence.

At the heart of much directorial fraud in railway companies lay conflict of interest. Directors often had personal interests in companies that were not altogether compatible with their role as shareholders' trustees. What was best for shareholders was not always best for directors. If, for example, a company were failing, shareholders' interests might best be served by winding-up the firm before liabilities got out of hand. The directors, however, would be out of employment, and might therefore struggle on with the result of further losses for shareholders.

Directors also had numerous opportunities to profit at their company's expense. They could award contracts out of favoritism to friends or relatives who would then "kick-back" payments to their patrons. Directors might sell personal property to their companies at extravagant prices. George Hudson, for example, sold 2,800 of his own Great North of England shares to the York, Newcastle and Berwick Railway of which he was chairman for a personal profit of £7,000. The market value of these shares was £21, though Hudson paid himself £23 10s per share.[71]

Different railway lines sometimes had almost identical boards of directors, though the interests of the different lines could be wildly at variance. Such was the case of the North Wales Railway and the Richmond Railway that came before the House of Lords in 1849. The North Wales Railway had lent £25,000 to the troubled Richmond Line on the flimsiest of security. The loan was a reckless use of shareholders' money, but the directors benefited since most of them were also on the Richmond board.[72] Hudson, the Railway King, was himself chairman of four railways with divergent interests. The falsity of Hudson's position became apparent in his various dealings with the Great Northern Railway. Two of Hudson's lines, the Midland and the Eastern Counties, were bitter rivals of the Great Northern while his other lines, the York and North Midland and the York, Newcastle and Berwick, wished to affiliate themselves with the Great Northern.[73] Men like Hudson profited from multiple directorships, but shareholders were ill-served by this juggling of interests.

Opportunities for fraud and chicanery, as well as the general lining of professional pockets depended upon the Railway Mania continuing unabated. White-collar crime thrived in a bull market where promotion followed promotion in a veritable Niagara of new companies. Above all else, the ball had to be kept rolling by launching fresh projects for expansion. Yet, as a few killjoys began pointing out in the autumn of 1845, the Mania could not be kept up indefinitely.

In October 1845, *The Economist* argued that the nation did not possess sufficient capital to pay for all proposed railway construction.[74] Even that capital already authorized by Parliament seemed impossible to raise. Parliament had authorized the creation of £59 million of new railway capital in 1845 and £132 million more in 1846, although the total annual income of the whole kingdom was estimated at no more than £200 million.[75] In November 1845 *The Times* estimated that the cost of an additional 620 new railway schemes was £563 million, or more than two-thirds of the total National Debt. This money could not be raised, *The Times* maintained, without "the most ruinous, universal, and desperate confusion."[76]

The construction of railway lines was proceeding faster than new traffic, while overspeculation guaranteed a steady stream of bubble promotions. Many proposed lines were redundant. According to *The Economist*, "we see nine or ten proposals for nearly the same line, all at a premium, when it is well known that only one can succeed, and the rest must, in all probability, be minus their expenses."[77] Such unrestrained speculation led *The Times* to characterize the Railway Mania as "a tale of national delusion."[78] Unfortunately, few investors heeded the handwriting on the wall.

In 1846 the Mania fizzled out. Over subscription had taken its toll and investors now sold shares to meet calls on other shares. Hundreds of proposed lines collapsed as their scrip became unsalable.[79] During the panic, Peel pushed through legislation requiring scripholders to meet before their Bills' third reading and decide whether or not they wished to continue the schemes. This Act facilitated the abandonment of new lines and prevented unscrupulous promoters from pushing through railways to the detriment of shareholders and the benefit of themselves. At this time, T.S. Duncombe also proposed stricter publicity requirements for railways, most of which the House acceded to. In the future, railway promoters had to inform Parliament of the source of their legislative deposit, the amount of shares retained by the provisional committee, and the amount of money (if any) that committee members paid on shares allotted them.[80]

As there is no sight like hindsight, the English public now regarded the Railway Mania as a monstrous plot for the extortion of money. After the crash, a number of newspapers and journals printed cartoons which showed savage, anthropomorphic trains devouring shareholders.[81] Literary depictions of the Mania were equally harsh. Mention has already been made of Robert Bell's *Ladder of Gold* (1850). In 1851 Emma Robinson dissected railway speculation in her allegorical novel *The Gold Worshippers*. Robinson tells the story of the railway magnate Humson and his accomplice Lawless who lead the Gullibul family to financial ruin.[82]

In his *History of the English Railway*, John Francis argued that "no other panic was ever so fatal to the middle class. It reached every hearth, it saddened every heart in the metropolis. Entire families were ruined."[83] No doubt there was much personal suffering. Even the Brontës in distant Haworth burned their fingers on shares of Hudson's York and North Midland Railway.[84] Yet it is important to remember that total losses were spread out over thousands of shareholders. In many cases shares had not been fully called-up. Numerous lines collapsed on which only a small part of the proposed capital had been subscribed.

The disappearance of so many bubble schemes at first seemed a blessing to the surviving railways. After a year or two, however, it became clear that the nation's traffic would not sustain the high dividends to which railway shareholders had grown accustomed. Investors also had difficulty meeting further calls and many had to sell shares in order to repay bankers' advances with which those very shares had been purchased. By the late 1840s railway share values had dropped precipitously. The twelve principal railway companies had paid an average dividend of 7.6% in 1846. By 1848 the average dividend had fallen to 5.3% and by 1849 to 3.2%. During the early 1850s, dividends hovered around the 3% mark.[85] As companies paid smaller dividends, irate shareholders began to scrutinize accounts more closely, and, in the late 1840s Committees of Investigation were set up at a number of railways. These committees uncovered an alarming amount of fraud and mismanagement, especially at the firms managed by George Hudson.

Hudson was the subject of major shareholders' investigations at the York and North Midland, the York, Newcastle and Berwick, and the Eastern Counties. In 1849 the York and North Midland Railway's Committee of Investigation released its report detailing Hudson's crimes. Under his chairmanship, no proper books and accounts had been kept and records of much company business reposed in Hudson's mind alone. Without company sanction, Hudson and the other directors had appropriated thousands of shares for themselves. Hudson also overstated traffic accounts and understated working charges so as to pay some £84,000 in unearned dividends. In 1845 Hudson resold 2,500 tons of rails to the Company for nearly twice the amount he had purchased them, for a personal profit of £14,000. The Company demanded from Hudson the return of dividends paid him on misappropriated shares and profits from the rail transaction. After years of squabbling and negotiation, Hudson returned £72,000 to the Company.[86]

The 1849 Report of the York, Newcastle and Berwick Railway told a similar tale. In 1845 Hudson, although entitled to only 900 shares in the original Newcastle and Berwick Line, appropriated 10,000 shares for himself, selling them for a profit of £145,000. In addition Hudson purchased for himself with company funds 2,300 shares in the Sunderland Dock Company. Hudson and his friends received dividends on shares they held without ever having paid the requisite deposit and calls. Some £26,000 meant to purchase shares in the Great North of England Company found its way into Hudson's bank account, allegedly by "error," and Hudson kept back another £30,000 intended for land purchases. Between 1844 and 1848, the Railway's books were falsified to the extent of

£122,000 in order to inflate the revenue account beyond its true state and pay higher dividends than were earned. Hudson also resold several tons of rails to the York, Newcastle and Berwick for a personal profit of £38,500. The Company eventually recovered £140,000 from Hudson, though only after numerous legal proceedings.[87]

The Eastern Counties' investigators also pilloried the Railway King in 1849. The Committee exposed Hudson's extravagant inflation of dividends to the horror of the financial community.[88] Investigators also found among the 1846 accounts, the sum of £7,600 listed as "Parliamentary Expenses." When questioned about this item, the directors replied that the money had been disbursed "for services rendered, and in a manner which did not leave them at liberty to give particulars, as they could not be given without implicating other parties." This was immediately interpreted as a confession of Parliamentary bribery, though the Commons later concluded that the money had been expended by Hudson and his fellow directors in an unauthorized attempt to merge with the London and York Railway.[89]

The revelations which emerged from these inquiries brought about Hudson's financial downfall, social disgrace and eventual exile from England. The nation's wrath now fell upon its former hero, as Hudson was made the scapegoat for all the crimes of the Railway Mania. That Hudson was unfairly singled out for blame was clear to many of his contemporaries. Carlyle declared: "One sordid, hungry *canaille* are they all. Why should this, the chief terrier among them, be set upon by all the dog fraternity?"[90] David Morier Evans argued that "numbers of persons equally guilty escaped public contumely, simply because they had not the misfortune to be found out."[91] Even *The Times* acknowledged: "Neither the other officials, nor the shareholders, must hope to escape censure under the cover of a personal onslaught upon Mr. Hudson. The system is to blame. It was a system without rule, without order, without even a definite morality."[92] Hudson's legitimate accomplishments were all but ignored by aggrieved shareholders thirsting for revenge. Yet the fact remains that George Hudson embodied many of the worst business practices of his day.

The Railway Mania had left a residue of great bitterness, though its financial legacy was even more significant. Railway share prices remained depressed throughout the 1850s. This was partly due to factors such as insufficient traffic and the injudicious location of lines, though most of the depreciation was related to the piratical policies of directors during the mid-forties. According to David Morier Evans: "For this depreciation reference must be made to the means taken by proprietors to enable them to divide among themselves millions of pounds sterling in the way of premiums, to the creation of nominal capital far exceeding the actual outlay, and to the exhaustive effects resulting from the highest allowable dividends being paid irrespective of legitimate receipts."[93]

For decades after the Mania, there was a tremendous loss of public confidence in railway building. Having been burned once, investors were wary of new lines, and for twenty years after the crash, promoters had the greatest trouble raising capital for new railways. Unfinished lines lacked the proper security to obtain bank loans and could only issue debentures (loan securities) to one third of their share capital and only after half that capital had been paid up and expended. Ironically, the very difficulty of raising new capital from the share market and banks led railway companies to resort to even more unorthodox methods of finance during the 1850s and 1860s.[94]

Promoters evaded the restrictions on debenture issue by falsifying their share capital. Railways now issued shares with nominal values greater than their real value, and then issued debentures to one third of the nominal capital. Railways were thus able to secure more funds, although debenture holders were led to believe that a company's security was greater than it really was, for much of the security (capital) existed only in name.[95]

During the 1860s, railway promoters also circumvented the 1844 prohibition on loan notes[96] by utilizing new credit instruments known as Lloyd's Bonds. A Lloyd's Bond was an acknowledgment by a company of a debt due to a contractor or merchant, with an agreement to pay the debt with a certain interest at a future date. Lloyd's Bonds were little more than glorified I.O.U.s, but the holders of these bonds used them as negotiable securities to raise money. The issuance of Lloyd's Bonds was not illegal, but their use was considered reckless and unethical by many in the financial community.[97]

Undoubtedly the most imprudent form of post-Mania railway finance involved paying contractors in the shares of a new line. Contractors would raise money on these "securities" (if shares in an unfinished line can be so-called) by discounting them through questionable firms known as Finance Companies. This form of speculative finance was to have disastrous consequences in the 1860s.[98]

Railway fraud obviously did not die with the Mania itself. Indeed, continual fraud was hardly surprising as promoters and directors were still largely unsupervised and auditing provisions remained weak. George Hudson and his ilk had ready successors after the crash.

In 1855, for example, the Eastern Counties Railway initiated an investigation which uncovered widespread fraud and mismanagement involving its Chairman David Waddington and other officers of the company. Ironically, Waddington had become Chairman in 1851 with the promise to rescue the railway from Hudson's corrupting influence. The accountants Quilter and Ball had a different story to tell. Their examination of the company's books showed that Waddington had paid dividends out of capital à la Hudson. In 1855 alone, Waddington authorized a dividend of more than £55,000 although company revenue for the year was only £19,000. He even abandoned the Permanent Way Fund for the upkeep of the line and improperly applied the money for dividends. Waddington increased company debt through loans obtained illegally without shareholders' knowledge or permission. Under his administration there was no competitive bidding for contracts. Contracts for materials went at exorbitant prices to companies in which Eastern Counties directors had interests or to relatives of directors.[99]

Slipshod bookkeeping and auditing were hallmarks of Eastern Counties' management. Nathaniel Davis, Treasurer of the railway, often deposited company funds into his own private bank account for the payment of company debts. He kept no books detailing these operations, and, while no one suspected him of fraud, there were no safeguards against this. The clerk in charge of the Stores Department, Mr. Williams, also used his private bank account for purchasing, and Williams overcharged the company thousands of pounds. Somewhere between £10,000 and £40,000 was lost in this manner; the embezzlement could not be calculated more precisely since records were horribly kept. Williams purchased timber from his brother-in-law at inflated prices and the books of the Stores Department seem never to have been audited. Waddington also kept back certain books from the auditors but these worthy gentlemen never objected. Indeed, the auditors were so lax in their duties that they only visited the company twice in the half-year for a few hours at a time.[100]

Perhaps the most notorious company fraud of the 1850s involved the embezzlements of Leopold Redpath, Registrar of the Great Northern Railway. Over the course of ten years Redpath defrauded the railway of some £240,000. Redpath used his ill-gotten gains to maintain a lavish lifestyle including a town house in Regent's Park and a country house at Weybridge. He also gave generously to charities and served as a governor of Christ's Hospital and the Royal Society of St. Anne. Redpath's employers became alarmed when they learned of his extravagance since they knew it could not be supported by his £300 annual salary. In 1856 the Great Northern Railway launched an investigation which uncovered the full extent of Redpath's crimes. He was found guilty of embezzlement and transported for life.[101]

As Registrar of the Great Northern Railway, Redpath had access to the share books and share transfer deeds of the company. Redpath knew that once stock was entered upon the company's books, it could be dealt with almost like cash, and yet the company did not exercise the same care over its books as it did over coins. Redpath thus forged share transfers with fictitious names to create some £220,000 of fraudulent stock. Redpath sold much of this stock, though he kept some to receive dividend payments. Redpath's frauds were unwittingly assisted by the company's directors who cut back the clerks in Redpath's department in an attempt to save money.[102]

The company's auditors were oblivious to Redpath's defalcations. After Redpath had been swindling the railway for three years, the auditors presented the directors with the following statement:

Gentlemen, The accounts and books in every department continue to be so satisfactorily kept, that we have simply to express our entire approval of them, and to present them to you for the information of the shareholders, with our usual certificate of correctness.[103]

By 1854 the auditors were aware that dividend payments were not in accordance with the authorized capital upon which payments were due, but they continued to declare the accounts correct. It later transpired that the auditors had never examined the registration books, and moreover, had never conceived it their duty to examine them! The professional accountant William Deloitte had to be brought in to untangle Redpath's web of deception.[104] At the company's half-yearly meeting in March 1857, an irate shareholder asked:

Of what earthly use are auditors at all to us? It is manifest that they have been useless. I have, year by year, attempted to show what a miserable farce it is to have these gentlemen as auditors. When there is any real work to be done, they employ a professional auditor; and then these gentlemen come down and sign their names, declaring that they have nothing to do with the registration department. I say these gentlemen have manifestly neglected their duty.[105]

In the light of Redpath's fraud, a number of railway companies made radical changes in bookkeeping procedures. Most companies left the issue of share certificates in the hands of the Registration Department, but greatly increased the paperwork of that Department. The North Eastern Railway, for example, now required four separate books for entering certificates, each employing different clerks. The Midland Railway had its accountant keep a separate record of certificates as an independent check against the Registrar's books. William Grinling, Redpath's successor at the Great Northern, devised a system of cross checks, whereby transfers were checked against share certificates, the share register was checked against the balance books, and dividends were checked against the share register.[106] Some companies even kept a Forged Transfer Reserve Fund to provide for a possible Redpath. The London, Midland and Scottish Railway maintained just such a reserve until it was nationalized in 1947.[107]

While frauds such as Redpath's caused railways to better supervise employees, directors continued to remain largely unsupervised, and the feeble nature of railway legislation did little to hinder them from unauthorized borrowing or paying unearned dividends. In 1849 the Parliamentary Committee on the Audit of Railway Accounts had recommended standardized balance sheets for all railways as well as the publication of more rigorously detailed accounts. The railway interest lobbied against the Bill arguing (improbably, in the light of so many criminal revelations) that shareholders already had sufficient powers to supervise directors. The government capitulated to this pressure and let the Bill drop.[108]

Only after the Commercial Crisis of 1866 exposed the rottenness of much railway finance did companies reconcile themselves to greater publicity.[109] In 1868 the Regulation of Railways Act was passed, specifying for the first time uniform standards for published accounts. Balance sheets now had to make the all important distinction between revenue and capital. The more detailed contents of railway accounts gave directors less facility for manipulating company funds.[110]

The pattern of railway regulation was similar to that of business generally, with early government restrictions giving way in the mid-1840s to policies of *laissez-faire* and *caveat emptor*. In railway matters, however, the government became increasingly intrusive from the late 1860s. The unique and vital function of railways seemed to justify greater state interference than in other businesses, where the spirit of free trade remained unfettered until very late in the century.

The Railway Mania in all its excess exemplified the new scale of industrial finance and the new kinds of fraud which were to plague the modern English economy. The Mania and the corporations it engendered demonstrated the fraudulent possibilities of company promotion, share dealing and the day to day management of big business. Railway fraud was the harbinger of Victorian white-collar crime, and men such as Hudson and Redpath the prototypes of the criminal capitalist.

CHAPTER 3

Banking and credit fraud

For most of the Victorian period, the English banking system was riddled with fraud and mismanagement. Each wave of bank failures brought forth new revelations of criminal conduct. The financial crises of 1857 and 1866 and the collapse of the City of Glasgow Bank in 1878 were but the high-water marks in an age of widespread commercial dishonesty. By the late nineteenth and early twentieth centuries, improvements in bank management and accountancy had reduced the level of fraud, though by no means had eliminated it.

Banking lies at the heart of the modern commercial nexus. As Thomas Joplin, founder of the National Provincial Bank, wrote in 1827: "Banks are by far the most important of all our commercial establishments. They are the fountains of our currency, the depositories of our capital, and at once the wheels and pillars of our trade. Business to any great extent could not be carried on without them."[1] For the greater part of the nineteenth century, banks were the most important type of joint-stock company after railways. Between 1844 and 1868, 291 banks were formed. Banking promotions peaked in the early sixties, 36.4% of the capital offered to the public and 27% of subscribed capital was from banks and finance companies in the years between 1863 and 1866. In 1844 total bank capital and deposits for the nation amounted to some £139 million or 34% of national income. The bulk of these deposits was in the form of small sums from a very large number of customers. From the 1840s onwards, bankers held in trust for shareholders and depositors enormous sums of money which they invested in securities or lent to commercial enterprise.[2]

Despite their financial importance, banks were plagued by amateurish management throughout the nineteenth century.[3] Anyone could establish a bank, regardless of experience. Banking legislation was overwhelmingly concerned with the issuance of currency, and not with principles of sound management. The only attempt at regulation, the Joint-Stock Bank Act of 1844, effectively halted the promotion of new banks until its repeal in 1857, but did nothing to improve the operation of those banks already in existence.[4] Indeed, the 1840s and 1850s were the heyday of bank failures and bank fraud. Many banks did bad business – discounting doubtful bills and lending on questionable security. All banks tended to keep too little of their assets realizable. They lent out too much money, and, thus in times of commercial distress or panic, numbers of banks would fail. Directors had great latitude as to the investment of bank funds, and no responsibilities of public disclosure. The magnitude of deposits proved an irresistible temptation to many bankers who treated bank funds as their personal property. For most of the nineteenth century, English finance and English credit rested on the shakiest of foundations.[5]

The image of the upright and incorruptible Victorian banker is a recent invention. The respectable businessman was a rare character in nineteenth-century literature, where financiers were usually depicted as worshippers of Mammon.[6] In Victorian novels, the banker was more often than not a villain. A good example of this phenomenon can be found in Catherine Gore's 1846 novel, *The Banker's Wife*. Gore, a popular writer all but forgotten in this century, created the nefarious Richard Hamlyn, a banker whose "whole life was a system of semblance – of careful and consistent deceit." To bolster his ailing firm, Hamlyn embezzled customers' money, bringing ruin upon many quiet-living families. One character concludes that "the trade of banking incrusts a man's soul with yellow leprosy."[7] Mention should also be made of Bulstrode, George Eliot's disreputable banker from *Middlemarch*, and Dickens' fraudulent banker, Mr. Merdle, from *Little Dorrit*. Merdle, who is honored as the greatest financier of his age – the veritable "eighth wonder of the world" – is ultimately exposed as "the greatest Forger and the greatest Thief that ever cheated the gallows." Having deceived a gullible public, Merdle ends his infamous career by slitting his throat with a pen-knife.[8]

Such characterizations are almost mild when compared to the bankers of the Victorian stage. The banker was the stereotypical villain of melodrama – the forecloser of mortgages, the despoiler of widows and orphans. He appeared as a menacing presence in a black cape and top hat, twirling his black mustachio with one hand and brandishing a notice of eviction with the other. Typical of the genre is the grasping banker Gideon Bloodgood in *The Poor of New York*, a melodrama by the Anglo-Irish playwright Dion Boucicault. In the play, Bloodgood saves his insolvent firm by stealing $100,000 from a dying man. No tender feelings hinder him from his pursuit of riches. We later learn that Bloodgood corners the market in flour, raising bread prices and reducing thousands to starvation.[9] Although such portraits were drawn with broad strokes, they reflected a popular mistrust of the financier and were based on a real incidence of white-collar crime.

In the 1840s, some of the most alarming bank frauds involved savings banks. Savings banks had existed as early as the eighteenth century, but at that time they were private philanthropic institutions. In 1817, to encourage thrift among the lower classes, the government passed an Act which empowered the National Debt Commissioners to pay 4% interest on all sums deposited with them by savings banks.[10] From time to time Acts were passed lowering the interest and restricting the amount of money a person could deposit, as it was discovered that middle-class persons were monopolizing the banks. By the 1840s there were some 500 government savings banks in the United Kingdom with one million depositors and total deposits of £30 million.[11] The Act of 1817 had intended that deposits be invested in government securities, but in practice managers had sole control of bank funds. This system resulted in a large amount of fraud and a false sense of security among depositors.

One of the earliest frauds to come to light was that of George Haworth, manager of the Rochdale Savings Bank. At Haworth's death in 1849 it was discovered that over the course of ten years he had systematically embezzled £71,000 from the bank. Haworth had been a wool trader and an agent for Guinness who always claimed that he acted as manager "as a matter of charity." It appears he was the charity. Altogether he absorbed nearly two-thirds of bank deposits. Haworth's estate brought in £16,000 and trustees subscribed £17,000, reducing depositors losses to £38,000. Of the sufferers, 1,014 were women, 539 laboring men, 191 sick clubs, and 1,184 under twenty-one years of age. Haworth had avoided detection by keeping two sets of books – one for the money he handed over to the trustees and one for the money he kept.[12]

Following the revelations at Rochdale, the government ordered the examination of all savings banks. In 1852 a Parliamentary return disclosed that some £160,000 had been lost to eighteen savings banks as a result of fraud between 1844 and 1851.[13] Investigation also uncovered an extraordinary carelessness in management and book-keeping. Trustees, it was found, seldom if ever supervised managers. Books submitted each year to the National Debt Office contained a number of glaring mistakes which nobody ever checked. Ledgers from the Cuffe Street Bank, for example, listed 320 accounts of between £100 and £150. Total deposits were then given as £13,173 when they had to have totaled £32,000 at the very least.[14]

Notwithstanding the warnings of the 1852 Report, savings bank fraud continued. In 1853 William Wheeler Yelf, manager of the Isle of Wight Bank, was found to have embezzled over £8,000 through forged checks. Had the trustees ever compared the forgeries against the bank ledger, the fraud would have been discovered. The trustees even allowed Yelf, a Wesleyan preacher, to inspect the bank's books – which he invariably pronounced sound.[15]

Depositors in savings banks believed that their money was guaranteed by the government, but in fact the guarantee only covered money received by the trustees. If the bank's manager embezzled money before it had been handed over to the trustees, that money was unprotected by law.[16] In response to savings bank frauds Gladstone sponsored an Act in 1861 which established a system of Post-Office Savings Banks to afford small depositors a safe outlet for thrift. Accounts could be between 1s and £150, interest was at 2.5%, and deposits were unconditionally guaranteed by the government.[17]

While the public had been alarmed by savings bank fraud, it was even more distressed by extensive crimes at the large banks of deposit. The 1840s and 1850s were a period of widespread bank fraud and of mismanagement amounting to fraud. As *The Economist* observed in 1857:

When a bank fails, if it be a private partnership, it always turns out that some of the parties have wasted the depositors' money in speculations, altogether extraneous from the business of the bank, or in a long course of extravagant living; – if a joint-stock concern, in nine cases out of ten the directors have abused their trust, and have made the money of the shareholders and depositors subservient only to their own uses.[18]

Since effectual supervision by the entire board of directors was difficult if not impossible, the bank's business often fell into the hands of a single manager or a few of the directors. In such cases, there was no effective check against fraud.

In 1840 the Commercial Bank of England failed with liabilities of £2 million. Irresponsible directors had used bank funds for their private expenses, bad debts had been treated as assets and dividends were paid when the bank was losing money. In 1841 the Marylebone Bank failed with liabilities of £85,000. It was discovered that the dishonest manager had misappropriated bank shares and embezzled at least £12,000 of bank money. The Bank of Manchester failed in 1842 with a loss to shareholders of £1 million. Indolent directors had left the bank's affairs to the manager who then embezzled the bank's entire capital and reserves. The North of England Joint Stock Banking Company failed in 1847 for £2,200,000. Incompetent and dishonest directors had squandered the bank's capital and deposits on reckless speculations and the insolvent businesses of friends. A false appearance of prosperity was maintained by issuing dividends. In 1851 directors of the Sunderland Bank were found to have taken up the bank's entire capital of £132,000 for their personal use. In 1855 directors of the Shropshire Banking Company discovered that the manager and chief cashier had embezzled some £200,000 over the course of thirteen years, keeping the deficiencies secret by means of false ledgers and false balance sheets.[19] This litany of frauds and failures illustrates an utter disregard for principles of sound banking. Apart from outright embezzlements, advances were made against inadequate security, incomplete accounts kept, and unearned dividends paid out. The exposure of dishonest banking heightened in the mid-fifties, at which time there were a number of enormous frauds.

The first of these large frauds, and the most shocking to contemporaries, was that of Strahan, Paul and Bates, a centuries old, highly respected firm of private bankers. In 1855 the bank failed for £750,000. The partners, William Strahan, Sir John Dean Paul and Robert Bates were subsequently charged with misappropriating customers' money to cover their losses. At the trial it was revealed that the firm had been insolvent for a number of years, owing mainly to bad debts from collieries. In 1854 the partners had tried to raise loans on securities which depositors had lodged with them for safe-keeping. Failing this, the bankers actually sold over £100,000 of these securities. All three men were convicted and sentenced to fourteen years transportation. In pronouncing judgment, Mr. Baron Alderson observed: "A greater and more serious offense can hardly be imagined in a great commercial city like this. It tends to shake confidence in all persons in the position you occupied, and it has shaken the public confidence in establishments like that you for a long period honourably conducted."[20] Perhaps the most bizarre detail of this case was the fact that the writer Catherine Gore had been the ward of Sir John Dean Paul – the father of the convicted banker and former head of the firm. Shortly after Gore published her novel about a fraudulent banker, the younger Paul embarked on his own criminal career. Gore herself lost £20,000 in the failure of the bank.[21]

Only two months after the Strahan, Paul and Bates trial, the nation was shocked anew by the exposure of John Sadleir's frauds at the Tipperary Joint-Stock Bank. As director of the bank, Sadleir had embezzled some £200,000. Another £400,000 was lost when the bank suspended payment. Sadleir had come to London in 1846 as an agent for Irish railway schemes. Augmenting his directorship of the Tipperary Bank, Sadleir became Chairman of the London and County Bank and the Royal Swedish Railway. Elected to Parliament, he was a spokesman for business interests and was eventually appointed a Lord of the Treasury. As it later transpired, Sadleir had built his vaunted financial reputation on a series of monstrous impostures. Besides his embezzlements from the Tipperary Bank, he issued fictitious shares in the Swedish Railway to the extent of £150,000. While a member of the Irish Encumbered Estates Commission, Sadleir also forged title deeds to a number of properties. Rumors of his misfeasance had forced his resignation from the Treasury and the London and County Bank, and the crash of the Tipperary Bank in January of 1856 laid bare his crimes. Sadleir immediately committed suicide, his career inspiring Dickens to create the character of Mr. Merdle.[22]

Embezzlements at the Tipperary Joint-Stock Bank had been concealed from shareholders by a series of false balance sheets representing the bank to be in the most flourishing condition. In a letter written to his brother in December of 1855, Sadleir detailed the creative bookkeeping which at the time was practiced not only by himself, but by most banks:

My Dear James, The accounts should be made out treating the paid-up capital as £100,000 on the 31st of December, 1855 . . .
By this means the present English shareholders will double their present holdings in the Tipperary Bank, and I dare say the balance of the £100,000 of stock will be quickly taken up.
Now, I know many of the English joint-stock banks, in order to give a good appearance to their balance, have constantly trebled the amount of their balance, &c., by making a series of entries, whereby they appeared to have assets and liabilities to four times the amount they really possessed or had. This has always been kept very quiet, and what at first was a kind of fiction became gradually to be *bona fide*.[23]

Upon the faith of such false statements, a number of small tradesmen and farmers became shareholders in the bank, and, in consequence, were completely ruined.

On the very heels of Sadleir's demise, the Royal British Bank failed amid revelations that the bank manager, Hugh Cameron, and two directors, Humphrey Brown and Edward Esdaile, had wasted the bank's resources in unsecured loans to themselves and their friends. Sadleir had implicated the Royal British directors in a letter which was published after his suicide and which caused a run on the bank. It transpired that Cameron, Brown and Esdaile had kept a separate ledger into which they entered certain accounts. From this bank within the bank, the men made advances to themselves and their friends without regard to security. On becoming a director in 1853, Humphrey Brown opened an account at the bank for £18 14s upon the faith of which that same day he borrowed £2,000. Brown was eventually indebted to the bank for £70,000. At the time of the failure, the directors had exhausted the entire £158,000 subscribed by the shareholders along with £500,000 of additional debt. As one contemporary observer noted, the directors "suddenly and unexpectedly found themselves in the all but uncontrolled command of unlimited funds, and the temptation to use them for their own private purposes was irresistible."[24]

In effect there was little difference between the actions of the Royal British Bank directors and the crimes of Sadleir or of Strahan, Paul and Bates, though *technically* the Royal British directors had not embezzled bank funds – they had made "loans" to themselves. Cameron, Brown and Esdaile could only be tried for the lesser crime of issuing false reports since, in the course of their activities, they had falsified balance sheets and bribed an auditor with £2,000. The men received sentences varying from one year to three months, most of which were never served in their entirety. In pronouncing sentence, Justice Lord Campbell regretted to say that in mitigation of the offense "it was said that it was a common practice."[25] Once again shareholders had been duped by their lack of accurate information regarding a bank's affairs. As the *Bankers' Magazine* concluded, "the history of the Royal British Bank proves how utterly futile is the dependence upon directorial reports, published and audited accounts, or even the payment of respectable dividends, as the criterion of the prosperity or the solvency of a joint-stock bank."[26]

In the spring of 1857 two more important bank frauds came to light. Henry Salmon, manager of the Falkirk Branch of the Commercial Bank of Scotland, committed suicide upon the discovery that he had embezzled over £25,000 through the use of duplicate books.[27] W. Petrie Waugh, director of the London and Eastern Banking Corporation, fled abroad when it was discovered that he had "borrowed" from the bank £244,000 – almost the entire subscribed capital – to support his insolvent brick works. Thousands were lent to other London and Eastern directors on the flimsiest security and false statements were released to shareholders claiming that the bank's capital was invested in good securities.[28]

The escalating bank frauds of the 1850s culminated in the Banking Crisis of 1857. The Crisis originated in the United States, where railway securities fell dramatically in 1856, bringing down a number of American banks. In turn this led to the failure of British banks and bill brokers who held American securities. The Crisis was particularly severe in northern cities which had strong links to the American market. The collapse of major banks in Scotland, Liverpool and Newcastle in the autumn precipitated a nationwide panic which peaked in a run on banks in England and Scotland.[29] In the aftermath of the Crisis, investigations revealed an alarming amount of banking fraud. At the time, David Morier Evans noted:

Cases of mere overspeculation form the most agreeable part of the picture; the darker portion being filled with the records of fraud, and of a recklessness which was equivalent to fraud. A long succession of firms could be passed in review, in which assets and liabilities seem like so many figures, selected for no other object than that of illustrating a strong disproportion.[30]

A Parliamentary Investigation of the 1857 Crisis focused on the failures of three major banks: the Western Bank of Scotland, the Northumberland and Durham District Bank and the Borough Bank of Liverpool. In a report issued in 1858, the Commons catalogued a litany of abuses including fictitious bills, false reports, manufactured dividends and advances made on doubtful security.[31] The Liverpool Bank was the first to fail, with losses of almost £1 million – mostly in bad bills. Only three of the bank's twelve directors knew anything about the bank's affairs, and even these three paid scant attention to business. Discounting was left almost wholly to the manager, who loaned out the bank's money with no attention to proper security. To conceal a state of insolvency, the bank paid dividends out of capital. £50,000 was distributed to shareholders in 1857, although the bank was then operating at a loss.[32]

The Northumberland and Durham District Bank of Newcastle failed in November of 1857 with losses of £2,600,000. Almost £1 million of the bank's liabilities was debt from the Derwent Iron Company – a firm in which the bank's managing director, Jonathan Richardson, held a key interest. £400,000 in bad debts were listed in the bank's accounts as assets. To further produce an illusion of prosperity, dividends were paid out of capital.[33] In describing the bank's management, one contemporary declared that "acts of such stupendous folly have been rarely witnessed beyond the walls of a madhouse."[34]

Like the other banks, the Western Bank of Scotland also gave out too much money on inadequate security. The bank's entire capital and then some – almost £2 million – had been lent to only four firms, all of which became insolvent. One of the firms, MacDonald and Company, had £260,000 in bills lodged with the bank which were represented to shareholders as assets, although a confidential memo among directors said that this sum was irrecoverable. A shareholders' Committee of Investigation found that the Western Bank had repeatedly paid dividends out of capital, including a dividend of 9% only months before the bank failed. The directors also pursued the foolhardy policy of taking out life insurance on its debtors as a means of (eventually) recovering bad debts. In this way tens of thousands of bank funds were tied up in premiums to insurance companies. Not surprisingly, the Committee of Investigation concluded that "the directors of the bank have been much to blame in neglecting to perform the ordinary duties incumbent upon them on the acceptance of such a trust."[35]

As has been noted, many bank failures, both during the 1857 Crisis and before, were the result of credit abuses. Bankers sometimes betrayed their positions of trust by utilizing banks' credit facilities for themselves and their friends. In other cases, banks were defrauded by outside merchants and businessmen who borrowed money under false pretenses, often by means of fictitious bills of exchange or false collateral. The increased use of paper securities such as commercial bills, letters of credit and dock warrants expanded the opportunities for financial fraud, and the abuse of these credit instruments was a perennial problem during the Victorian era.

The principal instrument of credit during the nineteenth century was the bill of exchange. In its simplest form, a bill of exchange was a promise of payment between two parties. The person responsible for payment was the acceptor and the person to be paid the payee. Payment could be on demand or, as was more common, at some future date. A tradesman, for example, would give a merchant a bill in exchange for goods, the goods would be sold, and money from the sale would go to the merchant when the bill fell due. Bills were fully negotiable, and our hypothetical merchant might well transfer his bill at a discount to a third party, or endorser – so called because he would endorse the bill by writing his name across it. Bills could be endorsed indefinitely, changing hands many times before payment was due.[36]

Besides having a commercial function, bills could also serve as financial instruments when sold as a means of raising money or offered as collateral for loans. With the growth of banking, the use of bills of exchange was greatly facilitated and discounting bills became a major avenue for the investment of bank funds. Banks bought bills to accommodate businessmen, and for this service, charged interest, or "discount." The larger the bill, or the longer the time before it fell due, the greater the discount banks charged. Early in the nineteenth century, brokers specializing in bills of exchange emerged as a distinct group in the money market. Bill brokers advised bankers what bills were safest to accept and they borrowed money from banks to discount bills themselves. To raise money, banks would sometimes rediscount their bills through brokers. By the mid-nineteenth century, large bill-broking firms like Overend and Gurney were an integral part of English finance, providing bankers with both a channel for investment and a source of funds.[37]

Victorian businessmen were quick to avail themselves of the innovations in credit. As Walter Bagehot observed in *Lombard Street*: "In modern English business, owing to the certainty of obtaining loans on discount of bills or otherwise at a moderate rate of interest, there is a steady bounty of trading with borrowed capital, and a constant discouragement to confine yourself solely or mainly to your own capital."[38] Bagehot gave the example of a merchant trading on his own capital of £50,000 being undersold by a merchant trading with £10,000 of his own capital and £40,000 borrowed at 5% interest. Supposing that both men make a 10% profit, or £5,000, the borrower has actually made a 30% profit on his own capital. He can then forgo some profit, lower his prices, and outsell the other merchant. Under such conditions, credit facilities were much in demand.

The proliferation of credit during the Victorian period generated a number of problems. Creditors were often at difficulties in determining the solvency of prospective borrowers. In an economy of national scale, businessmen were not intimately known to all with whom they did business, and information as to credit-worthiness was easily manipulated. Borrowers could mislead lenders with falsified financial statements, fraudulent securities or even with a mere appearance of respectability. Credit remained a fragile entity highly dependent on trust. In Bagehot's words, "credit is a set of promises to pay – will those promises be kept?"[39]

Perhaps the most common form of fraudulent borrowing was the false accommodation bill, as described by Herbert Spencer in *The Morals of Trade*.[40] Under this method, two traders conspired to raise money by accepting bills for one another for "goods received" when in fact nothing had changed hands. The bill broker or bank which discounted the bills was thus deceived that the bills were backed by collateral. Such securities were known in City parlance as "pig-upon-bacon" bills. When these bills fell due, if the conspirators did not have money to pay, they would repeat their fraudulent transactions. So long as money was cheap, it was easy to keep up the charade. Indeed, an increased number of bills, bearing respectable endorsements, created confidence and facilitated further extensions of credit. The whole process, however, required constant maintenance to pay interest on due bills, and it encouraged reckless speculation to realize money. Unfortunately such unorthodox financing was all too common, causing one observer in the 1860s to lament: "Those persons who have not been behind the scenes of that great mercantile theatre called the City during the last three or four years, will find it extremely difficult to believe how much falsehood, how much paper credit, and how little substantial foundation, appertain to a vast number of our mercantile houses."[41] Some borrowers obtained credit on thin air, others on varying degrees of inadequate security – almost all did so beyond their ability to repay.

A remarkable example of credit fraud from mid-century can be found in the actions of MacDonald and Co., a firm of Glasgow muslin merchants. MacDonald's created a vast array of fictitious bills meant to represent genuine trade as a means of obtaining money. The firm found acceptors for its fictitious bills from a confidence man in London who specialized in providing men of straw for such transactions. MacDonald's then discounted these bills with bankers and brokers to the extent of hundreds of thousands of pounds. The crash of the Western Bank of Scotland in 1857 was largely due to its extension of credit to MacDonald's and other firms which employed false accommodation bills.[42]

In 1860, the bankruptcy of the nation's largest leather company, Streatfield, Laurence and Mortimore, revealed that a great deal of the English leather trade had been conducted on a system of fictitious credits. Streatfield's failed for £980,000 bringing down thirty other leather firms with total liabilities of almost £3 million. For years these firms had employed agents to draw up and accept fictitious bills. The Leather Crisis revealed how easily credit fraud could become institutionalized.[43]

Another credit instrument which proved vulnerable to abuse was the dock warrant, or title to merchandise stored in warehouses. Dock warrants facilitated the movement of commodities and could also be used as collateral for loans. It was this latter, financial, function which presented unscrupulous traders with opportunities for fraud. During the 1850s, for example, Joseph Windle Cole borrowed hundreds of thousands of pounds upon warrants representing non-existent goods. Cole also duplicated genuine warrants to increase his borrowing potential. In the words of D.M. Evans, so complicated were these frauds that: "Cole kept a strong force of clerks, whose business it was to check the double lists of warrants, so that no duplicates of similar goods should fall into the same hands, to intermix the warrants, genuine and fictitious, and to advise him on loans falling due."[44] Cole was only exposed when some creditors discovered his warehouses were empty. At Cole's trial the commercial world was further astonished by the revelation that David Chapman, a partner of the famous discounting house Overend and Gurney, had known of Cole's frauds for some time but kept silent. In a telling illustration of Victorian business ethics, Chapman had concealed Cole's crimes in the hopes of reimbursement for Overend and Gurney which had advanced some £400,000 to Cole and his accomplices.[45]

Credit fraud flourished in a world of imperfect financial information. It was often difficult for bankers and brokers to assess the quality of bills presented for discount or securities pledged as collateral. Many bankers, however, did not even attempt to evaluate securities, especially during times of easy money when investment outlets were eagerly sought after. Dishonest traders soon realized that discount houses and banks lent money on securities without thoroughly examining the documents tendered, except to see that they were properly signed and endorsed. As long as interest on the loans was repaid, the securities were virtually ignored. The Western Bank of Scotland, for example, had typically failed to examine most of the bills it discounted. Although bills discounted for MacDonald and Company in 1857 bore acceptances from 124 different parties, only thirty-seven of them had been inquired into by the bank. Twenty-one of these inquiries resulted in negative evaluations of the acceptors, but the bank still declined none of the bills.[46]

Witnesses before the Commons Banking Committee in 1858 complained that a system of "open credits" was developing, whereby country banks advanced money without collateral or security.[47] According to the eminent accountant John Ball:

The great bulk of failures that have come under my notice have originated from the circumstances of bills having been accepted by houses in the country to a very large extent without receiving any previous value for them, but trusting to the standing of the houses on whose account they were accepted to provide for them when they should become due.[48]

London discount houses also recklessly rediscounted the bills of country banks solely upon the banks' endorsements, with no reference to the quality of the bills.[49] The abundance of money available for lending was only matched by the carelessness with which it was lent.

The 1858 Report of the Select Committee on Banking made it clear that the public had no real guide to the solvency of banks. False balance sheets and manufactured dividends gave the lie to the ideal of safety through publicity. Kirkman Hodgson, a director of the Bank of England, admitted to the Committee that, in the absence of honor and integrity on the part of bank directors, the law gave the public no protection.[50] The British government, however, was increasingly reluctant to intrude itself into company affairs. The principles of *laissez-faire* which had triumphed in railway legislation and the Company Acts of 1855 and 1856 also made themselves felt in banking matters. Rather than strengthening the audit or appointing government bank inspectors, Parliament hoped to offer bank shareholders a greater measure of protection through the limitation of liability. In 1857 joint-stock banks were given the same privileges of limited liability that had already been extended to most other types of joint-stock enterprise.[51] Most established banks, however, declined to limit their liability arguing that their goodwill rested on unlimited liability. New banks also hesitated to lessen their liability for fear that they would be unable to compete for customers with the older, unlimited banks.[52]

Despite their unlimited status, and despite the high incidence of fraud, banks were never at a loss for shareholders. Risks ran high, but so too did dividends. According to figures published by *The Economist*, between 1847 and 1857, the London joint-stock banks issued dividends that averaged 10%. The highest single dividend was 22% by the London Joint Stock Bank in 1857.[53] This was at a time when 3% was considered a reasonable return for one's investment and 5% a good return. Clapham has noted that "ghosts of fraudulent joint-stock banks haunted the Victorian mind."[54] While this is undoubtedly true, investors' fears do not seem to have affected their actions.

After 1862, when banks were put on the same footing as other joint-stock companies, there was a boom in new promotions. Between 1863 and 1866, 108 banks and finance companies were incorporated.[55] The Finance Company, the latest and most significant development in the money market, represented almost half of these new promotions. Modeled on French banking innovations, especially the *Credit Mobilier*, finance companies specialized in long-term credit.[56]

The chief impetus for finance companies came from the railways, which were experiencing great difficulty attracting investors on account of the shocking revelations and general depression of share prices following the Railway Mania. The lag time between the promotion of new railways and profit from completed lines also continued to deter investors, who wanted a quick return for their money. In many cases railway companies were unable to complete their lines with the subscribed capital, and the only security they possessed was the partially completed line. Banks would not advance money in such circumstances, but finance companies were not so scrupulous. A railway would deposit bills drawn upon its unfinished lines with a finance company, and upon that "security" would obtain the money needed to finish the work. Finance companies, however, did not give out cash; they acted as intermediaries between debtors and the general discount market. The railway, or its contractor, would have to draw up another set of bills upon the finance company; these would be accepted and taken elsewhere to discount. For such a transaction, a finance company would charge as much as 10% – a handy profit for the mere use of its name.[57]

By their very nature, finance companies dealt in securities unacceptable to banks. Long-term lending on promissory bills was the most fragile of credit transactions. As *The Economist* argued: "A bill of exchange drawn in reality against an unfinished work is a pure speculation on the possibility of that public work yielding a dividend on its cost, and finding purchasers in detail for its bonds and shares is not therefore a proper instrument in any sense for Lombard St. purposes."[58] The boards of the new-fashioned finance companies were largely inexperienced in banking matters, and their ethical standards were not always of the highest caliber. Albert Grant, one of the less reputable company promoters, pressured debtors of his finance company to take up its shares if they wanted their loans extended.[59] Almost all finance companies lent recklessly and indiscriminately. Again, *The Economist* lamented:

. . . lenders are running about after borrowers. So many Banks and Credit Companies are beginning work, that they are at a loss for customers to begin upon. Petty contractors, makers of Welsh railways and so forth, are obtaining large advances from new institutions; and we confess to great doubts whether such advances ought to be given, or whether they will ever be repaid.[60]

The house of cards collapsed in 1866. The money market had lost confidence in the evanescent credit transactions of the finance companies, unsecured bills could no longer be discounted, contractors failed, and the panic became a full-fledged commercial crisis with the failure on Black Friday – May 11, 1866 – of the renowned discount house Overend, Gurney and Company.[61] The 1866 Financial Crisis destroyed most of the finance companies outright. In the wake of the failures, aggrieved shareholders condemned the free and easy policies of their boards of directors. Albert Grant, for one, was forced to pay large sums to his company to avoid legal proceedings. Others were not so fortunate, and in February 1869, the six directors of Overend and Gurney were indicted for defrauding shareholders of £3 million.[62]

The trial of the Overend and Gurney directors centered on allegations that they had concealed from shareholders the true state of the company's affairs. After the 1866 crash, it was revealed that the old, private bill-broking firm Overend and Gurney had fallen on hard times during the 1850s due to a series of bad loans. In an attempt to stave off ruin, the business was floated as a public, limited company in 1865. Due to the firm's celebrated reputation, the floatation was fully subscribed, bringing in millions in new capital. The prospectus, however, had not disclosed the insolvency of the old firm. This sin of omission led shareholders to resist paying claims of almost £5 million against the now bankrupt company on the grounds that they had become members due to false information. The courts eventually rejected the shareholders' plea, and, to add insult to injury, the directors were acquitted of fraud. The shareholders only had moral force on their side, the directors the inadequate provisions of company law which failed to specify the contents of prospectuses. Overend's shareholders consequently lost millions of pounds, and the company's debts were not fully discharged until 1893.[63]

The Financial Crisis of 1866 represents a watershed in the English banking community. During the period from the 1840s through the 1860s, banks had the highest attrition rate of any type of joint-stock company. Of the 291 banks formed between 1844 and 1868, only 49 or 16% remained in operation at the end date.[64] The instability of the banking system was compounded by problems of fraud and misfeasance. From the 1870s onwards, however, English banks were generally better run than their early Victorian counterparts. A number of developments after mid-century helped increase banking security and reduce the level of fraud. Improved accounting methods made it more difficult for bank employees to conceal embezzlements and the tradition of amateurism in bank management was giving way to a new professionalism.[65]

The banking frauds and failures of the mid-Victorian period were the legacy of careless administration. Too often boards of directors viewed their positions as sinecures, abdicating their collective responsibility to a few among their number or to a single bank manager. A majority of a bank's directors might be completely ignorant as to the solvency of their bank or the validity of the audit. Such cases of directorial neglect, however, were becoming rarer after 1866. By the seventies, most banks had working committees of directors who supervised the manager, investigated large transactions and familiarized themselves thoroughly with bank business.[66]

Bankers were becoming more concerned with professional expertise as was reflected in the appearance of banking textbooks and formal courses of study. In 1872, for example, the Gilbart Lectureship in Banking was established at King's College, London to promote sound banking practice. By the end of the decade this lecture series attracted attendance of five hundred a year, and similar programs began appearing in other cities.[67] A better educated and more active class of bankers obviously contributed to a more secure banking system. Although most bank failures had been due to bad banking rather than dishonest banking, fraud had certainly thrived in an atmosphere of inefficiency and indolence. As the profession became more competent, dishonesty also decreased. By 1873, Walter Bagehot felt justified in claiming that bank fraud was "a rare and minor evil."[68] Bagehot's claim must be tempered, however, since the most notorious bank fraud of the nineteenth century occurred only five years later.

The catastrophic failure of the City of Glasgow Bank in 1878, amid revelations of fraud and mismanagement, cast a pall over the entire financial establishment and called into question the supposed improvements in banking practice. The City of Glasgow was one of the nation's largest banks with 133 branches, 1,800 shareholders and deposits of over £8 million. After the crash it transpired that the bank had bad debts totalling £5.8 million. In what seemed like a throwback to an earlier era, the directors had lent millions to family and friends with no regard to security. The board then concealed the bank's insolvency through a campaign of misinformation.[69]

The City of Glasgow Bank's manager, R.S. Stronach, and six of its directors, Lewis Potter, John Stewart, Robert Salmond, John Innes Wright, William Taylor and Henry Inglis, were indicted for publishing false balance sheets. At the trial the bank's accountant admitted that Stronach and Potter had first instructed him to falsify the balance sheets in 1876. The other directors pleaded ignorance of the bank's affairs, but their testimony demonstrated an extraordinary dereliction of duty on their part. Robert Salmond, for example, confessed: "My attendance at the examination of the books was more a matter of form than anything else . . . The manager was perfectly aware that I did not examine the books or accounts, and the other directors acted as I did myself. We confided in the statements of the manager."[70] The directors nonetheless signed the balance sheets, in effect giving their imprimatur to false accounts. For three years prior to its failure, the bank's balance sheets understated the figure of advances, treated bad debts as "securities held," and listed a fictitious reserve fund. The bank even falsified its bullion reserves to allow a fraudulent extension of bank notes. So cunningly had this deception been practiced that on the bank's last day of business its £100 shares were quoted at £236.[71]

The full extent of misrepresentation by the City of Glasgow Bank is illustrated in Table 2.

The jury found all the defendants guilty. Stronach and Potter were sentenced to eighteen months imprisonment, the other direc-

Table 2 *City of Glasgow Bank: fictitious elements in balance sheet of June 1878*[72]

1 Understatement of outstanding drafts	1,393,000
2 Understatement of monies advanced	3,521,000
3 Overstatement of cash in hand	219,500
4 Overstatement of stocks and bonds	926,800
5 Non-existent reserve fund	450,000
6 Overstatement of earnings	125,900

tors to eight months each. This was small consolation to the bank's proprietors whose position of unlimited liability beggared many of them. A third of the 1,800 shareholders were bankrupted by the call to pay £500 per £100 stock held. Only 269 shareholders could meet a second call of £2,250 per £100 of stock. Investors nationwide were thus confronted with the horrifying possibilities of unlimited liability, and bank shares experienced a sudden drop in value. An Act was then speedily pushed through Parliament in 1879, enabling all existing joint-stock banks to readily limit their liability.[73] The City of Glasgow Crash once again raised questions about the competence of bank officials, and earlier efforts at the professionalization of banking were intensified after 1878. It is no coincidence that the Institute of Bankers, the first professional qualifying body for bank employees, was established in 1879. The Institute organized lectures and published papers that promoted sound banking principles. More importantly, the Institute of Bankers sponsored a rigorous course of professional study, issuing certificates to successful candidates of its examinations. By the century's end, membership in the Institute numbered some 4,000, and bank employees eagerly sought Institute certification.[74]

Professional banking standards and higher levels of expertise were reflected in improved banking practice during the late nineteenth and early twentieth centuries. Most banks were keeping greater reserves than they had at the time of the mid-century crises, and they were also diversifying their holdings to prevent themselves from becoming tied to only a few merchant houses or a single industry. Furthermore, English banks at the end of the century rigorously investigated bill brokers and other borrowers to ensure that they possessed adequate capital. Unlike their frequently lackadaisical predecessors, bankers of the eighties and nineties actually checked the quality of securities pledged against loans.[75]

The trend towards greater banking stability was accentuated by the amalgamation movement. During the 1880s and 1890s, banking mergers resulted in a few large banks with branches over the whole of England. By 1918, the "Big Five" – Barclays, Lloyds, the Midland, the Westminster and the National Provincial – held deposits of over £1,307,000,000, or about 62% of the total deposits in England and Wales.[76] With amalgamation, the lending of bank funds became centralized at the head office, usually resulting in more conservative (and less reckless) loan policies. Large banking systems could also utilize surpluses from profitable branches to cover losses (including fraud) at other branches.[77]

The advantages of a centralized banking network were made clear by the Baring Crisis of 1890. During the 1880s, the respected banking house of Baring Brothers had locked up millions in Argentine securities which became unmarketable. In 1890 the bank was on the brink of suspending payment, when the leading banks met at the Bank of England and guaranteed to meet the liabilities of Baring's in order to prevent panic and widespread commercial failure such as that precipitated by the crash of Overend and Gurney in 1866 or the City of Glasgow Bank in 1878. The successful resolution of the Baring Crisis accelerated bank amalgamations and further contributed to the growth of central banking.[78]

English banking experienced a growth spurt late in the nineteenth century, but banking fraud seemed to be on the decline. Deposits in English banks increased from some £457 million in 1884 to £648 million in 1904, and the total number of bank branches grew from 2,075 to 4,621.[79] Yet, unlike the earlier banking booms of the 1830s and 1860s, this later boom was not accompanied by revelations of fraud and embezzlement. Banking defalcations were undoubtedly less common in an era of professional management, improved accountancy and financial stability. Increased banking stability meant less fraud, but it also meant less *exposure* of fraud. For it was largely through bank failures that revelations of fraud had come to light earlier in the century. Bank fraud had not completely vanished, it had become less visible.

Banks engaged in fraudulent activity of a subtler kind by the late nineteenth and early twentieth centuries. The notorious embezzlements of earlier decades had given way to crimes of misrepresentation: deceptive publicity, withholding information, false balance sheets, etc. Crimes of misinformation had always existed in banking practice, but, with the decrease of large-scale embezzlement, these crimes predominated.

Poor standards of data presentation existed throughout the Victorian period and well into the twentieth century. The Company Acts had prescribed no uniform balance sheets for bankers, and the law was equally imprecise about the contents of annual published accounts. After the Baring Crisis, many banks began publishing monthly returns to reassure customers of their solvency. More frequent publicity, however, did not mean better publicity, and the contents of balance sheets remained at best vague and at worst misleading.

Most monthly statements actually gave the public a false impression of bank assets.[80] The problem of deceptive balance sheets was explained by *The Cornhill Magazine* in 1897:

Banks call in money from the discount market to make a brave show in the monthly balance sheets which most of them publish. These monthly statements by the banks were thought to be a valuable step in the direction of healthy publicity, but the proceeding has degenerated into a farce, since it is well known and admitted that the banks call money in from the discount market for this express purpose – "window dressing," as it has been felicitously termed – so that statements arrived at by such devices give no clue as to the strength of the banks on ordinary days, when considerations of financial decency do not compel them to cover monetary nakedness with a garment of hastily called-in cash.[81]

Banks would also understate profits in their balance sheets, holding back money in "secret reserves" to pay dividends in lean years. The public was not informed when dividends were paid from reserves and was thus led to believe that profits were higher than they actually were.[82]

Deceitful practices such as window dressing and secret reserves were more difficult to correct than embezzlement. However unethical such behavior might be, it was not always outside the letter of the law – which was notoriously unclear with regard to matters of publicity. Not only were legislators reluctant to intrude themselves into business matters, but they also had difficulty keeping pace with financial (and criminal-financial) advances. Bankers could also hide behind a wall of moral ambiguity, arguing that incomplete information was not misinformation. The Overend and Gurney directors, for example, had included only truthful data in their prospectus. They had simply omitted certain unflattering details – i.e. £4 million of bad debts. Some directors believed that they falsified accounts for the good of the bank, and many others took refuge in that most common excuse for unethical business practice: "everyone else does it."

In the early decades of the twentieth century, the most damaging bank frauds occurred at small banks, principally savings institutions that appealed to small investors. Small banks could still be in the hands of a single banker, and at many of these institutions managerial amateurism lingered on. The failures of the Charing

Cross Bank in 1910 and Farrow's Bank in 1920, and the criminal trials of their directors demonstrated to the English public that the age of bank fraud had not altogether ended.

The Charing Cross Bank had been founded in 1886 by Alfred William Carpenter to cater to small investors, and advertised interest rates of 6 to 10% caused deposits to grow by leaps and bounds during the 1890s. Carpenter, however, had foolishly sunk most of the bank's funds in an unsound Canadian development scheme. By 1904 the bank's earnings could not meet interest payments, so Carpenter began paying interest from new deposits, in effect, robbing Peter to pay Paul.

The bank's downfall came about through a bit of poetic justice. In 1909 Carpenter suspected a branch employee of embezzlement and brought in an accountant to investigate. The accountant found no evidence of embezzlement, but he did uncover Carpenter's frauds and reported them to the Director of Public Prosecutions. In 1910 the Charing Cross Bank was forced to close with a loss to shareholders and depositors of over £2 million. Carpenter was convicted of fraud and given two years imprisonment.[83]

Even more alarming to the investing public was the strange history of Farrow's Bank. The bank had been founded in 1907 by two self-styled "philanthropists," Thomas Farrow and William Crotch, for the express purpose of providing banking facilities for persons of small means. Farrow, a lay preacher, and Crotch, a writer of spiritual tracts, possessed no banking experience whatsoever, but they did have support from Nonconformist churches which they cultivated by spending £9,000 a year on advertisements in religious journals. Farrow and Crotch also cultivated a spirit of fellowship among their shareholders and depositors whom they christened "Farrovians."[84]

Farrow was more fool than rogue, though in his simplicity, he aspired to financial distinction. In 1911, Farrow published a pretentious pamphlet, *Banks and People*, in which he of all people condemned amateurism in English banking.[85] At a shareholders' meeting in 1916 Farrow actually claimed that his bank was becoming a rival of the Big Five! All this bluster concealed incompetence and a state of utter insolvency. In 1914 alone, the bank's salaries and wages amounted to more than five times its total earnings.[86]

The bank was only kept open through an elaborate system of fraud. Farrow and Crotch, assisted by the bank's accountant,

Frederick Hart, paid interest and dividends out of capital and deposits, and wrote-up assets to conceal insolvency. In 1911, for example, the bank purchased a building estate for £23,350, but listed it on the books as an asset worth £81,000. A £230 investment in the Gazeland China Clay Company was valued in the 1912 balance sheet at £150,000![87]

The bank's apparent success attracted the attention of a group of American financiers, Norton, Read and Company, who in May 1920 opened negotiations to acquire controlling interest. Mr. Read first had the accountant Henry Morgan inspect the books of Farrow's Bank, and Morgan soon discovered that something was amiss. When confronted with Morgan's findings, Crotch exclaimed: "Well, the game is up. We have been sitting on this for years, hoping against hope until you turned up, and we thought our troubles were ended, instead of which they were really beginning."[88] Norton and Read pulled out of negotiations with Farrow on the grounds of misrepresentation. Read then contacted the Board of Trade and a prosecution was mounted against Farrow, Crotch and Hart.[89]

During the trial in June of 1921, the accountant Gilbert Garnsey of Price, Waterhouse and Company was brought in to explain the bank's creative bookkeeping. Garnsey found among the 1915 accounts a damnable paper in Hart's writing listing "profits required" at £309,298. That very sum was then provided by writing up one of the bank's assets, the Dreadnought Cement Company. As the judge affirmed: "The problem seems to have been approached upside down. It was not a question of finding out what the profit was, and then allocating it, but of first allocating what they wanted to allocate, and then finding the balance to make it up."[90]

The pious bankers were suitably repentant, but they did offer their excuses. Crotch explained that the first year they fiddled the books they were just a little short and believed that business would turn around. Each year they added to their crimes believing that some miracle would set things right.[91] Farrow pleaded that he was not an accountant, but "an idealist, an organizer, and an optimist."[92] Farrow and Crotch were sentenced to four years in prison, Hart to one year. The bank's loss was around £2,200,000 and many of its 4,000 shareholders (who included a large number of spinsters, clergymen and clerks) were impoverished.[93]

The case of Farrow's Bank was considered remarkable in the 1920s and as such highlighted the general soundness of English banking at the time. Considerable progress had been made since the Victorian period in bank management and accountancy, though not in public disclosure. The 1931 Parliamentary Committee on Finance and Industry found the problem of monthly and year-end window dressing by banks to be still very serious. The Committee likened bank's published statements to a "stage army" in which the same resources did duty many times over. Legal requirements for publicity and standards of data presentation were still notoriously low.[94]

During the three decades between the Bank Acts of 1844 and the City of Glasgow Crash, the British banking system experienced an unusually high level of fraud. Amateurish management, coupled with the "hands off" attitude of Parliament, gave bankers great facility for misusing or misappropriating shareholders' and depositors' money. Too many Victorian bankers ignored the distinction between *meum* and *tuum*, as the propertied classes learned to their sorrow. The situation only improved late in the century, when the more honest and competent men began to see the disastrous consequences of giving the rogues and fools a free hand. The professionalization of banking contributed greatly to the decrease in bank failures and frauds.

CHAPTER 4

Stock fraud

The proliferation of shares, bonds and securities of all kinds during the nineteenth century radically changed the nature of investment. Property as an essentially physical possession – land, plate, jewelry – gave way to the more intangible resources of income and interest from capital investment. The proprietors of joint-stock companies or holders of government bonds, for example, were entitled to a "flow of income" from their capital. Investments of this sort were responsible for the phenomenal growth of the English economy, but were especially vulnerable to manipulation by unscrupulous persons. The theft of shares or misuse of an investor's capital was not readily detectable so long as the accustomed flow of income was maintained. Worthless paper securities could also be passed off as representing valuable goods or profitable trade. Furthermore, the principal securities market – the London Stock Exchange – was a poor intermediary between investors and new share issues, failing to shield the public from fraudulent company promoters.[1]

The growth of stockholding and a securities market was originally tied to the National Debt, which increased from a mere £5 million in 1698 to £71 million in 1749 to £497 million in 1800. For over a century most stock transactions involved government securities, and company shares were not even listed on the Exchange until 1811.[2] The Railway Mania of the 1840s magnified the importance of company shares and railway share dealings increased Exchange membership from a few hundreds before the Mania to 864 in 1851. The Mania also led to the creation of a dozen new Provincial Stock Exchanges in 1844 and 1845.[3] Continued company promotion during the 1850s and 1860s caused the membership of the London Exchange to top one thousand in the midsixties. The floatation of numerous foreign loans and foreign companies during the 1870s brought Exchange membership to 2,000 by

1878 and the boom in industrial promotions during the 1890s led to further growth. By the early twentieth century the London Stock Exchange had over 5,000 members. Company shares so overshadowed government securities in the second half of the nineteenth century that, by 1914, the funds amounted to only 5% of quoted securities.[4]

Members of the public could not buy or sell shares directly on the Stock Exchange, but had to conduct their business through the agency of an Exchange member. The tremendous volume of business conducted on the London Stock Exchange led to the separation of its members into the categories of broker and jobber. A broker was a member who acted as an agent for an outsider, buying or selling shares for that person. A jobber was a member who acted as an intermediary between other members. The role of a broker was akin to that of a retailer, the jobber to that of a wholesaler. Others have likened the relationship to that between solicitor and barrister. Jobbers often specialized in certain types of securities, so that a broker wishing to deal in American railway shares for his client would seek out jobbers specializing in those shares.[5]

The London Stock Exchange was governed by a thirty-member, annually elected Committee of General Purposes. The Committee, which was created in 1802 to regulate transactions in domestic securities, had become a body of international importance by mid-century. The Committee had the power to grant quotations of new stocks, that is, to allow the shares of a new company or loan to be traded on the Exchange and the price of those shares to be listed on the official Stock Index.[6] Unfortunately, in authorizing quotations, the Committee exercised very little concern for the investing public with the result that fraudulent firms were in no way hindered from operating on the Exchange.

High levels of stock fraud gave the Exchange a bad reputation with the general public. Among London cabbies, "thieves' kitchen" was slang for the Stock Exchange.[7] In 1849 the financial writer John Francis observed: "the Stock Exchange is seldom named, out of the City, but with contempt; and a Stock Exchange man is, like the monied man in the early reign of William, despised by the landed, and looked down upon by the mercantile, aristocracy."[8] This view had changed little by 1876, when *Blackwood's* noted: "Without taking a specially gloomy view of the world in general, we see that at least in its financial department and on the Stock Exchange, the powers of evil for the time are decidedly in the ascendant."[9] A number of fraudulent share issues during the 1860s and 1870s gave rise to two Parliamentary investigations of the Exchange: the 1875 Select Committee on Loans to Foreign States and the 1878 Royal Commission on the Stock Exchange.[10] The Reports of both Parliamentary bodies concentrated on problems involving pre-allotment share dealings and the granting of official quotations.

Most critics of the Exchange agreed that quotations were too easily obtained. In granting quotations to foreign loans, for example, the Committee of the Stock Exchange made no attempt to ascertain the solvency of the borrowing government. To secure quotation for a loan, it was only necessary to prove that the government in question had actually authorized the loan. However reckless the terms of the loan, or however unlikely that a loan would be repaid were not matters considered by the Exchange when it granted a quotation.[11] The 1875 Committee wondered why large loans had been raised on the London Exchange for Honduras, Santo Domingo, Costa Rica and Paraguay during the 1860s and 1870s only to have those countries default on payment. The political and economic instability of Latin America did not surprise many in Parliament, but the irresponsibility of the Stock Exchange did.[12] Brokers and financiers were only interested in making profit for themselves; the loss on bad loans was borne by investors who were ensnared by loan-mongers promising them a huge return on their capital. In the opinion of the *Contemporary Review*: "The ways of 'high finance' are not exactly immoral, but completely non-moral. The great loan dealers never ask whether it would be good for an applicant for money to have it. They merely look to see if they can make the operation of lending pay themselves."[13] The Stock Exchange failed conspicuously in its duty to mediate between new loan issues and the English public.

Joint-stock companies also found it easy to have their shares quoted on the Exchange. For companies to secure quotations they had only to lodge certain documents (e.g. prospectuses, Articles of Association) with the Committee of the Stock Exchange and to inform the Committee that two-thirds of their share capital had been allotted to the public.[14] These strictures were of little effect, however, as the Committee never investigated documents tendered for company quotation. Only if allegations of fraud were made was any company investigated.[15] When asked by the 1875 Committee if the machinery of the Stock Exchange was sufficient to detect fraud among those parties seeking quotations, the broker Sir Henry James answered:

There is nothing in our rules to enable us to do so. If the fraud were flagrant, and testified to, and brought to our notice, we should take notice of it, directly, of course; or if money were not going in the direction indicated, we should immediately take notice of that; but unless it was something of that kind we should not.[16]

It was not uncommon for promoters to falsify documents given to the Exchange Committee so as to receive a quotation for their shares. The Chairman of the Stock Exchange Committee, Samuel De Zoete, told Parliament in 1875: "We find in the case of companies where we impose certain restrictions, and require certain returns to be made before granting a settlement or quotation, we have not the slightest doubt that constantly they are fitted and concocted for the purpose."[17] One such fraud involved the Eupion Gas Company in 1874. There were no applications on the part of the public for shares in this company, but to secure a quotation, the promoters induced people to make dummy applications. The promoters then used their own money to represent shareholders' deposits. The same money was also deposited and withdrawn many times over in the company's bank account in an attempt to represent a large volume of application deposits. So lax was the Exchange Committee in its examination of company documents that it did not even notice that the "deposit money" was withdrawn by the promoters as soon as it was paid in.[18]

The Royal Commission on the Stock Exchange concluded that official quotation gave companies a "spurious stamp of genuineness."[19] In so concluding it echoed the findings of the 1875 Committee which had argued that the Stock Exchange "gives, by granting a quotation, a certain prestige to a loan which neither the very slight and superficial investigation on which the grant of a quotation is founded, nor the nature of the tribunal seem to warrant."[20] Most members of the public assumed that only genuine securities could be traded on the floor of the London Stock Exchange and that the Exchange guarded investors against fraudulent issues. Few assumptions regarding the world of finance were so thoroughly wrong.

The buying and selling of a new company's shares before those shares had been fully allotted to the public was another source of much stock fraud. Pre-allotment dealings were meant to demonstrate the popularity of a new company's shares and thereby attract investment, but these dealings were the most artificial of all stock transactions. In effect some brokers were offering to sell shares they did not have, but hoped to acquire after allotment, while others were offering to buy shares that they had no intention of acquiring merely to drive up the price of those shares. Company promoters often sent brokers into the market with offers to buy the shares of whatever companies they were promoting, thus tricking the public into believing there was a genuine demand for those shares.[21]

Once promoters had created a fictitious market, they secretly held back their shares in the hopes of driving the price even higher. Dishonest firms, such as the Peruvian Railway Company in 1865, pretended to issue more shares to the public than they really did. The promoters then had brokers bid for their shares on the Exchange, and, since no shares were available, the prices skyrocketed. In effect the promoters had secretly cornered the market in their own shares and could virtually dictate the price at which they would be sold. If the Stock Exchange Committee could prove a dishonest corner in shares, it would annul dealings in those shares. Yet, since these transactions were secret and usually carried out through the agency of third parties, the guilty were seldom brought to account.[22]

Pre-allotment "rigs" were to plague investors throughout the nineteenth century. In fact, frauds involving share dealings in embryo companies became so widespread during the 1860s that the Committee of the Stock Exchange outlawed all such transactions in 1864. Nonetheless, pre-allotment dealings continued unabated; they simply took place outside the Exchange. In 1865 the Committee reversed its decision for fear of losing business to outside brokers.[23] The 1878 Report of the Royal Commission on the Stock Exchange concluded that, were it not for specious dealings in shares before allotment:

. . . the greater part of the fraudulent and worthless companies by which the public has been defrauded would have found it impossible to succeed in attracting public confidence; and that conversely the system placed great facilities at the disposal of those who promoted such companies for entrapping the public, which nothing is likely to diminish in the future so long as the system prevails.[24]

The Commission recommended that all pre-allotment share dealings be banned, but neither the Stock Exchange Committee nor the legislature followed suit. These dealings were never prohibited, though informed opinion was against them and they declined towards the end of the century.[25]

Rigging the market would not have been possible without the collusion of brokers on the Exchange, though in fairness to some, promoters often concealed their rigs by operating through men of straw. Yet even in cases where brokers were complicitous in rigging the market, guilt was most difficult to prove. Brokers could always plead ignorance to the base motives of their transactions, claiming to be the innocent dupes of company promoters. Rarely did the Stock Exchange discipline its members for share rigs and the law courts only began addressing the problem late in the century.

Strictly speaking, a company's purchase of its own shares was legal, unless expressly prohibited by its Articles of Association or when a *conspiracy* to defraud the public could be proven. In 1892, for example, the promoter of the Steam Loop Company was found to have defrauded investors through the creation of a fictitious market in his company's shares.[26] In this case conspiracy was established by producing in court a series of letters from the promoter, Mr. Scott, instructing brokers to create an artificial price for Steam Loop shares.[27] Most company promoters, however, were more careful in covering their tracks so that successful prosecutions for share rigs were very rare. In 1898 *The Economist* condemned the loopholes in commercial law that accommodated unscrupulous promoters:

. . . unless conspiracy can be proved, which is usually an exceedingly difficult matter, the operation of "making a market" in shares is legal, although it generally takes the form of a flagrant attempt to deceive gullible people into the belief that practically unsalable shares are being actively dealt in, and that the premiums quoted are real and not, as they almost invariably are, utterly fictitious. If a practice of this kind is legal, as we must assume it to be, then no time should be lost in making it illegal.[28]

During the nineteenth century the law of the land had little impact on the Stock Exchange which was virtually a law unto itself. The Exchange considered its own rules and regulations sufficient government and resisted all interference on the part of the law courts or legislature. The Committee of the Stock Exchange was the court of final appeal for its members and one of the Exchange rules even stipulated: "No Member shall attempt to enforce by law a claim arising out of Stock Exchange transactions against a Member or defaulter, or against the principal of a Member or defaulter, without the consent of such Member, or of the creditors of the defaulter, or of the Committee."[29] The Exchange was almost contemptuous with regard to Parliament, often ignoring those Acts which attempted to regulate share transactions. In 1875 the Chairman of the Stock Exchange candidly remarked to the Foreign Loans Committee: "We disregarded for years and years Sir John Barnards's Act, and we are now disregarding Mr. Leeman's Act."[30]

The Stock Exchange defended its insularity by claiming that its own rules and usages provided adequate protection against fraud, though, as we have seen, this was hardly the case. Not only was the Exchange careless in granting quotations and regulating share dealings, but its conduct with regard to its own membership was far from exemplary. The London Stock Exchange had no entrance requirements for its members save those of entrance fee and recommendations from three current members. An applicant's recommenders had further to pledge to pay £500 to creditors should the applicant default within four years of his admission.[31] The Committee made no difficulties when screening applicants as can be measured by the fact that, between 1886 and 1903, 3,854 members were admitted to the London Exchange and only 39 applications were denied.[32]

In 1902 the Exchange attempted to improve the basis for membership by requiring that applicants must serve as clerks in the Exchange for at least two years previous to becoming members.[33] Opposition to this rule was fierce among brokers and it was repealed in 1904. Some firms had even evaded the rule by entering candidates as clerks in their books while those men were actually attending university.[34] Membership remained more a matter of whom one knew than of what one knew.

The Stock Exchange was particularly lax with reference to defaulters. Those members who were unable to meet their pecuniary engagements were expelled from the Exchange, though news of a broker's default was seldom communicated to the outside world. Defaulters thus had little trouble setting themselves up as outside brokers and dealing with a public ignorant of their expulsion. Defaulters also found it easy to gain readmission to the Exchange once they had compounded with their creditors. Between 1867 and 1877, for example, 265 brokers were expelled from the Stock Exchange as defaulters, 116 later applied for readmission and 105 obtained it. The Royal Commission on the Stock Exchange found such a percentage "excessive."[35]

The seeming nonchalance of the Stock Exchange was largely based on its fear of outside competition. The Exchange resisted passing tighter entrance requirements or stricter operating rules lest business go to outside brokers or to overseas exchanges in Paris and Amsterdam.[36] Competition from outside brokers was the bane of the London Exchange. Outsiders did not bear the responsibilities or costs of Exchange membership and their dealings were not subject to the supervision, however slight, of the Exchange Committee. Resentment of outside brokers intensified in the late nineteenth century as securities investment grew in importance. In 1885, for example, the Stock Exchange placed advertisements in the press warning the public against trading with brokers who were not members of a recognized Exchange. The following year the London Exchange denied outside brokers access to information from its stock-tapes.[37]

The Stock Exchange's campaign against outside brokers, although grounded in professional exclusiveness, called attention to a sector of the economy that was riddled with fraud. For while many outside brokerage houses were perfectly respectable and honest firms, many others were "bucket-shops," that is, dishonest businesses unloading worthless goods onto the public. In a 1901 advice book, *How to Invest and How to Speculate*, C.H. Thorpe warned investors to avoid all outside brokers. Especially dangerous were those dealers who sent out advertisements in the mail with extravagant claims as to profits made in their previous deals. These confidence men often announced themselves as members of old, established firms, though they frequently changed their names and addresses to keep ahead of the police.[38] Twentieth-century bucket-shop operators were the direct descendants of nineteenth-century "alley-men" – a species of financial vermin D.M. Evans delineated in 1845:

They are a description of people including the lowest of the low among the outside speculators, who traffic in the letters and shares of railway, or any other joint-stock company that may happen to fall into their hands. They frequent the purlieus of Capel-court, the Auction Mart, and the adjoining lanes and alleys, and principally consist of broken-down merchants' clerks, decayed tradesmen who have lost money by speculation, and others, whose pretensions to honesty and character it would be difficult to describe.[39]

The vastness of the English share market, the demand for profitable investments, and the absence of regulations governing brokerage allowed a steady stream of confidence men – high and low – to operate on the fringes of the stock markets well into the twentieth century.

The growth in shareholding after the First World War heightened the problem of bucket-shop frauds. Disreputable brokers, often referred to as "share-pushers," defrauded the investing public of millions of pounds during the 1920s and 1930s, sparking a Parliamentary Inquiry in 1937.[40] The *modus operandi* of share-pushers was to persuade investors to give them money or good securities in exchange for securities which proved to be worthless. Share-pushers acquired shares by either registering dummy corporations or by purchasing the shares of moribund companies. There was never a shortage of worthless stock since at any time there were thousands of firms which had ceased business but had not yet had their names removed from the Stock Index. In some cases share-pushers asked investors to join a pool to raise money for the purchase of a certain commodity or stock which was then to be sold for profit. Imaginary lists of past pools and supposed profits would be sent out, often promising returns of 50%.[41]

Share-pushers operated behind a facade of respectability, advertising themselves as "Stock and Share Dealers" and maintaining posh offices in the City near the Stock Exchange. These confidence men sent out circulars to the public with investment advice and offers to sell shares for which "some confidential information of their certain rise in value" was claimed. Share-pushers sometimes baited their traps by claiming to have purchased certain shares for customers and sold them for a profit. No such deals had taken place, but this induced some persons to send in money for other transactions.[42]

Share-pushing firms utilized modern advertising and sales methods, blanketing the market with thousands of circulars and soliciting business over the telephone. Share-pushers employed "postal publicity" firms to draw up mailing lists for them of known shareholders. Lists of as many as 500,000 shareholders were easily obtainable. If firms received answers to their solicitations, they immediately sent out professional "touts" to meet with prospective victims. These touts were usually well-dressed men in fancy auto-mobiles who were expert at conning people out of money or securi-ties. Some victims related that they were "fairly hypnotized" into parting with property.[43]

Victims of share-pushing were drawn from all segments of the propertied classes, though persons with the least experience in finance such as widows, spinsters and clergymen were especially vulnerable. The Board of Trade concluded:

. . . the desire to "get rich quickly" which is deep-rooted in the minds of many, coupled with the lack of prudence and experience in many persons and their curious reluctance to seek any advice before parting with money or securities – all these have conduced to the infliction of very serious losses.[44]

One witness estimated the annual loss due to share-pushing at £5 million. The "takings" of a single firm could be enormous. Edward Guylee, for example, made over £130,000 through the sale of shares to the bogus "Amalgamated Electrical and Lighting Equipment Company." Between 1929 and 1930, Jacob Factor received £1,600,000 for worthless shares.[45]

The Committee on Share-Pushing alleged that English-speaking aliens were heavily involved in touting, though Edward Smithies' examination of cases from London and the southern counties found that share-pushers were mainly English and included a number of well-connected persons.[46] During the 1920s, for example, Lieutenant-Colonel Edmund Octavius Eaton – a penniless adven-turer in the south of England – specialized in buying up small, worthless companies and selling their shares through the mails. William Preston, a university graduate and son of a solicitor, was operating as a share-pusher near Chancery Lane in 1930, having already spent nearly twenty years in prison for a series of forgeries. A policeman recognized him from his prison days, followed him to his offices and found evidence of his newest fraud. Most share-pushers, however, were never caught. When they felt that the police were on to them, or when complaints were made against their firms, they simply disappeared, assumed new names and offices and began business anew.[47]

No rules or regulations guided the transactions of outside brokers. Anyone could act as a broker, as dramatized by the notorious case of an ex-convict who upon his release from Dart-moor Prison set himself up as a stockbroker in a northern town and proceeded to defraud his clients. In England, unlike most other European nations, brokers did not have to pass examinations, serve a probationary period, or even pay a surety.[48] In the opinion of Parliament, "so long as anybody, however impecunious or impoverished he may be, can call himself a 'stockbroker,' there will be grave and obvious risk of losses inflicted on the ignorant public."[49]

Investors were at a real disadvantage when dealing with stock-brokers, both inside and outside the Exchange. The public lacked good sources of information regarding the securities market, and stock prices were easily manipulated by unscrupulous brokers. False information, the bane of the Stock Exchange in the early nineteenth century, was still a problem at the century's end.[50] In 1885, for example, a hoax involving foreign bonds startled the financial community. A forged letter on official paper addressed by Gladstone's private secretary to the secretary of the London Stock Exchange claimed that a settlement had been reached with the Chilean government in favor of holders of Peruvian bonds. The letter was posted on the notice board of the Exchange causing the bonds in question to rise sharply in value. In 1900 a false telegram was placed on the notice board giving favorable news concerning the Australian Broken Hill Company so that the price of its shares nearly doubled before the forgery was discovered.[51]

The introduction of stock-tape machines in the 1880s was seen as an improved means of proliferating securities information, though stock prices on the tape were often of dubious quality. Price quo-tations on the stock-tape were provided by the Exchange Telegraph Company, an independent firm in no way controlled by the Com-mittee of the Exchange. Brokers found it very easy to get prices from sham transactions quoted on the tape.[52] In 1898 the *Nineteenth Century* criticized the Exchange Telegraph Company, arguing that the firm:

. . . has to rely upon servants who cannot exercise discretion, and upon information which it cannot test; hence many a quotation gets upon the "tape" which its providers would probably not admit had they the time, opportunity, and knowledge to check them. The way in which newly issued shares are boomed on the tape, often before they are offered to the public, is little short of scandalous.[53]

Prices from the stock-tapes found their way into the newspapers and were disseminated to a public which assumed such prices bore the imprimatur of the Stock Exchange Committee.

Investors were especially vulnerable to fraudulent data when dealing in the shares of overseas companies or foreign loans. Foreign investment scandals had prompted government inquiry in 1875, and the problem lingered on.[54] While xenophobes concluded that there was "an easier standard of financial morality among Indians, and half-breeds, and curly-headed negroes,"[55] the real problem lay closer to home. Stockbrokers, company promoters and merchant houses which dealt in foreign shares could make the most extravagant and deceptive claims regarding their securities with little fear of contradiction. Even the most cautious investors could hardly saunter off to the jungles of Latin America or the deserts of Australia to examine the *bona fides* of a railway or gold mine that might not even exist.

Stock and share prices are essentially a reflection of public confidence. As such they are extremely vulnerable to any news which might enhance or diminish that confidence. In an age of poor financial information when spurious evidence was easily passed off as genuine, investors had little protection against fraud. This problem was compounded when investors trusted, as they generally did, such unreliable sources as the Stock Exchange. As the financial writer Anthony Pulbrook explained in 1906: "The public imagine that by buying through the Stock Exchange securities quoted on the official tape issued from that institution they are protected from joining anything not thoroughly genuine."[56] Pulbrook went on to warn his readers: ". . . shares on the Stock Exchange are not guided by their intrinsic value but by the law of supply and demand and that for all practical purposes shares may be regarded as counters for gambling purposes."[57] Yet all players in this game were not equally at risk. The cards were clearly stacked in the dealers' favor.

Investors were at the mercy of the "experts" who controlled the market in stocks and shares. Large numbers of upper and middle-class Britons lived off dividends from shareholdings and interest from government bonds. These securities were often lodged with brokers and solicitors who specialized in managing their clients' investments. The immense value of stocks and bonds held by these trustees proved too great a temptation for some persons, while the intangible nature of such securities made their misuse or misappropriation difficult to detect.

A typical case of stock fraud from the mid-Victorian period involved William Lemon Oliver, a broker on the London Exchange. In 1858 Oliver was found to have fraudulently converted customers' securities to his own use. Among his crimes, Oliver had forged share transfers for £5,000 of Canadian government bonds left in his safe-keeping by Caroline Dance. Miss Dance never suspected that her bonds had been sold, since Oliver regularly paid her the accustomed amount of dividend, and the fraud was only discovered when she asked for the securities and Oliver procrastinated. Oliver had used the stolen funds to meet losses from share speculations and for this crime was sentenced to twenty years penal servitude.[58]

Later in the century the Barton frauds again dramatized the vulnerability of the investing public. Samuel Barton, a trustee for an inheritance which included large quantities of London and North Western Railway stock, forged the signatures of the other trustees and transferred the stock to buyers. Barton's frauds went undetected for ten years since he made the usual dividend payments, and only came to light in 1886 when Barton absconded. New trustees brought a successful lawsuit against the railway company which was required to reinstate to them the fraudulently transferred stock. Unfortunately, those persons who had purchased the stock from Barton were deprived of it without compensation, although they had acted in good faith and were entirely innocent of fraud. The Barton case caused much alarm among the nation's investors, any of whom unwittingly might have acquired, or might yet acquire, stolen shares.[59]

Brokers, bankers and other trustees had little trouble misusing the securities of their clients.[60] Especially at risk were minors and single women, though all types of propertied people remained ignorant of basic finance and trusted solely to the discretion of their brokers and solicitors. As long as respectable dividends were maintained, investors seldom inquired after the securities themselves and only discovered that their capital had been tampered with when their trustees could no longer keep up the game. Trustees often convinced themselves that they were only "borrowing" clients' securities to extricate themselves from "temporary" financial difficulties and that they would return any stocks or bonds so used. Such was the belief of the bankers Strahan, Paul and Bates in 1855 as it was of the sharebroker Sir Arthur Wheeler in 1931 when he fraudulently converted £23,000 of clients' stocks to repair losses to his firm from the 1929 crash.[61]

Dishonest trustees were the bane of the affluent classes and proved a favorite literary theme for Victorian and Edwardian writers. Trollope's *Three Clerks*, for example, tells the story of Alaric Tudor, who, as trustee for the young Miss Golightly, sold out £10,000 of her government bonds to pay calls on his own railway shares. The great harm of such crimes, Trollope seemed to argue, was that they undermined "that trust which the weaker of mankind should place in the stronger."[62]

The problem of trust was later explored by the dramatist and Fabian Socialist Harley Granville Barker in his 1905 play *The Voysey Inheritance*.[63] In this work, the solicitor Mr. Voysey speculated with clients' money that was supposed to be invested in good securities and utilized the profits to maintain a lavish lifestyle for himself and his family. On learning of these frauds, one of Voysey's sons remarked: "The world's getting more and more into the hands of its experts, and it certainly does require a particular sort of honesty."[64]

Stocks were bought and sold by thousands of Britons who placed their trust in the honesty of the experts. These investors were mostly unversed in the ways of high finance, they lacked good sources of advice and information, and they had few protections offered them by Parliament or the Stock Exchange. "Buyer beware" was cold comfort to those persons defrauded by dishonest brokers or enticed by misleading stock quotations. The motto of the Stock Exchange, "my word is my bond," was a pretty sentiment, but it accorded very little safeguard to English investors.

CHAPTER 5

Company fraud: promotion

The greatest opportunities for white-collar crime probably occurred during the promotion of new companies.[1] British company law was the most permissive in all of Europe and gave promoters great latitude in their operations.[2] The ease with which a limited, joint-stock company could be created was remarkable. Seven persons had only to take up one share each in a concern to achieve incorporation. They might have no real stake in the company, but they could sell its shares to the public, have themselves or their friends appointed directors, and trade on the firm's capital in the most reckless manner with no personal liability beyond their own small shareholding. In 1867, only ten years after the liberalization of company law, Parliamentary hearings were held to inquire into the alarming incidence of company fraud.[3] Many witnesses complained that promoters were taking advantage of the law's leniency. The company promoter David Chadwick admitted "there are radical defects in the Act [Companies Act, 1862], and that too great facility is afforded to the promoters of companies who wish to palm off something unsound on the public."[4] The Master of the Rolls, Lord Romilly, was more blunt:

In a great many cases which have come before me, I am satisfied that the company was formed for the purpose of being wound up, and that the original promoters had no other object than just to put a company on foot which they were satisfied could never be carried into any profitable execution, for the mere purpose of afterwards winding it up in the Court of Chancery. In these cases the creditors are paid nothing; but all that takes place is, that a few deluded individuals are induced to take shares, and their payments are divided among some of the promoters of the company and the lawyers who are employed to wind it up.[5]

Frauds of this sort, all too familiar from the Railway Mania,[6] had intensified with the coming of limited liability in 1855 and the

Finance Company Mania of the early sixties.[7] The boom in foreign loan floatations during the 1870s brought forth further revelations of financial fraud.[8]

Company fraud flourished in periods of intense financial growth. The speculative booms of the 1840s, 1860s, 1890s and 1920s afforded promoters their greatest opportunities for fraud. During upswings in the business cycle, investors were more confident and trusting in the disposal of their capital. Disreputable promotions found it easy to hide themselves among the crowded field of new companies. The *National Review* commented on this phenomenon in 1898: "By force of sympathy good shares drag bad ones of the same class up along with them, and thereby assist the wiles of the unscrupulous promoter. The better the market the easier it is to foist new stuff on it, and the hotter the boom the worse it is certain to be abused in the end."[9] Speculative manias engendered the most impulsive optimism, causing many people to seize upon any investment opportunity (however improbable) that came their way. Company promoters exploited this mad rush to get rich quick.

Promotion frauds included a wide range of deceptive practices, some more severe than others. The worst examples were those promotions got up merely to defraud gullible investors. It was quite common for a group of swindlers to buy up a bankrupt factory or a worked-out coal mine and float it as a limited company. A prospectus was issued making the most extravagant claims for the business, shares were allotted and deposits collected. The company would then mysteriously fail, leaving the unfortunate shareholders in the lurch. Few shareholders were willing to expend more money in the uncertain attempt to gain legal redress.[10] Outright swindles of this sort were the most dramatic case, but they were probably always a minority of all promotion frauds.

Most frauds were of a subtler kind. Actual businesses were sold to the public, but the vendors made distorted claims, concealed unpleasantnesses and generally pulled the wool over investors' eyes. As the *Journal of Finance* argued in 1899:

. . . the number of downright criminal promoters bears hardly a sensible proportion to those who are absolutely dishonest, but cunning enough to keep just within the law. It is those people who are the most dangerous element; they mislead the public, yet they are not punishable. They have brought the art of deceiving credulous shareholders to great perfection. They bring into play a hundred different subtle devices to conceal ugly truths or to suggest rosy falsehoods.[11]

The state of the law with regard to company promotion was so vague that many utterly deceptive practices were not illegal.

As a measure of financial dishonesty, the economist H.A. Shannon estimated that one sixth of all new promotions during the nineteenth century were fraudulent. Shannon's estimate is based upon the high percentage of insolvencies during the first five years of incorporation – some 17% for the period 1866–1883. "It may be admitted generally," he asserts, "that companies which so failed, failed from fraud or gross mismanagement amounting to fraud."[12] Clapham does not attempt to quantify company fraud, but he agrees that the percentage was high.[13] Whatever one's guess, and the precise figure for company fraud is certainly unknowable, there is little doubt that it was a serious problem. Of course the great majority of English businesses were honestly run, as Parliament made clear in its Reports on Company Law in 1895 and 1898.[14] This truism, however, requires an important qualification, as supplied by Shannon:

It is acceptable to common sense that fraudulent companies are short-lived and honest companies more long-lived. Hence, fraudulent companies coming into existence, new and short-lived, will arithmetically form a small proportion of all companies in existence mostly old and honest. But, compared with the flow of companies coming into existence at the same time, fraudulent companies will form a high proportion . . . The dead as well as the living must be remembered.[15]

In England company promotion can be said to begin with the Railway Mania, but the professional company promoter really came into his own during the 1860s. Railway companies had tended to promote themselves without the assistance of outside vendors. With the company legislation of 1856 and 1862 and the resultant upsurge in joint-stock floatations, there was a greater need for financial intermediaries between the merchants, industrialists and inventors who desired to incorporate their businesses and the English public who wanted investment outlets for their capital. The promotion of a company required advertising skills and share-dealing expertise which many businessmen did not possess. In France, Germany and other continental states, investment banks supervised the majority of joint-stock floatations. In

England, however, investment banking never developed fully, and most companies went public through the agency of an individual promoter who would purchase the business, assemble a board of directors, draw-up a prospectus and advertisements, and resell the company to the public through the issuance of shares.[16]

Almost from their first appearance, company promoters had a bad name. At mid-century D.M. Evans wrote:

> The man who assumes as a calling the constitution of joint-stock associations, is most frequently looked upon as a doubtful character, who, if even to be trusted, requires looking after. He is not like an individual who, bringing a great system to bear, and having carried it out, obtains a leading appointment, and continues in the service of the company; but, in the character of "company-monger," he is merely the person who, having the idea entrusted to him, endeavours to get together a body of men who are willing, by their names and influence, to set the scheme in motion.[17]

In other words he was a salesman, and given to all the flash and impertinence of modern commercialism. It was believed by many that promoters would sell any company, however defective, so long as they could turn a personal profit. In the opinion of the *Journal of Finance*, "a preponderating majority of them will stop at nothing, not even criminal acts, in the pursuit of their delusive schemes."[18] The images most frequently applied to promoters were those of predator and parasite; in popular parlance they were "vampires," "bloodsuckers," "wolves" and "vultures." The *National Review* typically expressed this sentiment in an article published in 1898: "The trust or company-monger pure and simple, who is neither producer nor distributor, but is content to make his own dirty profit out of the ruin and impoverishment of other people, is nothing but a blood-sucker, in that he benefits nobody but himself."[19] A harsh judgment, to be sure, but one that is not without some foundation in reality.

The most notable feature of fraudulent promotions was misleading or deceptive publicity. There were little or no legal guidelines as to the content of prospectuses and advertisements with the result that these documents were singularly uninformative. Most prospectuses contained lurid promises of success rather than substantive financial data. Worthless or failing businesses concealed their insolvency by dwelling on past performance or future hopes, assets were shamelessly overvalued, and liabilities overlooked. The Overend and Gurney crash in 1866 revealed the full possibilities of such deception. The prospectus for the 1865 Overend's floatation had failed to list several million pounds of bad debts which were transferred to the new public company by means of a secret contract with the old private firm.[20] Parliament responded with a hastily drafted amendment to the 1867 Companies Act requiring prospectuses to list all contracts. There was considerable confusion, however, as to what constituted a contract, and some promoters evaded the new requirement by means of a waiver clause.[21]

The use of guinea-pig directors, so popular during the Railway Mania, remained another favorite device for enticing investment. Investors often applied for shares in a new company on the faith that certain distinguished persons advertised as directors had a real stake in the company, when in fact they had been paid for patronizing the firm. There was never a shortage of impecunious peers willing to lend their names to a prospectus in exchange for cash payment.[22] More audacious promoters used famous names without permission. A particularly impertinent case was that of John Stanley Humphery, who in 1843 promoted the bogus City of London Convalescent Fund, Pension Society and Savings Bank by claiming Queen Victoria and Prince Albert as patrons and the Duke of Wellington as a director. Humphery was eventually brought to trial for fraud, and when he claimed that his bail was excessive, the judge countered that "if the prisoner knew so many illustrious persons he should have no trouble finding the money."[23]

When distorted publicity failed to excite interest in a new company, promoters organized share rigs to artificially inflate the value of company stock.[24] Promoters would buy up their own shares using either the company's capital or borrowed money, thus creating the illusion that their shares were in demand. In 1878 the Royal Commission on the Stock Exchange condemned the practice, citing a number of disturbing examples. In 1864, for instance, promoters of the Australian and Eastern Steam Navigation Company drove up the price of their stock by having brokers purchase in the open market 19,000 of the company's 27,000 shares.[25]

In all this double-dealing promoters were assisted by the permissive nature of company law and the Stock Exchange rules. The Registrar of Joint Stock Companies was merely a scribe for recording new promotions; he had no discretionary powers in granting or denying incorporation as did the Registrar of Friendly Societies. Likewise, the Committee of the Stock Exchange erected few barriers in the granting of official quotations to new share issues. There were no institutional procedures for determining the *bona fides* of English companies. The primary check on promotional fraud was the integrity of the individual promoter.

Clearly all promoters were not bent on illicit profits. The best practice was represented by men such as David Chadwick. Chadwick was active during the 1860s and 1870s, promoting at least forty-seven limited companies between 1862 and 1874 – most of them being floatations of private industrial firms. Before agreeing to float a business, Chadwick, who was also an accountant, would examine the firm's books over a number of years to assure himself of the venture's credibility. As a result of his scrutiny, Chadwick's floatations were unusually long-lived for Victorian promotions. His business methods were also above reproach. He charged a commission of only 1% for converting businesses into public companies, shares were offered through private circulars and prospectuses sent to known investors, directors held large numbers of shares, and share rigs were not permitted.[26] Unfortunately Chadwick's methods were not typical of Victorian company promoters who were usually more concerned with personal gain than with the creation of viable public companies.

Among the most notorious of the early company promoters was Albert Grant. Grant would promote anything if he thought that it would bring him a profit and most of his floatations were trash foisted on a gullible public. Grant did not wait to be approached by industrialists or traders, but rather sought out businesses to be converted or invented wild schemes of his own to promote. Once a company was floated, he washed his hands of it. Grant's methods were characterized by fraud and deceit, yet, so lax were the requirements of commercial law, that during his active career between 1863 and 1877 he avoided criminal prosecution altogether.[27]

Grant was first active during the Finance Company Mania of the 1860s. In 1864 he created the Credit Foncier and Mobilier of England, a firm which financed Grant's numerous promotions.[28] He specialized in forming foreign railways, mines and public utilities. Most of his floatations led to legal disputes and allegations of fraud. In 1866, for example, Grant attempted to attract investment to the Marseilles Land Company by purchasing 27,000 of the company's 80,000 shares.[29] The Marseilles firm had been purchased by Grant for some £400,000 but was resold to the public for more than

£1 million. The difference of over £600,000 went largely in promotional fees to Grant and his cronies. According to *The Economist*: ". . . Mr. Grant had got so much into the habit of handling large sums that he gave away £10,000 to one person, £15,000 to another, and in fact distributed sums of this magnitude with as much ease as other people would have given half crowns."[30] Grant concealed his exorbitant profits by loading the purchase price of his promotions with overvalued assets.

By the early 1870s, Grant's promotional techniques were subject to growing public scrutiny. In 1871 Grant floated the Emma Silver Mining Company of Utah with a capital of £1 million. In reality this was a small, unpromising mine which failed within a year, paying investors only one shilling per £20 share. Grant, however, had puffed the concern in the press, at one point predicting annual profits of £800,000.[31] It later transpired that Grant wrote the money article for *The Times* while the financial editor, Sampson, was on holiday, and that he used this opportunity to puff shares in the mining company. An aggrieved shareholder by the name of Rubery sued Grant and Sampson for the recovery of his investment, claiming that he acquired the shares because of the puffs in *The Times*. Rubery won his case in 1872 and Sampson lost his position at *The Times*.[32]

In 1875 the Parliamentary Committee on Loans to Foreign States criticized Grant's 1871 floatation of the Paraguay Loan. It appeared that Grant and his fellow promoters bought back £300,000, or nearly one third, of the loan to artificially raise the price and attract further subscription.[33] Foreign promotions like the Paraguay Loan, the Emma Silver Mines and the Marseilles Land Company gave Grant tremendous leeway for distortion with little fear of contradiction. Investors had small opportunity to examine the *bona fides* of enterprises in distant lands and Grant traded on their ignorance. He applied to people of slender means; having lists compiled of clergymen, widows, retired army officers and other small investors, he sent them his circulars. Not only were these people lacking in business acumen, but they were ill placed to fight him in court should it come to that.[34]

The public contributed millions to Grant's various promotions, much of which went to fuel his vaunted social ambitions. In 1873 he purchased lands near Kensington Gardens on which he built a lavish mansion. He amassed a huge art collection and patronized charities. In 1865 and 1874 he was elected M.P. for Kidderminster. In 1868 King Victor Emmanuel made Grant an Italian baron for services involving the Milan Improvement Company which had cleared slums in the city center and built an elaborate shopping arcade. Remarkable achievements for a man who had begun life in Dublin as Abraham Gottheimer, the son of a poor Jewish tradesman from central Europe.[35] Grant's success, however, proved as transitory as most of his promotions.

In 1874 Grant was unseated from Parliament for election bribery. Earlier that year he had purchased property in Leicester Square, made it into a park and presented it to the City of London. By this time Grant had become discredited in the City, and, during the presentation ceremony men with sandwich signs listing Grant's defaulting companies were paid to walk around the square. Some of the placards bore the memorable verse:

> Honours a King can give, honour he can't:
> And Grant without honour is a Baron Grant.[36]

By 1877 Grant was bankrupt and his companies in disarray. Thirty-seven of his promotions, which had a total capital of £25 million in 1872, were now worth only £5 million. Grant retired from the City in disgrace; hounded by his creditors, he was forced to sell his art collection and Kensington mansion.[37]

Scores of civil actions for fraud were pending against Grant in 1877, many of them related to his 1871 promotion of the Lisbon Tramways Company. The first of these suits to be heard, Twycross vs. Grant, became a landmark case in company litigation. The plaintiff, James Twycross, alleged that Grant had violated section 38 of the 1867 Companies Act by failing to disclose in the prospectus certain contracts – in particular, a secret agreement between Grant and the builders of the tramway to pay Grant £45,000. Hidden fees of this sort, in effect "kickbacks," were a common feature of company promotions so that much of the money which investors believed went for the purchase of land, machinery, patents or labor went in fact into the pocket of the promoter. Twycross, arguing that he would not have acquired shares in the tramway company had he known of the undisclosed contract, demanded repayment of his £700 investment. The courts found for Twycross, and in so doing, established the principle that promoters were fully responsible for information in the prospectus and that they must disclose all contracts which affected the new company in a significant, material way.[38]

The company frauds of the 1860s and 1870s, especially those involving finance companies and foreign loans, gave promotion a decidedly bad name.[39] The amoral atmosphere of the City was taken up by Anthony Trollope in his dark novel of 1875, *The Way We Live Now*. Trollope detailed the activities of financiers promoting an improbable Mexican Railway: "The object of Fisker, Montague, and Montague was not to make a railway to Vera Cruz, but to float a company . . . Mr. Fisker seemed to be indifferent whether the railway should ever be constructed or not. It was clearly his idea that fortunes were to be made out of the concern before a spadeful of earth had been moved."[40] The novel's central character, Augustus Melmotte, was almost certainly modeled after Albert Grant. In 1876, *Blackwood's* published the short story "The Autobiography of a Joint-Stock Company, Limited," that was also modeled on Grant's speculations. Imaginatively told from the company's point of view, the story began: "I was conceived in sin and shapen in iniquity, and became almost immediately the means of demoralising every one who came into contact with me, of deceiving those who trusted in me, and of crushing those who opposed me, until my own time came, and I fizzled out in a gutter of fraud like a bad squib."[41] The story went on to detail all the abuses of company promoters: fraudulent prospectus, dummy directors, share rigs and false accounts.

Not surprisingly, many sober merchants and manufacturers remained suspicious of incorporation until very late in the century. "To the serious industrialist," Clapham argued, "the words joint-stock company still connoted irresponsible management, defective finance – actual fraud."[42] The bulk of promotions from the 1840s through the 1870s involved railways, government loans, banks and utilities. English industrial firms did not enter the share market in a significant way until the 1880s and 1890s, at which time there was a promotional boom in home industrials. Domestic manufacturing firms quoted on the Stock Exchange increased tenfold between 1885 and 1907. This was a period of industrial amalgamation and numerous businesses saw incorporation as a means of raising capital for expansion and acquisitions. In other businesses, founders retired and a new generation less interested in entrepreneurship – and less distrustful of the City – transferred their firms to public ownership. New technical advances in electricity and the internal combustion engine – the so-called Second Industrial Revolution – also sought financing in the share market.[43]

The late-century company boom unhappily saw a resurgence of fraud and questionable promotion methods. The vogue for private businesses going public was often abused by entrepreneurs who used floatation as a last, desperate attempt to bolster insolvent firms. In such cases prospectuses were cleverly worded to gloss over liabilities and lure investors with rosy promises.[44] Private traders also found that they could avoid the bankruptcy courts and cheat their creditors by means of incorporation. Upon turning their businesses into limited companies, traders would secure most of the assets for themselves through debentures (loan securities), leaving as little capital as possible to be the company's property.[45] They would then trade under the corporate name and incur debts for which only the property of the company was liable. If the company failed, the traders, as debenture holders, had first claim on their companies' capital, while the creditors were left with nothing.[46]

The most novel abuse of limited liability involved one-man companies, where a single person would appoint six "dummies" to inflate the number of company members to the required seven. An individual could thus carry on trade with limited liability, incurring debts in the company's name rather than his own. In case of insolvency creditors could not sue the individual businessman in the bankruptcy court but had to approach him through the "company" in Chancery.[47] While many legislators and jurists felt that one-man companies were an abuse of commercial law, the courts upheld the practice in the landmark case Broderip vs. Salomon and Company. Aron Salomon was a leather merchant who had converted his business into a limited company in 1892. Salomon held £19,994 of the £20,000 capital in the form of debentures; the company's other six members were Salomon's wife and children who held £1 each. In 1893 Salomon and Company became insolvent, and the debenture holders (Salomon himself) swept up all of the capital. Broderip, an aggrieved creditor, sued Salomon for the recovery of his debt, arguing that the company was a sham. The lower courts felt that Salomon had perverted company law to cheat his creditors, but on appeal it was decided that the letter of the law had not been violated.[48] Gilbert and Sullivan burlesqued the case in their 1893 operetta *Utopia, Limited*. In the play the King of

Utopia has himself incorporated as a limited company to foil assassins – since one can blow-up an individual, but not a corporation![49]

The most significant white-collar crimes of the *fin de siècle* involved the promotion of large-scale, public companies. The renewal of the speculative spirit furnished promoters with almost unlimited possibilities for personal profit at the expense of the investing public. The escalation of company fraud during the 1890s also drew Parliamentary scrutiny and was responsible for tightening the permissive Company Acts of mid century.[50] A new breed of company promoter emerged during the late Victorian and Edwardian periods. These men, as exemplified by Harry Lawson, Ernest Hooley, Whitaker Wright and Horatio Bottomley, were flamboyant figures who lived in ostentatious vulgarity, made and lost fortunes, and through it all traded on public ignorance and gullibility. They were, not to put too fine a point to it, con-men on a gigantic scale.

Typical of the new breed was Henry J. Lawson, an inventor and industrialist turned financier. After an early career as a bicycle manufacturer, Lawson floated a number of finance companies during the 1880s. These firms included the London and Scottish Trustee and Investment Company, the Mortgage Loan and Discount Company and the Discount Banking Company of England and Wales. Little is known of Lawson's early promotions, but in no case were the companies successful. The next phase of Lawson's financial career was as a promoter of bicycle and automobile companies. From the late 1880s through the 1890s he floated the Rudge Cycle Company, the Humber Cycle Company, Beeston Cycle, Beeston Tyre, the Great Horseless Carriage Company, the British Motor Syndicate and Daimler Motors. Like his earlier promotions, Lawson's cycle and car companies also had inauspicious careers. His method of promotion was to buy up a company on the cheap, inflate its capital outrageously, puff it in the press and unload its shares on the public. Lawson did nothing to increase companies' earning powers, but to maximize his own profit, he routinely inflated capital by a factor of ten or more – most of the difference going to himself or his allies as promotional fees. When Lawson purchased the Daimler Motor Company in 1895 it had a working capital of £6,000, but when he sold it to the public the next year, the capital was increased to £100,000. Lawson's floatations were doomed almost from inception through inability to earn profits on their inflated capitals. Almost all of Lawson's companies failed or else experienced a sharp drop in share value after floatation. In 1897 *The Economist* observed, "very few company promoters have equalled Mr. Lawson in glowing promises, while fewer still have been associated with so many ventures that have signally failed in the matter of performance."[51]

The promoter *par excellence* of the nineties was Ernest Terah Hooley, the "Napoleon of Finance." Not since George Hudson had a financial star blazed so brightly in the City sky. A number of Hooley's early deals were made in conjunction with Harry Lawson, though Hooley soon surpassed Lawson in level of operations. Between 1895 and 1897, Hooley promoted twenty-six companies with a total capital of over £18 million, of which some £5 million was his personal profit.[52] Hooley acquired two country estates, and further satisfied his social ambitions by becoming a justice of the peace, the High Sheriff of Cambridgeshire, a Lieutenant of the City of London and the Conservative candidate for Ilkeston. It was all too brief. By 1898 Hooley declared bankruptcy amid revelations of deceptive practices, while many of his companies were in dire straits.[53]

The son of a Nottingham lace manufacturer, Hooley left the family business to become a stockbroker and later a company promoter. In 1895 Hooley participated in a number of cycle floatations with Henry Lawson. The next year Hooley moved to London and intensified his promotional activities. Hooley was quick to grasp the fiduciary nature of company promotion, realizing that success lay in inspiring public confidence and enthusiasm. He was a master of persuasion and publicity, though his methods quickly degenerated into duplicity and fraud. Hooley routinely published prospectuses and advertisements which made exaggerated claims, he bribed journalists and financial editors for favorable reviews, and secured titled directors through substantial cash payments.[54] According to the *National Review*, Hooley's system of finance: "was corrupt in its inception, and in every step in its progress it spread fresh corruption. Every person who aided and abetted in carrying it through must have known perfectly well that the sole object of it was to get an outrageous 'pull' out of the public."[55] Hooley even boasted: "Any fool can sell what buyers require, but I can make them buy what they don't want."[56]

Hooley, like Lawson, would purchase companies from their

owners (mostly with borrowed money) and resell them to the public with as much capital tacked on as possible. The beef-extract firm Bovril, for example, was recapitalized by Hooley in 1896 from £400,000 to £2.5 million, though neither its assets nor its dividend earning power was increased one penny. Management usually continued in the same hands, with the sole addition of a few ornamental directors.[57] How the new public companies were to earn dividends commensurate with their inflated capitals was no concern of Hooley's. As he later admitted: "I bought a business as cheaply as I could and sold it again for the biggest price it would bring. Some people might say that by this method I robbed the public of millions of pounds, but nevertheless I did not do anything against the law."[58] The obvious response to this boast was articulated by the *National Review*:

Technically there may have been no legal flaw in these gigantic shuffles, but anything more mischievous and contrary to the spirit of sound finance it would be difficult to conceive . . . If the moral sense of the nation were to permit such finance to be carried on, we should soon degenerate into a gang of blacklegs. There would be less honour or honesty in the City than there is on the racecourse.[59]

Those businessmen who placed their faith in Hooley's abilities soon regretted their decision. As *The Economist* observed, "in nearly every instance the companies which wholly or mainly owed their existence to his operations were so grossly overcapitalized that they were practically foredoomed to a career of unprofitableness and trouble."[60] Because of their bloated capitals, "Hoolified" companies had to pay out too high a proportion of their profits in dividends and were unable to plow back sufficient money for improvements or expansion. Hooley also stripped companies of their cash reserves before reselling them so that illiquidity was another problem.[61] Hooley's enduring promotions, such as Bovril and Schweppes, only succeeded in spite of his intervention. Bovril was hard-pressed to service its capital after Hooley's restructuring, let alone find additional money to expand its business. The company was only able to continue through a personal loan from the firm's founding chairman, J.L. Johnston.[62]

Hooley's system of finance could not be carried on indefinitely. It required great sums of money to grease the palms of the press and guinea-pig directors, and as Hooley's methods achieved greater notoriety, lenders were not so forthcoming or investors so trusting.

In 1898 Hooley declared bankruptcy, and his house of cards came tumbling down. Hooley had liabilities of over £400,000, though, typical of the man, his bankruptcy was itself a fraudulent affair. Hooley had made over his properties to his wife, and life at his Derbyshire and Cambridgeshire estates went on pretty much as usual. The press christened him the "splendid bankrupt."[63] When Hooley filed his petition only four of his dozen cycle promotions were marketable; the others were moribund or in liquidation. The surviving firms' original capital of £8.5 million was at a 60% discount. Hooley's legacy was a string of ruined companies and firms floundering through overcapitalization and the shrinkage of share values.[64]

After his bankruptcy, Hooley carried on fraudulent schemes, albeit on a smaller scale, for another forty years, becoming bankrupt again in 1911, 1921 and 1939 and serving jail sentences for fraud in 1912 and 1922. In 1900 Hooley brought out the Siberian Goldfields Development Company with a proposed capital of £1 million. Since he was still bankrupt, Hooley directed things behind the scenes. The company falsely claimed to have the Tsar's sponsorship, and, when the press uncovered Hooley's involvement with the business, the scheme collapsed. In 1901 Hooley joined forces with the Canadian swindler J. Carling Kelly in promoting the Sapphire Corundum Company to work Canadian mines. The *Pall Mall Gazette* exposed a number of embarrassing facts about the company, the directors resigned and the banks refused to handle the company's funds. Hooley narrowly evaded criminal prosecution, improbably claiming to have been Kelly's ingenuous tool.[65] In 1904 Hooley and his old friend Henry Lawson were tried at the Old Bailey for defrauding a publican with regard to share deals in the Electric Tramways Construction Company, a firm which existed only on paper. Hooley escaped conviction, but Lawson was given twelve months imprisonment for publishing false reports about the company.[66]

Hooley's luck began to run out in 1911. That year he again became bankrupt, but this time around he had to sell his estates and had few assets to salt away. In 1912 Hooley was sentenced to twelve months imprisonment for defrauding George Tweedale of £2,000 through crooked property deals. Tweedale was a young man who had inherited £27,000 in 1909 and within two years been induced by Hooley to part with £21,000 of that sum.[67] In 1922

Hooley was again convicted of fraud for share dealings in a small cotton mill and given three years imprisonment.[68]

No sooner had Hooley's star fallen than it was replaced by that of Whitaker Wright, a mining company promoter whose career was equally spectacular, short-lived and fraudulent. After Wright's fall in 1900, *Blackwood's* summed up his promotional style: "Everything was swagger and no room was left for business. Swagger directors, swagger offices, swagger bankers, a swagger house at the West End, a swagger palace down at Surrey, a swagger yacht at Cowes, swagger entertainments – all matched each other. The whole thing was a gorgeous vulgarity – a magnificent burlesque of business."[69] Wright had left England at an early age and embarked on a career as a mining assayer in America where he made and lost a fortune. Upon his return to England in 1889 he set himself up as the promoter of imposing mining companies, exploiting the Australian and South African mining booms. Like Lawson and Hooley, Wright was a master of overstatement and showmanship, but his special contribution to promotional fraud was the abuse of holding companies and interlocking directorships.[70]

In 1894 Wright launched the West Australian Exploring and Finance Corporation and in 1895 the London and Globe Finance Corporation. Both firms had capitals of £200,000 and acted as holding companies for Wright's numerous mining promotions. Wright's fortunes did not depend on the performance of his mining companies (many of which were dubious speculations), but on the continued infusion of fresh capital to keep the ball rolling. To this end, the West Australian and the London and Globe were combined in 1897 as the New London and Globe and refloated with a capital of £2 million. In 1897 the new company spawned the British America Corporation with a capital of £1.5 million and in 1898 the Standard Exploration Company also with a capital of £1.5 million. Thus, within four years, Wright's two holding companies with a combined capital of £400,000 had blossomed into three companies with capital of £5 million. Wright desperately needed the new money as his promotions and share dealings were in pretty deep water by 1898. Investors had gradually awakened to the fact that the millions they had poured into Wright's floatations were not going to earn them a splendid return, and the outbreak of the Boer War further depressed the share market.[71]

Rather than admit defeat, Wright concealed his losses through a series of inter-company share manipulations. Wright's three holding companies, the London and Globe, the British America and the Standard Exploration, traded assets and liabilities with one another for balance sheet purposes. In this way the companies manufactured sham assets to make themselves appear profitable and to encourage further investment. In 1899, for example, the Globe "sold" to the British America worthless International Nickel shares at 18s a share for a "profit" of £237,000. The British America then resold the identical shares to the Globe at 20s per share. No money ever changed hands, but the shares (which were not worth a shilling on the open market) did double duty as assets in the companies' published balance sheets. Some of the shares traded between the Wright group were from companies that only existed on paper. By means of such frauds, Wright's balance sheets for 1899 and 1900 concealed a state of complete insolvency.[72]

Despite Wright's frauds, the shares in his mining companies fell sharply in 1900. Wright made enormous purchases of these shares in an attempt to rally the market but this did not happen and Wright was unable to pay for the shares when called upon to do so. His crash in December of 1900 brought down twenty Stock Exchange firms which had bought the shares for him. Wright fled to the United States but was extradited and tried in 1904 for issuing false balance sheets. Upon receiving the maximum sentence of seven years, Wright committed suicide by swallowing cyanide.[73]

The last and most audacious of the great Victorian swindlers was Horatio Bottomley. Bottomley's criminal career lasted nearly thirty years; first charged with fraud in 1893, he was not effectively brought to justice until 1922. During the intervening years Bottomley achieved great fame as a financier, politician and journalist. Despite his financial notoriety he was sent to Parliament by the voters of South Hackney in 1906, 1910 and 1918. Between 1906 and 1921 he published the popular paper *John Bull* from which he launched a number of his disreputable schemes. Bottomley outlived many a scandal through sheer force of personality. He was a genuine working-class hero, cultivating an air of impudence and addicted to horse racing, show girls and champagne. Throughout a long and checkered career, Bottomley used his celebrity to attract interest to his fraudulent promotions.[74]

After an early career as a court reporter, Bottomley was involved in promoting a number of publishing companies during the 1880s.

These ventures ended in bankruptcy and allegations of fraud against Bottomley, though nothing could be proved since accounts were poorly kept and certain key books were found to be missing. Bottomley then embarked on a series of more ambitious mining promotions in the manner of Whitaker Wright. Between 1894 and 1900, he promoted dozens of mines, including the Associated Gold Mines of West Australia, Nil Desperandum Gold Mines and Lake View South Gold Mines. These companies were notoriously short-lived, but Bottomley kept money coming in by resorting to the much abused financial technique of "reconstruction." Every year one or more of Bottomley's mines went into liquidation only to rise phoenix-like in a slightly different form. Shareholders of the old company would be told that the only chance of making money was in floating a new and improved company to take over the liabilities of its predecessors. They would be offered shares in the new company for a small consideration, say half their investment in the old company. If shareholders protested, they might receive some money back, but more often they would be ignored or told that their capital had been lost. Some Bottomley companies underwent as many as eight reconstructions, but this process depended on the speculative fever continuing unabated. When money became tight in 1899 the snowball stopped rolling, and Bottomley ceased his operations altogether at the time of Whitaker Wright's disgrace, though he emerged from the business a millionaire.[75]

Bottomley entered the newspaper business in the early years of the twentieth century, publishing first the *Sun* in 1902 and then launching *John Bull* in 1906. He used his papers to promote his political ambitions and to project a populist image of himself as "Tribune of the People" and champion of the "bottom dog." Bottomley also exploited the criminal possibilities of journalism, extorting money from individuals or businesses in return for suppressing negative stories. During this period Bottomley also began a long association with Ernest Hooley, assisting the bankrupt promoter in a number of shady deals. In 1905, for example, the two men floated the defunct (traffic-less, water-less) Basingstoke Canal as the "London and South Western Canal" – renamed to conjure up associations with the South Western Railway.[76] Bottomley was adept at pushing worthless shares, but with each new swindle his list of enemies grew.

In 1908 Bottomley lost a civil action brought by the heirs of one of his dupes and he was forced to repay £50,000. Bottomley declared bankruptcy in 1912 to ward off other claimants, but not before salting away his assets à la Hooley. Although he continued to live in his accustomed splendor, the bankruptcy hearings exposed too many of Bottomley's disreputable methods forcing his resignation from Parliament. In the years before the First World War, Bottomley contented himself with running a series of lotteries in *John Bull*. The schemes were registered in Switzerland to avoid the ban on domestic lotteries and the lucrative prize drawings rigged by Bottomley.[77]

Bottomley's public reputation revived somewhat during the war. He was active in the Anti-German League and *John Bull* struck a chord of defiant jingoism. A powerful orator, Bottomley was much in demand at recruitment drives, though his detractors mocked his pompous style and christened him "Hotairio." In 1918 he was returned to Parliament having campaigned on the slogan "Business, Brains, Bottomley" and the promise to punish the Germans. Bottomley's wartime patriotism was to prove his undoing. In 1918 Bottomley promoted the Victory Bond Club to encourage the purchase of the government's newly issued Victory War Bonds. Since the bonds were beyond the reach of the working class, Bottomley's scheme allowed people to send in small contributions which were pooled to buy bonds. Each pound sent in entitled a person to one chance at annual prize drawings for the accumulated interest. In this way Bottomley raised nearly a million pounds, though only part of the money went for the purchase of bonds. At least £150,000 went into Bottomley's pocket – the precise embezzlement was never discovered as accounts were poorly kept and certain incriminating documents destroyed.[78]

The war bond swindle was finally exposed through a bit of poetic justice. A fellow con-artist and sometime Bottomley ally, Reuben Bigland, publicized the fraud because Bottomley refused to back Bigland's scheme for converting water into gasoline. In 1920 Bigland published a pamphlet entitled *The Downfall of Horatio Bottomley, M.P.* in which he accused Bottomley of embezzlement. According to Bigland:

The British Government has allowed one of the greatest crooks ever born of woman to issue as one pound shares nearly one million of these pieces of common blue paper, thus permitting this editor of a well-known weekly paper to assume the right to hold this huge sum *alone*, with *no trustee*, *no auditor*, and a secretary only in name, with no one to say yea or nay if he cares to draw Ten Thousand Pounds to have a flutter at Ostend, on his horse Aynsley, or on the roulette table in the Casino.[79]

Bottomley felt compelled to sue Bigland for libel, but libel was not proven, and in 1922 the Public Prosecutor initiated proceedings against Bottomley for the fraudulent conversion of trust monies. He was found guilty and sentenced to seven years penal servitude.[80]

Infamous promoters like Horatio Bottomley and Ernest Hooley demonstrated the possibilities of company fraud on a gigantic scale, though many of their techniques were imitated by a host of other, less celebrated financiers. It has been noted that "further down the scale were men whose names have not even survived, hovering on the fringes of the financial scene, coalescing into groups to promote one or two schemes and then splitting up and disappearing again into obscurity."[81] It little mattered whether a would-be promoter had the financial resources of a Hooley or a Wright. By late century company promotion had become so pervasive that a whole network of subsidiary services and firms had grown up to assist promoters. Many of these agencies were not at all scrupulous about whom they assisted, fostering *bona fide* and fraudulent promotions with equal enthusiasm.

Advertising firms had been active since the 1860s, serving as middle-men between promoters and the press. The expense of inserting prospectuses and other advertisements in the London papers and provincial journals could be considerable and the papers expected cash payment in advance. Fly by night promoters seldom had the necessary money, but some advertising agents would pay the expenses of publicizing their schemes on a gamble. If the new company "took" and the public bought shares, the advertising agent would receive double the cost of the ads.[82] Promoting syndicates undertook the entire costs of floatation from the printing of the prospectus and stamp duties on memoranda and contracts to the law costs and accountant's charges connected with registration. These syndicates then charged the company a lump sum which often overstated the real costs of registration and publicity.[83] By the 1920s promoters were also assisted by postal publicity firms which sold to them lists of thousands of known shareholders.[84]

Financial agents assisted promoters in marketing shares and many such agents were undiscriminating about the quality of securities they sold. To take one case, the London solicitor Edward Beall accommodated Hooley by circularizing his clients with Hooley's prospectuses and recommending these companies as good investments. Beall received a commission of one shilling for every share his clients applied for in Hooley's companies, though of course the clients knew nothing of Beall's interest.[85] The most disreputable agents operated under assumed names and frequently changed offices to elude detection. Charles Singleton, for one, ran a series of fraudulent brokerage firms during the 1890s, working in concert with shady promoters. In 1890 Singleton conducted his business as Jacob B. Morrison and Company, in 1891 as both J.C. Hanson of the Metropolitan Stock and Share Association and T.V. Lawrence of the Empire Finance and Stock Corporation. At the time of his arrest in 1893, Singleton was known as A.F. Baker.[86] Even legitimate brokers were active in pushing shares. According to the *Journal of Finance*, some brokerage firms "depend largely upon acting as brokers for new companies . . . That they are not at all fastidious is shown by the fact that there has not been a single company amongst the swindles of recent years without its broker."[87]

Promoters were also assisted in their share issues by underwriters, or businessmen who guaranteed to take-up large blocks of shares in new floatations. Underwriters would then sell the shares to the public for which they would receive a commission, but if the shares proved unmarketable, the underwriters had to buy them themselves. Promoters favored underwriting as it transferred the risk of floatation to other parties. During the nineteenth century, however, underwriting was illegal as it was considered tantamount to issuing shares at a discount, though the ban was ignored by many promoters.[88] Underwriting was legalized in 1900 provided that the practice was disclosed in a company's prospectus. The advertisement that a company was underwritten actually inspired public confidence as it was assumed that underwriters would not undertake their risk unless they had thoroughly examined the company in question. Unfortunately, many underwriters were no more discriminating than brokers with regard to the quality of their wares. As capital issues grew larger during the twentieth century, underwriting grew in importance though not in soundness.[89] Securing good and reliable underwriters was a constant problem for honest promoters. Often companies had to pay underwriters heavy commissions, and if the issue was not successful, the underwriters disappeared, or in City parlance, proved themselves "duds."[90]

Company promoters and their various allies understood that publicity was key to a successful floatation. Thus investors would be bombarded on all sides with circulars, advertisements and press reports extolling the virtues of a new company in the rosiest terms possible. The most important document inviting subscription to a new company was the prospectus which set forth the company's purpose, the names of its directors and the amount of its capital. Ideally prospectuses should provide detailed financial information on the nature and value of companies' assets, though this was not required by law and in practice was rarely done. In the words of *The Cornhill Magazine*: "The large majority of them are interesting only as examples of audacious impudence, and as giving lamentably emphatic evidence of public gullibility: they seldom give one-half the information which anyone in his senses would require before investing in a new company, and yet it must be inferred that they do not display, or conceal, their charms in vain."[91] Promoters had advanced the art of prospectus writing to such levels of superficiality that potential shareholders remained ignorant of vital information. Estimates of future profits were dangled before investors' eyes while real assets were overvalued and past profits lumped together to conceal downward trends.[92]

According to Hooley, the public only read the front sheet of a prospectus to see the names of the company's directors and that to catch investors' attention a prospectus should advertise well known or titled directors, dubbed by Hooley "front sheeters."[93] These guinea-pig directors were the most celebrated aspect of promoters' window dressing. Their names were used to guarantee the respectability of a new company, although they usually held no financial interest in the undertaking, were shielded from liability and often completely ignorant of business matters. Great care was taken in assembling a distinguished board of directors. "A judicious promoter of companies," wrote *All the Year Round*, "is obliged, if he wishes to bring out a really good thing, to arrange his board as a bouquet-maker does his flowers."[94] Ideally, a directorial bouquet would have contained peers of the realm, country gentlemen, bankers, Members of Parliament and retired army officers. According to Hooley, "the average Briton dearly loves a lord, or if he is not to be had, a baronet, knight, or hon. will serve, while colonels and majors have their special uses."[95] Hooley claimed that the "front sheet" of the Dunlop prospectus cost him £100,000; Lord DeLaWarr cost so much, Lord Albemarle so much, and so on.[96] Whitaker Wright also paid thousands to secure Lord Loch and the Marquess of Dufferin and Ava as directors of the London and Globe.[97] Titled directors were invaluable publicity tools, ensuring that a company was mentioned in the society columns or gossip pages of the papers in addition to the money article. The use of guinea-pig directors was discredited somewhat after the fall of Hooley and Wright. Cartoons at the time pictured peers in sandwich boards advertising companies and a sign hung outside the House of Lords proclaiming "Peers for Hire."[98]

Promoters also traded on their own celebrity, and to this end fashioned images of themselves as powerful, wealthy and successful businessmen. By living showy, dramatic lives and indulging in conspicuous consumption, men such as Ernest Hooley, Whitaker Wright and Horatio Bottomley proclaimed their success and projected an air of confidence. Hooley in particular was master of the theatrical gesture, as in 1897 when he presented gold communion plate to St. Paul's Cathedral for the Queen's jubilee and then mentioned the gift in his company advertisements.[99] Hooley's exploits were even celebrated in popular song, as the following verse from a music hall ballad attests:

He walks into the Stock Exchange, and everybody there
Cries "Look out! Here comes Hooley, the famous millionaire!"
He can buy a share for tuppence and sell it for a pound
When he's bought St. Paul's Cathedral, he'll buy the Underground.[100]

This was the most valuable sort of publicity, reflecting as it did unsolicited public confidence in a promoter's money-making skills.

Promoters were well versed in the ways of journalism and cultivated close ties to the press. A number of financiers even owned newspapers which they used to puff their own companies. For a time Albert Grant was proprietor of a morning paper, the *Echo*, and the financier Edgar Vincent owned the *Statist* between 1892 and 1898.[101] In 1893 the disreputable financial agent Edward Beall established the *Financial Gazette* in partnership with the printer James Meeking. Beall wrote financial articles in the paper extolling the virtues of the London and Scottish Bank and other companies which he was involved in promoting. Meeking had previously printed the *Financial Critic* and the *Financial Lancet* in conjunction with other businessmen.[102] Horatio Bottomley had a long and profitable association with the press. During the 1890s Bottomley owned the *Joint Stock Circular* which puffed his mining promotions. In 1903 he ran the *Sun*, and between 1906 and 1922 his popular paper *John Bull* was the source of many Bottomley frauds.[103]

During the late nineteenth and early twentieth centuries, the financial press in Britain increased at a tremendous rate, reflecting the increases in joint-stock floatations and share dealings. In 1874 there were only 19 financial papers in all of the United Kingdom. This number rose to 32 in 1884, 50 in 1894, 92 in 1904 and 109 in 1914.[104] In addition to the quantitative upswing, financial journalism in England experienced significant qualitative changes. The "new financial journalism" which emerged in the 1880s and 1890s was livelier in style and more advisory in tone than the sober mid-Victorian money article. New papers such as the *Financial News* and its rival *The Financial Times* claimed to provide good investment information, exposing bad companies and steering investors toward good ones. In truth, however, the new journalism was riddled with fraud.[105]

Mercenary publishers such as Harry Marks exploited their positions of trust for illicit profit. Marks, who had apprenticed on American papers, brought "Yankee bounce" to British journalism with his creation in 1884 of the *Financial News*, London's first financial daily.[106] In the muck-raking tradition Marks' paper searched out fraudulent schemes; its biggest coup was the discovery of municipal corruption at the Metropolitan Board of Works in 1888. Through such revelations of fraud, the *Financial News* gained a credibility that it did not deserve. As a critic of Marks argued: "By the exposure of a few dubious cases, the opinion is engendered in the public mind that the *Financial News* is a genuine friend of the investor, and this makes it all the easier and safer for its proprietors and editor to play other games, where the interest of the investor is the last consideration that would ever occur to them."[107] Harry Marks was open to bribery from company promoters, accepting £17,000 from Ernest Hooley to puff the New Beeston Cycle Company. Marks also puffed concerns in which he was interested. In 1886, for example, Marks secretly promoted the worthless Rae Gold Mining Company, advising his readers to buy its shares at the same time that he was unloading his own holdings onto the market.[108]

Bribery of the press was widespread. In 1898 the *Nineteenth Century* complained: "That the City has a large number of 'reptile' journals, which will praise – and for that matter also condemn – anything as long as they are paid for it, is by this time well known to anyone who is not a tyro in finance. But unfortunately investors are mostly tyros in finance."[109] Three years later the financial journalist Charles Duguid criticized the sham financial press in his cautionary book, *How to Read the Money Article*. According to Duguid: "The pen is mightier than the sword, and sometimes, unfortunately, the purse is mightier than the pen. The writer of the money article, from the highest to the lowest, is subject to the frequent temptation of those financiers who would have him withhold his criticism or praise his wares."[110] The usual cash bribe was between £100 and £200, though bribes could sometimes reach into the thousands. A subtler method of buying influence was for the promoter of a new company to offer journalists a "call" on its shares, that is, the right to buy them at a guaranteed low price. Duguid asserted that these methods were so common that they were even pursued "by respectable men of business, who seem to regard the matter as an ordinary incident of commerce, and who sometimes take offense at the refusal, however delicately expressed." He goes on to relate that "there have been wagers in the City as to how long a certain financial editor would stand on his pedestal of honesty; such is the state of affairs."[111]

The most corrupt newspapers actually blackmailed promoters with demands of payment in return for the suppression of negative stories. Shady characters like Ernest Hooley were especially vulnerable to blackmailing journalists. During his bankruptcy proceedings in 1898, Hooley complained:

I have promoted companies that I have not made a single penny out of, because the newspapers took all the profit. I have paid one alone £40,000. A single article in another cost me £10,000. As soon as it is known that a company is coming out I am besieged by them and their representatives. They come quite openly and say, "Well, what are we going to get out of this?"[112]

Even honest businessmen submitted to the system, preferring being mulcted to the risks of bad publicity. Horatio Bottomley specialized in attacking companies in *John Bull* until placated by payments.

Payment might be in cash, or in the form of extensive advertising in the paper at inflated prices. Some victimized companies would quiet Bottomley by appointing him "special investigator," a sinecure for which he normally received £500 a year. Usually there was no foundation for Bottomley's attacks, but their nuisance value was so great that most firms would rather pay than fight.[113]

The financial press had a symbiotic relationship with company promoters which ill-served investors. Promoters needed publicity while newspapers and journals depended on promoters for advertising revenues. As *The Economist* put the dilemma in 1913, newspapers' "revenue is not derived from the readers they serve, but from the advertisers, and sometimes it is impossible for them to fulfil their duty to their readers without offending advertisers and losing revenue."[114] It was a common practice for papers to editorialize in favor of companies that advertised heavily and the line between advertisements and stories was not always drawn with much precision. Company promoters often paid reporters to cover company meetings or dinners given by the directors, though newspapers were not in the habit of labeling these stories advertisements.[115] The blurring of boundaries was rendered even more problematic when Reuters, the well-known news agency, entered the business of placing advertisements for companies just before the First World War. In its circulars to businessmen, Reuters declared: "In connection with any forthcoming issue of capital that you may contemplate, we are in a position to initiate and carry through a special preliminary Press propaganda to secure for the emission a successful reception of the investing public."[116] The agency could, in effect, disguise advertisements as news stories. Obviously standards of journalistic ethics were not well articulated during the Victorian and Edwardian periods, though the situation varied widely from paper to paper – usually depending upon the character of the publisher or editor. *The Economist* had always been above reproach. Not so *The Times*, though its lapses were few and far between.[117] The worst practice, as represented by papers like *John Bull*, persisted into the 1920s.

The acquisitive atmosphere of the City continued to find literary expression during the late Victorian and Edwardian years and images of the businessman showed a persistent mistrust of financial endeavor. The darkest picture was probably drawn by George Gissing in his 1897 novel *The Whirlpool*. Gissing's narrative is set in motion by the failure and suicide of the dissolute promoter Bennet Frothingham whose fraud serves as a metaphor for a society driven by greed and deceit. The Fabian dramatist Harley Granville Barker examined the embezzlements of a trustee in his 1905 play *The Voysey Inheritance*, concluding that the world was governed by "a particular sort of honesty." Joseph Conrad's 1913 novel *Chance* included a portrait of the financier deBarral, a promoter of dubious banking schemes. After deBarral's collapse, the book's narrator remarks: "I won't say in American parlance that suddenly the bottom fell out of the whole of deBarral's concerns. There never had been any bottom to it. It was like the cask of the Danaides into which the public had been pleased to pour its deposits."[118] The illusory, insubstantial nature of speculative finance fitted well with Conrad's pessimistic vision of modern society.

Other artists approached the City with a lighter, more humorous style. Comic portraits of pushing businessmen can be found in Arnold Bennett's novel, *The Card* (1911), and John Galsworthy's play, *The Skin Game* (1920). H.G. Wells betrayed a bemused appreciation for the audacious frauds of Mr. Ponderevo, the snake-oil salesman turned company promoter of his 1908 novel *Tono-Bungay*. The pantomimes and burlesques of the London music halls also delighted in poking fun at business types. Miss Julie Mackey had a great success at the Palace with her comic ballad "Terah-rah Hooley-ay" which celebrated the rise and fall of Ernest Terah Hooley to the strains of "Ta Ra Ra Boom De Ay."[119] Gilbert and Sullivan expressed musically the fraudulent possibilities of the joint-stock company in their operetta *Utopia Limited*:

> Some seven men form an Association
>   (If possible, all Peers and Baronets),
> They start off with a public declaration
>   To what extent they mean to pay their debts.
> That's called their Capital: if they are wary
>   They will not quote it at a sum immense.
> The figure's immaterial – it may vary
>   From eighteen million down to eighteenpence.
>   I should put it rather low,
>   The good sense of doing so
> Will be evident at once to any debtor.
>   When its left for you to say
>   What amount you mean to pay,
> Why, the lower you can put it at, the better.[120]

The style of W.S. Gilbert's libretto could hardly differ more from that of George Gissing's novel, but the two men's views of the City had much in common. Whether the tone was satirical or sardonic, the world of commerce was shown to be essentially amoral and self-serving.

The First World War had put a brake on new promotions, but the post-war years saw a frenetic return of joint-stock floatations. "Hard-faced men who did well out of the war" launched the nation on another decade of speculation.[121] The company manias of the 1920s were devoted to industrial amalgamations and the financing of new technologies such as radio and synthetic fibers, but they also gave rise to frauds and questionable methods of finance which were to culminate so disastrously in 1929.

The company boom of 1919–21 reflected the renewed confidence of the immediate post-war years and many of the floatations at the time were grandiose schemes for industrial amalgamations. The amalgamation or trust movement dated from the late nineteenth century, but earlier mergers had not relied so heavily on the public share market for financing.[122] Amalgamations were seen as the key to the "rationalization" of British industry, allowing for the more efficient use of resources, labor and technological "know-how" so that Great Britain could better compete with the large-scale economies of Germany and the United States. While there is much to be said for this belief, the promotion methods of many post-war amalgamations ill-served the British economy.

The amalgamation movement became the justification for a number of financial shams. Reckless promoters would combine several worthless or unrelated companies, inflate their capital, christen them a "trust" and unload their shares on the public. The *Nineteenth Century* complained that such amalgamations were focused "not on the 'rationalization' of an industry, not on the more economic and efficient creation of real wealth, but on the promoting of profits."[123] Many industrial combinations displayed no commercial logic as in Clarence Hatry's 1919 creation, Amalgamated Industrials, an odd mixture of businesses in shipbuilding, cotton spinning, the coal and iron industries and pig farming.[124]

Clarence Hatry was the first promoter to exploit the lucrative possibilities of business combinations, though his methods of finance rendered him one of the most notorious financiers of the 1920s.[125] Having begun his career as an insurance broker, Hatry acquired the Commercial Bank of London in 1916 to finance industrial amalgamations. Not all of Hatry's combinations demonstrated the illogic of Amalgamated Industrials, but nearly all of them were ridiculously overcapitalized in the manner of Hooley's promotions of the 1890s, and, like Hooley's companies, they struggled to service their inflated capitals. British Glass Industries, created by Hatry in 1919 with a capital of £3.6 million, had to write down its capital to £900,000 in 1924, but still failed two years later. Jute Industries, a 1920 combination of Scottish jute companies, only survived by decreasing its capital from £4.5 million to £1.6 million.[126] The high level of promotion could not be sustained beyond 1921 as the reality of the post-war industrial economy undercut the optimism born of victory. Hatry could no longer obtain fresh capital for his schemes and his bank collapsed in 1923 with liabilities of £3 million.[127]

The 1920s were a decade of slow growth for the British economy, but an economic upswing seemed likely in 1928 at which time there was another mania for joint-stock floatations. The mania was international in scope, fueled by a frenzy of speculative buying on the American Stock Exchange. In Britain, promotions again centered around industrial amalgamations as well as the creation of public companies in new industries such as safety glass, gramophones, radios, cinematography and artificial silk (rayon). The sad history of this speculative boom is too well known. Investors on both sides of the Atlantic bought shares on borrowed money in the hopes of reselling for a profit before their loans fell due, loans were obtained on inadequate security, and companies were sold for many times their original worth. Tremendous paper profits were generated through share dealings, but eventually loans fell due, sellers outnumbered buyers, and the house of cards collapsed. The panic began in America with the Wall Street Crash in October of 1929, and the London Exchange followed suit. In 1928 there had been 284 new share issues in Britain with a combined capital of £117,000,000. By 1931 70 of the companies had been wound up and the shares of 36 others had no value. The remaining companies were valued at £66 million, representing a loss to shareholders of over 47%.[128]

The English promotions of the 1920s were characterized by a number of reckless procedures, chief among them defective and fraudulent underwriting. A number of shoddy issuing houses had sprung up during the late twenties and were involved in dubious underwriting activities. If issues went well, the firms would make large profits, if not, they often defaulted on their obligations, wound themselves up, and started other issuing houses under different names. Many underwriters even contracted out their nominal responsibility to sub-underwriters who also frequently defaulted on their guarantees.[129] Both underwriters and sub-underwriters tended to operate on insufficient capitals so that they could not possibly support an issue which proved unmarketable. One underwriting firm active in rayon promotions took upon itself obligations of £292,000 when its own capital was only £30,000. The Fordham Trust, an issuing house with capital of merely £500, underwrote new issues totaling millions of pounds. Numerous cases came before the courts of penniless persons who speculated with underwriting. An official of the bankruptcy court described such practices as "a cankerous reflection on commercial rectitude."[130]

Another negative feature of the 1928–29 boom was the use of share pools and rigs to create an artificial demand for certain securities. Promoters frequently set up dummy corporations to purchase the shares of whatever companies they were pushing in hopes of "bulling" the market. The promoters of the Yorkshire Artificial Silk Company, for example, registered the Telford Trust with a capital of only £10. The Trust then bought up shares in the silk company to boost their popularity on the stock market.[131] Another common promotional technique of the 1920s was for promoters to place large buying orders with brokers in the provinces and then place orders to sell the same number of shares with other brokers. By doing this all over the country, promoters created the illusion that their shares were much in demand.[132]

The collapse of the share market exposed a number of gigantic company frauds, most notably those of Lord Kylsant at the Royal Mail Steam Packet Company[133] and Clarence Hatry at the Austin Friars Trust. Hatry had risen phoenix-like from his 1923 bankruptcy to participate in a new series of amalgamations during the late twenties. The second phase of his career, however, fared no better than the first and further illustrates how little English promotion had improved in nearly a century. In 1925 Hatry persuaded his creditors to provide him with £100,000 to start a new finance company – the Aylesbury Trust – to continue his promotion schemes, the profits from which would service Hatry's debts. The

Nineteenth Century later compared this transaction to the victims of a burglar financing the burglar so that he could steal from others to repay his original theft.[134]

Hatry sponsored a whole series of new amalgamations beginning in 1925 with the Drapery Trust, a combination of department stores. In 1927 Hatry's promotion syndicate, the Aylesbury Trust, was restructured as the Austin Friars Trust with its capital nominally increased to £300,000. In reality Austin Friars was insolvent almost from its inception, though the day of reckoning was postponed as long as Hatry could attract fresh capital through his promotions. Hatry exploited the latest company craze by floating in 1928 the Photomaton Group, a combination of firms that manufactured and distributed photo-booths. Like Hatry's earlier promotions, the Photomaton Group was ridiculously over-capitalized and was never able to earn sufficient profits to service its shares.[135]

Hatry's most ambitious scheme, and the one that was to prove his undoing, was his attempted purchase of the United Steel Companies and the United Strip and Bar Mills in 1929 to form a giant steel trust which he planned to float as Steel Industries of Great Britain. Hatry needed to secure £8 million to purchase the other concerns, and his difficulty in raising the money led him to fraud. The Austin Friars Trust duplicated securities in its possession so as to create additional collateral for bank loans. The head office of Lloyds Bank, for example, held 100,000 shares in Associated Automatic Machines on which it loaned Hatry money, while at the same time the St. James Branch of Lloyds held exact duplicates of those 100,000 shares on which it too had advanced money. Hatry also utilized companies which existed only on paper as collateral for loans. Almost £2 million was raised on securities from Iron Industries, a dummy corporation which had no business history, whose shares had never been traded and whose only asset was £2,000 in cash.[136] Hatry's most audacious fraud was probably his forgery of municipal bonds. Hatry had floated a number of municipal loans during the 1920s and he still held copies of bond certificates for Gloucester, Swindon and Wakefield which he now duplicated as security for additional bank loans.[137]

The downturn of speculation in the autumn of 1929 led to the exposure of Hatry's frauds. His crash in September, involving liabilities of nearly £14 million, further shook public confidence in the share market and contributed to the panic which overwhelmed Wall Street in October.[138] In 1930 Hatry was tried for fraud, convicted and sentenced to fourteen years imprisonment. In pronouncing sentence, Mr. Justice Avory characterized Hatry's crimes as "the most appalling frauds that have ever disfigured the commercial reputation of this country."[139]

Hatry's machinations dramatized the shortcomings of English finance. In 1931 the Parliamentary Committee on Finance and Industry criticized the amateurish nature of new share issues. During the entire period between the Railway Mania of the 1840s and the Great Crash of 1929, company promotion as practiced in Britain had been a poor intermediary between the business community and the investing public. The system contained a built-in conflict of interest between promoter and public, whereby the promoter benefited from selling a company for the greatest price he could obtain, frequently leading to overcapitalization, unprofitability and failure. Unlike most other commercial transactions, where there was a presumed equality between buyer and seller, the buyer of shares was at the mercy of the company promoter. As the Macmillan Committee argued in 1931: the individual investor can hardly be supposed to have himself knowledge of much value either as to the profitable character or the security of what is offered to him. How easily he can be misled in times of speculative fever by glittering – even tawdry – appearances is proved by the experience of 1928"[140] Lured by the presence of distinguished directors, bankers, auditors, solicitors and brokers on a company's prospectus, investors assumed that these experts had already examined the issue's *bona fides* and that they would not have lent their good names to anything questionable. Any or all of these agencies *could* have investigated the soundness of a new company before agreeing to act for it, indeed, one might argue that they had a moral obligation to do so. Unfortunately, they had no legal obligation. Likewise the Registrar of Joint Stock Companies and the Committee of the Stock Exchange exercised no discrimination with regard to the floatation of public companies. It was only natural that promoters would exploit the strategic position which the permissive nature of company law and commercial practice had given them.

CHAPTER 6

Company fraud: management

Once a company had passed through the uncertain process of promotion, it was still vulnerable to fraud on the part of those persons who managed the business for shareholders.[1] The vast assets of large corporations proved too great a temptation for many of those whose job it was to manage shareholders' money. The divorce of ownership and control in public companies also placed directors in positions of almost unlimited power *vis-à-vis* shareholders. The license of directors was further bolstered by investors' ignorance regarding business matters, the inadequacy of auditing and the permissive nature of company law.

Directorial abuse of power was greatest when authority was concentrated in too few hands. Ideally, managerial authority was to have been divided among several directors who were to act as checks on each other. In practice, however, there was nothing to prevent directors from conspiring with each other to defraud shareholders. In other cases a single, strong personality might emerge as leader, riding roughshod over other directors who were too timid, ignorant or lazy to protest. Too many directors, especially those of the guinea-pig variety, viewed their positions as sinecures. It was thus fatally easy for an aggressive businessman like George Hudson to gain complete control over his fellow directors, who were quite content to draw their salaries and leave the work to someone else.

That such dereliction of duty on the part of directors eliminated an important safeguard against fraud was dramatized in a number of notorious cases. At the trial of the City Bank of Glasgow directors in 1878, it was revealed that only one director was well informed about the bank's affairs.[2] During the bankruptcy hearings of the Liberator Building Society in 1893, most of the directors admitted that they knew nothing of the company's finance but had simply approved everything that the absconding chairman, Jabez

Balfour, enacted. The outraged registrar of the court finally complained:

I think we have had enough of this. Shall we ever come to anyone who will admit that he was responsible for anything that was done, or knew anything about it? . . . Each director comes here, and notwithstanding the fact that as a body they obtained immense sums of money from people, not one of them up to the present has admitted taking the trouble to read the important statements in the prospectus issued for that purpose.[3]

Another dramatic example of neglect occurred during the early twentieth century, at which time the directors of the City Equitable Fire Insurance Company gave one of their number, Gerard Lee Bevan, sole control over company investment with the result that Bevan purchased for the firm speculative shares in which he had a personal interest. These shares were flagrantly inappropriate investments for an insurance business and ultimately ruined the company.[4]

Dishonest directors had even less trouble exerting their control over shareholders. Many shareholders were ignorant of business matters and had few good sources of financial information on which to rely.[5] The overwhelming tendency of investors was to believe all that their directors told them. According to Herbert Spencer, many shareholders were by the very nature of their occupations and upbringing easily swayed:

A great proportion are incompetent to judge of the questions that come before them, and lack decision to act out such judgements as they may form – executors who do not like to take steps involving much responsibility; trustees fearful of interfering with the property under their care, lest possible loss should entail a lawsuit; widows who have never in their lives acted for themselves in any affair of moment; maiden ladies, alike nervous and innocent of all business knowledge; clergymen whose daily discipline has been little calculated to make them acute men of the world; retired tradesmen whose retail transactions have given them small ability for grasping large considerations; servants possessed of accumulated savings and cramped notions, with sundry others of like helpless character – all of them rendered more or less conservative by ignorance or timidity, and proportionately inclined to support those in authority.[6]

As long as a respectable dividend was paid, shareholders assumed that all was well.[7]

If shareholder opposition to the directorate manifested itself, it could usually be overcome. When directors anticipated trouble, they sometimes created false proxies to guarantee themselves a majority at public meetings. Directors might also "pack" meetings – that is, hire persons who were not shareholders "to make much noise and much show of hands." Crooked companies could avoid unpleasant confrontations altogether by holding meetings at inconvenient times and in out of the way locations. In 1901 the financial journalist Charles Duguid wrote: "It is amusing to note how hundreds of companies of the baser sort arrange to hold all their meetings at practically the same time within the period of a few days in December." Such gatherings were referred to by businessmen as "hole and corner meetings."[8] Recourse to such extreme methods of evasion was seldom necessary, however, as directors preferred subtler means of concealing unflattering information.

The obscurity of most published company accounts ensured that shareholders would remain in the dark regarding a company's poor financial performance or a director's financial indiscretions. Even many honest directors believed that shareholders, like children, should know no more than is good for them, and, like children, should be deceived for their own good.[9] The balance sheets and financial reports presented to shareholders at annual meetings contained the meagerest information. Balance sheets often lumped together assets so that the profits (if any) for a given year were not clearly discernible. According to the financial writer Hartley Withers: "Most quite intelligent people, faced for the first time by a balance-sheet, find in it a quite incomprehensible cryptogram, and it is only after many explanations and some practice that they can attempt to read any meaning into it."[10] A witness before the Parliamentary Committee on Company Law in 1928 described balance sheets as "models of obscurity" and the distinguished accountant Sir Mark Webster Jenkinson argued that "backers of horses have better information available than speculators in shares."[11]

Directors had great latitude in their valuations of a company's assets and the practice was often abused by directors who would write-up the book value of certain assets to project an image of false profitability or to conceal trading losses. A flagrant example of this sort of fraud can be seen in the activities of Farrow's Bank during the 1910s. Dudley Docker also grossly overvalued the assets of his Metropolitan Carriage Wagon and Finance Company before selling it to Vickers in 1919.[12] In other cases directors doctored balance sheets to show that their company was losing money. This would bring about a fall in share prices, enabling directors to purchase the shares at a heavy discount. The use of falsified balance sheets to "bear" the market had been pursued by numerous railway companies during the 1840s and 1850s.[13] Directors often defended obscurity in accounts as a necessary protection against competitors, and they even justified the fraudulent enhancement of balance sheets as well-intentioned attempts to save a company's credit or to protect shareholders.[14] During the 1920s one director frankly admitted that "the balance sheet is the Company's shop window into which we put as much of the profits as is necessary to display."[15]

Shareholders were completely at the mercy of directors with respect to the disclosure of information. From the 1840s through the 1920s, the accounting requirements of company law were ineffectual. The Companies Act of 1862 stipulated that "directors shall cause true accounts to be kept," but there was no mandatory audit for public companies until 1900. Even after 1900, the responsibilities of auditors remained largely undefined by the law. Directors could still insert anything regarding auditing in their Articles of Association, and, in most cases, the auditor was the mere nominee of the director.

Throughout much of the nineteenth century, the audit of company accounts was farcical. Before the 1870s most auditors were not professional accountants, and their methods of examining financial records were careless and haphazard. Auditors were often friends of the directors or else prominent shareholders; in some cases directors themselves conducted the audit. Furthermore, most audits were merely arithmetical checks of the books or comparisons of vouchers with recorded payments. Auditors seldom attempted to go behind the books and question the valuations or investigate whether paper assets had any real existence.[16] A witness before the Lords' Committee on the Audit of Railway Accounts in 1849 described audits as "mere moonshine as against dishonest directors."[17] In a scathing attack on amateur auditors, Charles Dickens argued that these "wooden guardians of property" almost assisted fraudulent directors. The financial criminal, Dickens contended:

. . . seems early to have analysed one of these highly curious productions of the mercantile world, and to have arrived at an exact estimate of its value. He found it to be composed of a little fussiness, a great deal of carelessness

and trusting simplicity, a small portion of hurried and divided attention
. . . He observed that this half-human, half-mechanical being had a settled
aversion to move off its chair, and seldom asked to be allowed to examine
any books or documents that were not voluntarily placed before it. He
observed that it had an almost superstitious reverence for figures, if they
appeared to balance each other, and showed no marks of erasure; and that
so long as these emblems or signs of things were provided in liberal
quantities, it never cared to inquire whether the things themselves had
any substantial existence.[18]

Auditors were usually businessmen fully occupied with their own
affairs who would stop by the companies they audited a few times a
year and literally glance over its books and vouchers.[19] Amateur
audits were most common during the first half of the nineteenth
century, though in some business circles they persisted into the
1890s at which time they were facetiously referred to as "biscuit
and sherry audits."[20]

Directors were only too ready to exploit the unrestrained atmosphere of the corporate world. In 1906 the financial writer Anthony
Pulbrook gave vent to this pessimistic view: "The author's experience of directors of companies is that, as a general rule, their ideas
of honour are not of a very high order."[21] The most sensational
directorial crimes involved the embezzlement of company assets.
Embezzlement was probably most common among banking companies, as these businesses always had large amounts of cash on
hand.[22] Victorian newspapers were filled with accounts of absconding directors and managers, offering their readers a capitalist mir-
ror to the *Newgate Calendar*. A particularly shocking fraud came to
light in 1877 when the aptly named William Swindlehurst was
convicted of embezzling funds from the Artisans' Dwelling Company – a prominent charitable institution.[23] Even the dearly
departed were not immune from victimization, for during the 1880s
the manager of the London Burial Company, which ran Highgate
Cemetery, embezzled some £300,000.

Less dramatic than outright embezzlements, though far more
common, was the misuse of company funds or the exploitation of
one's position as director for personal gain. A common abuse,
dating back to the Railway Mania was for directors to pay
dividends wholly or partly out of capital. By so doing, directors
placated shareholders, maintained the credit of the company,
raised share prices and even lured in further investment, but they

also drained the company of monies needed to operate its business. Some directors failed to maintain depreciation funds for the upkeep or renewal of equipment so as to pay out larger dividends. Directors' salaries were often based on a percentage of the dividend declared, so that it was in their personal interest to declare large dividends even when the company might be better served by plowing back profits.[24]

Directors' abuse of their borrowing powers was another serious problem for investors in joint-stock companies. Companies incorporated by special Acts (e.g. railways and banks) had restrictions placed on how much money they could borrow, but no such limitations were placed on companies registered under the Companies Acts.[25] Directors might borrow money far beyond a company's ability to repay. Failing companies sometimes borrowed as a way of paying dividends, raising share prices and enabling directors to unload their own shares. In practice shareholders could exercise little restraint over directors' borrowing, and creditors had no real knowledge as to how much of a company's assets were tied up in loans.[26] The most common means of borrowing was for a company to issue debentures, or mortgage stock secured on company assets. In many cases, however, unscrupulous directors backed their debentures with insufficient, or worthless, or unrealizable assets. Some directors employed crooked vendors who specialized in marketing counterfeit debenture stock. These vendors frequently advertised in papers the sale of debentures with a "guaranteed" profit of 50% and a promise to buy back the securities if the money was not realized in a year's time. When the time for payment arrived, the vendor would tell his unfortunate dupes that the tightness of the money market prevented his repurchasing. If victims proceeded to law, they would find that one could not recover on guarantees from persons who had no money.[27]

Directors profited in numerous ways by exploiting their positions of trust. They awarded lucrative contracts to friends and relatives in return for gratuities and sold personal property to their companies at inflated prices. A common fraud, known as "salting," entailed directors buying property at one price, selling it to shareholders at a much higher price, and then pocketing the difference. In 1877, for example, the directors of the Marseilles Land Company overcharged that company £600,000 for land purchases.[28] In 1893, when he was a director of the Hansard Union Publishing

Company, Horatio Bottomley bought a decrepit printing works for a few thousand pounds and resold it to the company through an intermediary for £325,000.[29] Directors also used their influence to employ company funds for the purchase of securities in which they held an interest. After the First World War, for example, Gerard Lee Bevan, in his role as director of an insurance company, purchased for that company's investment portfolio the shares of companies which he was promoting. Bevan hoped to boost the share values of his promotions, but he only succeeded in bankrupting the insurance company.[30] During the 1920s, Martin Coles Harman, the controlling force behind a series of companies known as the Harman Group, became a director of Morris and Jones, a Liverpool grocery company for the express purpose of persuading the grocery company to buy up worthless shares in his other companies.[31]

Perhaps the most lucrative source of illicit directorial profit was the use of privileged information before it became generally known. Directors and their friends could profit from such information if it were favorable by buying shares or if it were unfavorable by selling. Such "insider trading" has only recently been made illegal, but it was always held to be "a violation of the best City etiquette." There is frustratingly little evidence concerning insider trading during the nineteenth and early twentieth centuries, though informed sources maintained that the practice was widespread. According to H.B. Samuel, a solicitor who specialized in company affairs, the percentage of directors who engaged in insider trading during the 1920s was as high as 50%.[32] Then as now, such practices were difficult to trace since directors maintained secrecy by operating through nominees. Information remains the most intangible sort of evidence, defying our attempts to pin down its original source or to trace its progress.

The free and easy English business environment facilitated frauds and embezzlements at all levels within a company. The same laxity in bookkeeping and auditing that gave a George Hudson or a John Sadleir free rein over a company's funds, also allowed the lowliest clerk to dip into the till undetected. Clerical embezzlement was a serious problem for companies throughout the nineteenth century. In large corporations enormous sums of money passed through the hands of clerks who often had sole control over cash books and share registers and were in many cases poorly supervised.

Clerks in the billing departments of large companies developed ingenious ways of skimming off profits for themselves. During the 1840s, for example, John Mason, a clerk at the Board of Works in Ireland embezzled some £8,000 by altering checks which passed through his hands. In one case Mason altered a £141 check to £441 for a personal gain of £300.[33] Among the frauds of Leopold Redpath at the Great Northern Railway was the alteration of a stock coupon from £250 to £1,250.[34] Such frauds were made possible by slipshod bookkeeping as many companies did not write out the amount of payments in words upon checks and invoices. Another common clerical fraud involved paying the same bill twice; one check was sent to the creditor, the other misappropriated. The second payment could be receipted fraudulently or the creditor might be asked for a duplicate receipt on the pretext that the original had been lost.[35] Especially devious clerks inserted "dummy" names into wage books and then drew the extra salaries for themselves.[36]

Employees in companies' registry and transfer departments found it relatively easy to manufacture fraudulent stocks and shares. Clerks who kept the certificate books often had access to the company seal and blank share certificates. They could thus produce duplicate shares and sell them for their own benefit. During the 1830s a Treasury clerk, J. Beaumont Smith, created more than £270,000 of forged Exchequer Bills, prompting an official inquiry.[37] Leopold Redpath created over £200,000 of fraudulent stock at the Great Northern Railway in the 1850s. This sort of fraud was still very common in the early twentieth century and proved most difficult to detect since it did not require the alteration of a company's books. Manufactured shares could be sold for a rise and later redeemed before the next audit to maintain the original total of stock. If a director acted in collusion with a transfer clerk, detection was almost impossible.[38]

Clerical embezzlements were the subject of growing concern during the mid-Victorian era, at which time economic expansion and the proliferation of the joint-stock company increased the opportunities for such crimes. At the 1843 trial of an embezzling clerk, the judge observed:

... this case was only one out of 34 of a similar character comprised in the calendar of the present session. It was, therefore, absolutely necessary that a severe sentence should be passed, in order to operate as a warning to others, and prevent, if possible, the repetition of such offenses, which he regretted to say were increasing at an alarming extent.[39]

Clerical embezzlement was the most frequently tried of all white-collar crimes, with Victorian and Edwardian prosecutions numbering in the thousands.[40] These known cases, however, probably represented only a fraction of all such crimes. Many or most embezzlements probably remained concealed from the public because of employers' fears of scandal and bad publicity.[41] The concern for clerical honesty can also be measured by the prevalence of embezzling clerks in Victorian novels, exemplified by Uriah Heep in *David Copperfield* (1850), Carker in *Dombey and Son* (1846), and Alaric Tudor in Trollope's *Three Clerks* (1857).

The revelation of several extraordinary clerical embezzlements during the 1850s dramatized the vulnerability of large corporations to employee theft. In 1850, for example, the directors of the Globe Assurance Company were horrified to discover that one of their most trusted employees, Walter Watts, had embezzled over £70,000 from the firm during a six year period. As chief clerk in the cashier's department, Watts was custodian of the banker's pass-book and altered it as a means of embezzling money. Watts' *modus operandi* was relatively simple. An incoming check for £525, to take one example, would be recorded in the passbook as £25 and an already paid claim for £7 would be altered to read £507, leaving Watts free to pocket the £500. The receipt department had no effective check against fraud since the banker's passbook was the basis for the company accounts rather than the actual policies or claims. The audit could not have been very searching since Watts' books presented a mass of erasures and alterations which should at once have created suspicion. Watts' defalcations enabled him to augment his £200 yearly salary with an additional £10,000 a year. A passionate devotee of the drama, Watts led a double-life as a theatrical impresario, writing plays and leasing two London theatres – the Marylebone and the Olympic. He was sentenced to ten years transportation, but committed suicide while still in prison.[42]

In 1856 William James Robson, chief clerk in the transfer department of the Crystal Palace Company, was found to have embezzled some £27,000 through the fraudulent transfer of shares.[43] Shareholders often left their share certificates in the company's hands for safe-keeping and Robson sold these securities on the Stock Exchange. Robson's crime highlighted the negligent nature of much business organization, for he had sole control of the company's share register and transfer book and his superiors never seemed to have checked his work. At the trial, the company treasurer sheepishly admitted: "At every general meeting of share-holders a register was made up purporting to be a complete state-ment of the shares – it appeared to be complete. I looked at the total. I did not go into all the details personally or add up the shares."[44] Stockbrokers were also shown to have been careless in their transactions with Robson since they never questioned the fact that the names on the share certificates were different from the names Robson used as the seller of these shares.[45] Robson was sentenced to twenty years transportation and his crime alerted many companies to the possibilities of share transfer frauds. The same year as Robson's trial, an ad hoc investigation at the transfer department of the Great Northern Railway exposed a similar fraud by Leopold Redpath – for the staggering sum of a quarter of a million pounds.[46]

In 1860 the management of the Union Bank of London uncovered enormous embezzlements by their chief cashier William George Pullinger. Pullinger had served as a clerk in the bank since 1839, but upon his elevation to chief cashier in 1855, he found himself with unsupervised access to the bank's reserve at the Bank of England. Over a five year period, Pullinger extracted £263,000 from the balance at the Bank of England, using this money to speculate on the Stock Exchange. Pullinger pleaded guilty and was sentenced to twenty years penal servitude.[47]

The embezzlements of a Pullinger or a Redpath illustrated the upper limits of clerical fraud. Most known embezzlements, however, were considerably smaller. Rob Sindall's sampling of the Victorian criminal record found average embezzlements to have been only a few pounds.[48] Clerical embezzlements of over £1,000 were extremely rare.[49] Few clerks saw embezzlement as the path to great wealth or social advancement. Most embezzlers stole small sums in attempts to relieve the dull monotony and shabbiness of their lower-middle-class existences.

In many cases clerks received salaries similar to skilled laborers, and yet were expected to maintain a middle-class lifestyle. The necessary expense of a respectable wardrobe or children's educa-tion often meant pinching in other areas, especially diet and leisure activities. "An overcoat, but no breakfast" was the working-class assessment of the clerk. Mid-Victorian banking clerks began at around £50 per annum and seldom advanced to a salary beyond £250. Salary levels increased little during the nineteenth and into the early years of the twentieth century.[50] Since salaries were usually paid in quarterly installments, many clerks were continually in debt and the constant struggle to keep up appearances took its toll. Contemporaries often commented on the relationship between low wages and embezzlement.[51] John Francis, for one, contended:

> . . . it is a dishonour to commercial nature, that, considering the profits made by merchants, the daily intercourse they hold with their clerks, and the trust they are compelled to place in them, they pay in so small, and work in so great a degree. It is a most suggestive fact that, where the functionaries are remunerated the worst, the frauds are most numerous.[52]

Far more typical of the embezzling clerk than William Robson or Leopold Redpath was Thomas Hawkins, who in 1846 confessed to the theft of a few pounds from his employer because his salary was too low to support his wife and children.[53]

Not surprisingly, clerks were also lured into the world of speculation, sometimes beginning their defalcations to cover losses at the Stock Exchange. Clerks' occupations often familiarized them with company finance and share transactions, and they naturally sought to profit from their special knowledge. The problem of clerical speculation became apparent during the Railway Mania and was viewed with considerable alarm in the City.[54] At mid-century, the Committee of the London Stock Exchange, acting under pressure from the business community, forbade its members from transacting speculative business for clerks in private establishments or public companies without the knowledge of their employers.[55] In 1860 four brokers on the Exchange were suspended for one year for dealing with William Pullinger without informing his employer, the Union Bank.[56] Generally, however, the rule was not well enforced. During the 1870s, for example, the clerk Edward Barry invested £20,000 in shares with embezzled money and no broker ever challenged those transactions.[57]

Some contemporaries argued that clerks were driven to crime by the acquisitive spirit of the age and the poor standards of ordinary business ethics. The high premium placed on financial success by the Victorians and Edwardians may have made embezzlement seem less harrowing than the stigma of poverty or failure. In a sarcastic reference to Smiles' doctrine of "self help," Charles

Dickens likened embezzling clerks to self-made men who were simply responding to the ideal of their age:

Such men as Walter Watts, as William James Robson, as Leopold Redpath, and William George Pullinger are the purest examples of "men who have helped themselves." They started from very humble positions – were born with no directorial silver spoons in their mouths – were quick to discover the weakest point of the trading system in which they were placed – and, with one exception, almost ended by becoming convict millionaires.[58]

Other social critics believed that clerks were debauched by the low tone of commercial morality in which they worked. In 1913 the Reverend J.W. Horsley wrote:

How terribly common it is for employers to induce, and practically to force, employees to lie and deceive the public under penalty of losing favour or promotion, or even employment, is well known to those to whom shop-assistants and clerks come with their cases of conscience . . . In thousands of cases, religious principles having been thus outraged by employers, the practice of religion seems an hypocrisy, and is deserted in spite of early training and previous habit, and then, if the clerk or shopgirl eventually dips into the till the employer who has made this possible poses as an injured innocent and prosecutes![59]

Employers initially sought protection from clerical fraud through insurance. Banks, insurance companies and other commercial firms had a long tradition of expecting clerks to provide personal guarantees against fraud. Guarantees usually ranged from £100 to £1,000 and were in the form of pledges to pay on the part of clerks' friends or relatives. These sureties, however, would only cover small frauds, and, as the problem of embezzlement increased from the 1840s onwards, insurance policies began to replace personal guarantees. Insurance companies sold "fidelity guarantee" insurance to cover losses through embezzlement.[60] The demand for such insurance can be gauged from the records of one company, the Guarantee Society, which grew from 700 policies in 1848 to over 5,000 new policies a year by the late sixties.[61] Most fidelity policies would still not cover the largest embezzlements, and, before restitution was made, insurers usually required companies to prosecute the offending party and obtain a criminal conviction – an impossible requirement if the embezzler had absconded.[62] Insurance cushioned the blows of clerical fraud, but did nothing by way of prevention. Embezzlements only decreased in size and frequency in response to late-century improvements in auditing and managerial efficiency.

Clerical fraud was an important factor behind improvements in company auditing during the 1870s and 1880s. During these decades the practice of amateur audits gave way to professionalization and rigorous systems of internal bookkeeping checks. The London Institute of Accountants was founded in 1870 and the Institute of Chartered Accountants in England and Wales in 1880 as part of an effort to raise the standards of accountancy.[63] The National Institute established a program of study and a series of examinations to achieve certification. Members kept abreast of the latest innovations in accounting through lecture series and articles published in the journal, *The Accountant*. During its early years, much of the Institute's attention was focused on questions of fraud and embezzlement. In 1898, for example, the Institute sponsored an essay contest on the theme: "Frauds in Connection with Bookkeeping, and Methods to be used in their Detection."[64] So great was the Institute's impact that, by the 1890s, most company audits were conducted by professional accountants.

Annual audits improved markedly under the guidance of chartered accountants, but so too did the day to day techniques of corporate bookkeeping. Accountants assisted companies in setting up systems of continuous internal audits whereby bookkeeping responsibilities were divided among different departments that acted as checks on one another. Clerks were not allowed to monopolize certain ledgers but were periodically set to work on different accounts or in checking the work of their fellows.[65] Surprise inspections also diminished the level of fraud since embezzlers could no longer square their accounts in anticipation of regularly scheduled audits.[66] By the twentieth century large-scale embezzlements occurred only in those companies with poor systems of internal checks.[67] In 1902, for example, a ledger clerk at the Bank of Liverpool, Thomas Goudie, was able to embezzle £162,000 from the bank because he had free range over all of the bank's ledgers and account books and was even allowed to check his own work. The dismay with which the Goudie fraud was greeted in business and accounting circles and the harsh criticism leveled against the Bank of Liverpool's management demonstrated just how unusual and avoidable such embezzlements had become.[68]

Improved accountancy and auditing had reduced clerical

embezzlement, but had little effect on directorial fraud. In most cases auditors remained under the authority of company management and were unable to exercise their supervisory powers over directors' activities. By law, auditors were responsible to shareholders, but in practice they were answerable to the board of directors. Auditors were usually nominees of the board and were dependent on the board to keep their jobs.[69] As late as 1926 the Greene Committee on Company Law Reform heard testimony that many auditors experienced "terrific pressure" from directors to put a brave face on things and sometimes lost their jobs if they were too meticulous.[70]

Directors controlled the information on which a company's published accounts were based and they continued to enjoy great latitude in drawing up those accounts. The directorial abuse of information, that is, the distortion of published accounts so as to exaggerate company assets or to underplay or conceal liabilities remained a significant problem for public companies well into the twentieth century. Most serious company frauds of the late Victorian and Edwardian periods did not involve the embezzlement of company funds, but rather the fraudulent concealment from shareholders and creditors of negative information. Directors exploited new business developments such as subsidiary companies and secret reserves and perfected new techniques of "creative accounting" such as window dressing to assist them in their obfuscations.

The development of trust companies and interlocking directorships during the 1880s and 1890s lent itself to a number of abuses. The various companies in a single group could trade assets back and forth between each other to create paper profits and project a false appearance of affluence. Multiple company fraud was almost impossible to detect as each company in the group had a different auditor who only had access to the books of that particular company. Not until 1948 were trust companies required to publish consolidated balance sheets. Before that date, each member of the group could balance its accounts at slightly different times. The other companies in the group could then load the account of the company preparing its books with assets, only to be reciprocated when they prepared their own accounts.

The first person to exploit the fraudulent possibilities of intercompany finance was the property developer Jabez Spencer Balfour. The child of well-known temperance activists,[71] Balfour began his financial career in 1868 with the creation of the Liberator Building Society, an organization promoted to encourage thrift among the working classes and to assist the working man in acquiring his own home. Balfour drew heavily on his family's connections with temperance and nonconformist circles, advertising the Liberator in religious periodicals and employing missionaries and temperance workers as company representatives. The Liberator grew rapidly, receiving over £630,000 in shares and deposits by 1875 and over £1 million by 1878. A contemporary of Balfour, the financier Osborne O'Hagan, later commented on Balfour's rapid ascent in the business world: "His success had made him as vain as a peacock – imagining himself the born financier of the century – but with only a moderate amount of ability. His fellow directors and his associates took him, however, at his own valuation, and he was carried high up by the tide."[72] Balfour became the mayor of Croydon in 1883, having previously entered the House in 1880 as Liberal Member for Tamworth. He subsequently sat for Burnley and was looked upon in Parliament as an expert on company affairs.[73]

Despite the Liberator's slogan, "As Safe as the Bank of England," Balfour early on had launched the company on a series of speculative building projects. The main business of the Society was supposed to be lending money to members on long-term mortgages, but Balfour realized that far greater profits could be made by lending large sums of money to builders at higher interest rates than those undertaken by small home buyers. From its earliest years, the Liberator had been associated with two finance companies, the Lands Allotment Company and the House and Lands Investment Trust, which had almost identical directorships to the Liberator and, in effect, acted as one company. (See Table 3, below.) Unknown to the Liberator shareholders, their company by 1879 had lent the allied finance companies some £192,000. In 1880 the Liberator began lending money to J.W. Hobbs, a Croydon builder and friend of Balfour. By 1885, the Society had advanced Hobbs some £700,000. Hobbs was a poor manager and his business on the brink of insolvency, but rather than writing it off as a bad debt, Balfour and his associates created the Building Securities Company to purchase Hobbs' business and then Hobbs and Company to carry on that work. By 1892 the Liberator had lent out £3.5 million, though only £41,000 of that sum was to building society members. The remainder had been sunk in the Balfour group of companies.[74]

Table 3 *Interlocking directorships of the Liberator group*[75]

Directors	Liberator Building Society	Lands Allotment Company	House & Lands Investment Trust	Building Securities Company	J. W. Hobbs & Company
J. S. Balfour	1868–86	1867–85	1875–92	1884–92	1888–92
S. R. Pattison	1882–92	1867–92	1875–92	1884–92	1885–92
G. E. Brock	1885–92	1885–92	1879–92	1884–92	1885–92
G. Dibley	1897–90	1883–89	1883–87	1884–91	1885–92
Rev. D. Burns	1868–85	1876–96	–	–	–
L. B. Burns	1886–91	–	1886–90	1886–91	1886–90
R. Booth	1890–92	–	–	–	1892
F. H. Rocke	–	–	1890–92	1890–92	1892
F. Coldwells	–	–	1882–92	1891–92	–
J. T. Wright	1886–92	–	1883–92	1884–92	1885–92
M. Theobald	1868–87	1878–92	–	–	–

The several thousand shareholders and depositors of the Liberator Building Society remained blissfully ignorant of Balfour's reckless loan policies. These mostly humble investors believed that their money was spread out over small mortgages and gilt-edged securities. In fact the Society's capital was only backed by second, third and fourth mortgages on large, uncompleted building projects. By the 1880s the Balfour group had overextended its resources and was in a state of complete insolvency. Business was only kept up by a continual infusion of money from the Liberator which still attracted a mass of small deposits. Balfour relied on his supposed financial abilities to secure more funds, but the money market had tightened and in 1892 the crash came.[76]

Investigations subsequently uncovered a complicated system of bookkeeping fraud which had enabled Balfour to conceal the group's insolvency. Balfour had long been in the habit of listing the Liberator's floating assets (e.g. mortgages payable over many years) as money in the bank for balance sheet purposes. In 1875 the Registrar of Building Societies had objected to this optimistic accounting and the practice was discontinued. The Registrar's authority, however, only extended over those monies advanced to building society members and, as has been noted, the vast majority of the Liberator's capital had been loaned to other companies. In making up the balance sheets of the allied companies, Balfour calculated what a proposed building would be worth when completed and occupied and then treated that amount as if it were immediately realizable and available for distribution as dividends.[77]

Balfour's criminal genius reached its highest expression in his system of inter-company asset-juggling. At the close of each financial year, the various companies of the Liberator Group passed their properties from one to another with each company declaring a "profit" from the sales. In no case did money change hands; the profits were merely on paper. In September of 1882, for example, the Lands Allotment Company purchased the Ilford Estate in Essex for £52,000. In January that property was sold to the House and Lands Trust for a nominal profit of £8,000. Later that month the Trust sold the same property to Hobbs and Company for a "profit" of £74,000. These transactions were facilitated by the creation of even more allied companies: the London and General Bank in 1882, George Newman and Company in 1886 and the Real Estates Company in 1888. So successfully did Balfour create an illusion of profitability that the Liberator drew in £600,000 of deposits during its last year of existence.[78]

In 1892 Balfour fled to Argentina, where he successfully evaded extradition for three years. Upon his return to England in 1895 he was tried and convicted for the falsification of accounts and sentenced to fourteen years imprisonment. Balfour's associate J.W. Hobbs and the company solicitor, H. Granville Wright, had earlier been sentenced to twelve years imprisonment for the separate crimes of submitting forged tradesmen's bills and falsified wage sheets to the Liberator. The builder George Newman had also received a five year sentence for complicity in Balfour's frauds. The other directors of the Liberator group evaded prosecution since they were clearly Balfour's dupes, though they were strongly criticized in the press for their "scandalous dereliction of duty."[79]

In response to the Liberator frauds, Parliament passed the Building Societies Act of 1894, requiring societies to report all loans in excess of £5,000 and stipulating that auditors be professional accountants. As a result of the Act, a number of building society frauds were uncovered, though none on the scale of Balfour's.[80] A private relief fund was also set up to assist the victims of the Liberator crash many of whom had joined the society through the solicitations of clergymen. The relief fund lasted for more than twenty years, raising over £150,000 for several thousand of the neediest cases.[81]

Jabez Balfour had alerted the public to the criminal potential of company groups, though this type of fraud grew rather than diminished over the next quarter century. Indeed, in the absence of any system of consolidated accounts, the discovery of inter-company fraud was extraordinarily difficult. In 1910 the editor of the Accountants' Library Series concluded that fraud among company groups was very common:

There doubtless are legitimate advantages to be derived from the association of companies into groups, but it would hardly be over-stating the case to say that the experience so far obtained from such organizations is that at all events the majority of those that have gone into liquidation have been proved to be fraudulent almost from their inception.[82]

Whitaker Wright exploited multiple-company finance during the 1890s in an attempt to lure investment into his troubled mining promotions. Later, during the 1920s, Clarence Hatry manipulated the shares of subsidiary companies as a means of raising money for his takeover of United Steel.[83] In 1929 the insolvent British Cement Products and Finance Company manufactured a yearly profit of £250,000 through the bogus sale of shares to its subsidiaries.[84]

During the late nineteenth century a number of public companies, especially banks, developed a system known as "window dressing" which enabled them to exaggerate their cash assets in published balance sheets. Under this system, a company would call in short-term loans just before the drawing up of annual accounts so as to swell cash reserves. Once balance sheets had been published, the money would immediately be lent out again. Banks defended the practice as a legitimate demonstration of their liquidity, but critics charged that window dressing deceived the public by creating the impression that companies normally had large cash reserves when, in fact, they did not.[85] In some cases window dressing entailed the fraudulent understatement of liabilities or overstatement of assets, but since directors had few guidelines as to their valuations or the presentation of accounts, the criminal boundaries were not well defined.

The case of Gerard Lee Bevan in the 1920s helped fix the limits of acceptable window dressing. Bevan was a partner in the stockbroking firm Ellis and Company and in 1916 he became chairman of the City Equitable Fire Insurance Company.[86] Bevan pillaged the funds of the City Equitable to support his brokerage firm's speculative promotions – many of which were Clarence Hatry schemes.[87] By 1921 Bevan had loaned over £900,000 of City Equitable money to Ellis and Company, in effect wiping out the insurance company's capital. Bevan then concealed City Equitable's insolvency through a series of balance sheet manipulations. When the post-war investment boom ended, Bevan's investments fell and the City Equitable declared bankruptcy in 1922. Bevan fled to the continent but was eventually found in Vienna posing as a French artist and extradited to stand trial for fraud.[88]

The main charges against Bevan concerned his distortion of company accounts rather than his misuse of company funds. Specifically, Bevan was charged with issuing false balance sheets for the City Equitable Company in 1919, 1920 and 1921. These balance sheets allegedly understated the company's debts and listed certain government securities as assets which had only been acquired as temporary "window dressing." The most damning evidence against Bevan was that he had purchased £200,000 of Treasury Bills just before the publication of the balance sheets so that those securities would appear as company assets. The Treasury Bills were bought with borrowed money and were resold immediately after the preparation of the balance sheets. Bevan vigorously defended his actions, arguing: "Six-tenths of the balance sheets published in the United Kingdom showed more cash at the date of the balance sheet than the company was in the habit of holding during the major part of the year. Every big man knew perfectly well what was done."[89] Bevan may well have been following a common commercial practice, but he had the misfortune to be found out at a time when the nation was demanding stricter standards of accountancy.

Another directorial fraud of the 1920s, that of Lord Kylsant, highlighted a new form of "creative accountancy" as well as the courts' growing intolerance of such abuses. As director of the Royal Mail Steam Packet Company, Kylsant had over several years paid dividends out of a secret reserve fund so as to conceal the company's trading losses. It had long been a practice of public companies to hold back part of their profits for lean years. In 1886 the Royal Commission on the Depression found that some firms supplemented their dividends in bad years by diverting money from reserves.[90] No one questioned the integrity of this policy so long as shareholders were aware that the dividends did not represent current profits. Recourse to *secret* reserves, however, could easily lead to fraud since the public would assume that dividends represented profitability when in fact they only represented savings.[91] Such was the case of the Royal Mail.

The years 1915 to 1921 were extremely prosperous ones for the shipping business, and the Royal Mail had been able to set aside over two million pounds in a secret reserve fund which did not appear in the company's published accounts. After the economic downturn of 1921, Lord Kylsant dipped into the secret reserve to supplement the Royal Mail's falling profits and ensure the maintenance of the accustomed dividend. The company's business deteriorated markedly after 1925 and dividends for the years 1926 to 1928 had only been possible through recourse to the secret reserve. During these years both the shareholders and the general public naturally assumed that the Royal Mail was prospering. Lord Kylsant took advantage of this assumption in 1928 by issuing additional debenture stock in the company. In 1929 Kylsant requested a postponement of certain loan payments which the Royal Mail owed the Treasury and, as a condition of deferral, the government ordered an independent audit of the company's books. This investigation revealed Kylsant's financial juggling, and in 1930 he was brought to trial, along with the company auditor Harold Morland, for publishing false balance sheets. Kylsant was additionally charged with publishing a fraudulent prospectus in connection with the 1928 debenture issue.[92]

Both Kylsant and Morland escaped conviction on the false balance sheet charge due to rather technical considerations. In preparing the 1926 and 1927 balance sheets, Morland had amended the "profit" heading with the phrase "including adjustment of taxation reserves." The defense apparently convinced the court that such terminology was "perfectly well-recognized throughout the entire profession of accountancy to indicate exactly what had been done." It is obvious, however, that shareholders did not understand accounting jargon, though the prosecution failed to emphasize this point. Kylsant was convicted for the 1928 debenture issue as it was clear that no investors would have subscribed had they known that the Royal Mail had been losing money since 1921. Kylsant received twelve months imprisonment.[93]

In summing up the case Mr. Justice Wright commented darkly on the use of secret reserves:

If the shareholders had been told that this company had no earnings, because earnings are the life blood of a company – a company cannot go on indefinitely using the capital assets unless it is earning – surely they might have taken steps for the reconstruction and rearrangement of the company's affairs. It was never brought to the shareholders' knowledge what the position was.

Continuing, Justice Wright condemned the whole tendency of directorial autocracy and called for greater openness in published accounts:

Now it is a little astounding, and one cannot help wondering whether those who managed big companies did not forget sometimes that the body of directors of the company were the agents of the shareholders, that they owed them full information subject to proper commercial and reasonable necessities, and it was the shareholders' interest they had to study. They were not to regard shareholders as sheep who might look up if they were not fed.[94]

Secret reserves, window dressing and other forms of creative accountancy had been defended by their practitioners as well-intentioned attempts to preserve the business. Deception was practiced, directors averred, not to enrich themselves or to defraud shareholders, but to maintain the credit of the company. During the 1890s, for example, the chairman of the Millwall Dock Company increased the firm's book assets with fictitious entries for the purpose of inspiring public confidence in the company's ability to do its work.[95] In 1931 the broker Sir Arthur Wheeler justified his fraudulent conversion of securities as a temporary measure designed to safeguard clients' investments: "It would be a poor captain who would haul down the flag immediately a storm broke."[96] The judge, however, had a ready response for Wheeler: "You have to consider whether it is honest for a captain who knows his ship is sinking to invite passengers on board."[97] However pure a director's intentions in withholding information or manipulating securities, the end result was often financial ruin for investors. Had shareholders been given the true state of affairs in companies such as the Liberator or the Royal Mail they might have been able to salvage some of their capital.

By the 1920s the climate of public opinion favored greater frankness in disclosures, as illustrated by the Companies Acts of 1928 and 1929, and the prosecutions in 1930 of Lord Kylsant and Clarence Hatry.[98] The white-collar crimes of the Victorian and Edwardian periods had taught the nation hard lessons, not least of which was the inadequacy of *laissez-faire* in hindering company fraud. The experience of an unrestrained economy eventually produced a backlash in favor of greater state supervision and regulation of the market.

CHAPTER 7

Company law and the courts

The story of English company law during the nineteenth and twentieth centuries is the story of the rise and fall of *laissez-faire*. As we have seen, the various agents of English finance and trade operated under the most permissive commercial legislation in all of Europe, if not the world. From the mid-nineteenth century through the early decades of the twentieth, the law put few obstacles in the paths of white-collar criminals, trusting instead that the free market would regulate itself and that good business would drive out bad. The liberal outlook was taken up by the law courts which neglected business frauds and treated white-collar criminals with comparative leniency. Throughout much of this period, cultural perceptions of "criminality" remained focused on the "dangerous classes" while elite misconduct was seen as a relatively minor social ill. Experience, however, proved increasingly irreconcilable with classical economic theory and class prejudice. The speculative disaster of 1866, the fraudulent loan issues of the 1870s and the crash of the City of Glasgow Bank in 1878 brought to light a system of finance riddled with fraud. Thus, from the 1880s there was an ideological shift in favor of greater state regulation of the economy to protect investors. Thereafter, the movement for the reform of company law gained momentum with each new revelation of fraud. Balfour, Hooley, Wright, Bottomley, Bevan and Hatry all contributed to the weakening of free trade doctrines among legislators, the business community and the general public.

In 1844 the British Parliament attempted to regulate joint-stock company affairs for the first time.[1] The 1844 Act sought to lessen fraud by requiring companies to register certain documents with the government and to present shareholders with an annually audited balance sheet. The standards of accounting and auditing, however, were not set forth in any detail and the Registrar was given no powers of enforcement, but instead of strengthening the law, the government substantially weakened it through company legislation in 1856 and 1862, at which time the spirit of *laissez-faire* triumphed in company matters. The principle of governmental non-interference was to prevail until the twentieth century.

Between 1856 and 1900 there were no legal specifications as to the keeping of proper books and accounts, nor was there a mandatory audit for most joint-stock companies. The guidelines for prospectuses and advertisements were equally vague so that the public had little information on which to base its investment decisions. The proponents of classical economic theory argued that the market was self-regulating, that good reputations would drive out bad and that government regulation would only lull people into a false sense of security. As *The Times* stated the case in 1856:

In the face of all that has been shown of the effect of legislative attempts to keep men prudent by determining the modes in which they shall transact their business there are always a number of persons ready whenever any financial disaster occurs, to propose measures of control, the fact being wholly lost sight of that a multitude of regulations serves merely to confuse the general public and to give adroit schemes increased openings for evasion, while at the same time it begets a false confidence and extinguishes the habit of private vigilance.[2]

Individual responsibility was deeply embedded in the Victorian consciousness and undercut nineteenth-century attempts to tighten the requirements of company law. Often the victims of company frauds were chastised for failing to exercise proper judgment or for being blinded by their own greed.[3] Legislation, it was argued, could not protect a fool from his folly.

Not everyone in Victorian England rejoiced in the principles of classical political economy. Even so important a liberal as William Gladstone embraced *laissez-faire* with a sense more of resignation than enthusiasm. Writing to a friend in 1846, Gladstone observed: "I suspect that with regard to Joint-Stock Companies and Speculation we are a nation of children who will not allow our nursery maids to govern us."[4] During times of commercial panic or speculative disaster, the voices of paternalistic government were loud in their demands for company law reform. At the time of the railway panic, for example, Benjamin Disraeli asserted: "This system of letting everything take its course has been of late the fashionable one among the advocates of political economy; it is the course which we have been all latterly encouraged to pursue, but is one, Sir, which in my humble opinion, is hurrying on this country to ruin and degradation."[5] The widespread frauds of the 1860s and 1870s gave birth to Parliamentary Select Committees on Company Law Reform, but the legislature resisted stricter regulation, opting instead for half-measures and minor alterations in the law. The business community opposed law reform and was well placed to influence the course of legislation.

Between 1862 and 1900, there were numerous Companies Acts which amended the liberal provisions set down in 1856, but these alterations were mostly ad hoc attempts to patch-up holes in company law and did little to change the permissive tone of that law. Company law reform remained essentially reactive, responding piecemeal to new types of fraud or to especially serious cases, rather than re-evaluating the underlying principles of *laissez-faire* and *caveat emptor*.

Following the Financial Crisis of 1866, a Parliamentary Committee inquired into the possibility of overhauling company law. Numerous witnesses before the Committee expressed the opinion that promoters and directors abused the principles of limited liability since they often had no real stake in the companies with which they were associated. Some witnesses suggested that promoters and directors should be required by law to hold a substantial block of shares, though most businessmen opposed this idea and it was rejected by the Committee in its final report.[6] The accountant and promoter David Chadwick suggested that the Registrar of Joint Stock Companies have greater discretionary powers in granting corporate status, much like the Registrar of Friendly Societies, but this also was rejected by the Committee.[7] Some witnesses favored increasing the liability of directors along the lines of French *sociétés en commandite*, whereby shareholders' liability was limited but directors' liability was unlimited. The Committee resisted making this arrangement mandatory, but the resulting 1867 Companies Act gave corporations the option of unlimited liability for directors.[8] This provision had little practical effect, however, since directors were usually the ones who made decisions regarding a company's constitution and few of them desired to increase their own liability.[9] The 1867 Act also specified that a company's prospectus must include "the dates and names of the parties to any contract entered into by the company."[10] This requirement was drafted in response to the Overend and Gurney debacle,[11] but it proved inadequate as the names to contracts told investors nothing material about the contracts, and promoters often waived compliance through an escape clause.[12]

During the 1870s frauds involving foreign government loans and foreign companies gave rise to three Parliamentary inquiries, the most important of which was the 1877 Select Committee on the Companies Acts.[13] Robert Lowe, the moving force behind the 1856 Companies Act, sat on the 1877 Committee at which time he regretted the permissive nature of his earlier legislation. In its Report the Committee recommended the re-institution of provisional registration as laid down in the 1844 Companies Act as well as requiring a minimum subscribed capital to achieve complete incorporation.[14] By such means it was hoped that many frivolous and fraudulent company schemes would be weeded out, though Parliament rejected these recommendations as being too onerous on the business community. The 1877 Companies Act merely facilitated the reduction of share capital.[15]

The crash of the City of Glasgow Bank in 1878 renewed demands for the reform of commercial law, but once more Parliament held back from a major reworking of the Companies Acts. In 1879 another Companies Act was passed, yet its provisions were mainly concerned with problems raised by the Glasgow Bank frauds. The Act required a compulsory annual audit for banks and facilitated unlimited companies converting to limited liability as a safeguard for shareholders.[16]

The depressing history of fraud and chicanery detailed before Parliamentary Committees in 1867, 1875, 1877 and 1878 had little influence on resulting legislation. Despite an alarming incidence of fraud, legislators feared alienating the business community or hindering trade through the imposition of tougher company law. Parliament satisfied itself that its inquiries brought about greater awareness of fraud and would therefore hinder such practices. The 1875 Select Committee on Loans to Foreign States typically concluded: "the best security against the recurrence of such evils as they have above described will be found, not so much in legislative enactments as in the enlightenment of the public as to their real nature and origin."[17]

It is hardly surprising that nineteenth-century Parliamentary Committees merely tinkered with the 1856/62 Companies Acts.

The ideal of *laissez-faire* was well established by mid-century and underscored the case for benign neglect. Also, from a more pragmatic standpoint, large numbers of both Houses were directors of public companies and would not have benefited from a tightening of the law.[18] As Philip Cottrell has pointed out, the Select Committees on the Companies Acts often contained large City contingents.[19] The 1867 Select Committee on the Limited Liability Acts is a case in point. Of the seventeen M.P.s who sat on the Committee, ten were involved in finance and trade. Five of the ten were London merchants, three were bankers, one was a Liverpool shipowner and one was an industrialist from Bradford.[20]

The "experts" brought in as witnesses were also usually businessmen, accountants and lawyers who had a vested interest in maintaining the *status quo*. Many lawyers and accountants actually benefited from the large number of company failures and frauds. Liquidation, for example, might take several years for a large company, generating thousands of pounds in lawyers' fees and accounting expenses.[21] The economist H.A. Shannon argued that "as promotion and liquidation are lucrative fields of practice for them [solicitors and accountants], they are likely to over-estimate the deterrent effect on enterprise (and consequent social loss) that a tightening up in that law might have."[22] The whole process of selecting witnesses was rather clubby – committee members and witnesses both coming from the same elite circles of trade, banking and accounting.

The close links between the City and Parliamentary Committees on Company Law suggest a much cosier relationship between the governing elite and big business than we have been led to believe existed by historians such as Martin Wiener. Wiener's *English Culture and the Decline of the Industrial Spirit 1850–1980* argued that " the radical ideal of active capital was submerged in the conservative ideal of passive property, and the urge to enterprise faded beneath the preference for stability."[23] In other words, the English aristocracy remained aloof from business and industry and the entrepreneurial classes abandoned "the industrial spirit" and aped the aristocratic lifestyle. Wiener's thesis is contradicted by the hundreds of aristocrats who acted as company directors and the thousands who invested in company shares. Many of the highest in the land had links to the business world. The Duke of Wellington speculated in railway shares and socialized with George Hudson.

Later in the century Lord Salisbury was Chairman of the Great Eastern Railway.[24] Aristocrats may well have looked down on businessmen as social upstarts and vulgar money-grubbers, but this snobbery did not prevent them from working hand in glove with the world of commerce. Nor did anti-business sentiment prevent financiers from influencing the course of legislation with the ideas of economic liberalism.[25]

Laissez-faire seemed to justify itself as an economic philosophy in light of the spectacular mid-Victorian economic growth, but faith in the "invisible hand" faltered during the late-century trade depression. In the 1880s and 1890s, agricultural depression and the fear of German industrial competition led to demands for the re-imposition of protective tariffs. Domestically, the great increase in the securities market, especially industrial floatations, and the accompanying frauds brought about calls for more and better regulation.[26] The *Edinburgh Review* believed that the trade depression was brought on in part by reckless speculation which deterred genuine investors from dealing in Stock Exchange issues.[27] *Blackwood's* also saw a connection between unregulated companies and the commercial slump, and suggested that directors be held more accountable as trustees.[28] Many felt that the Companies Acts were abused by feckless promoters and frauds and that free-trading had become synonymous with free-booting.

Exposure of notorious frauds, such as the fall of Albert Grant in 1877 and the Glasgow Bank Crash in 1878, contributed to the erosion of free trade in company matters.[29] In the wake of the City of Glasgow failure the movement for company law reform picked up momentum. From the 1880s *The Economist* abandoned its long-standing espousal of free trade and threw its considerable influence behind the campaign for new company legislation.[30] The proponents of reform argued that while Acts of Parliament could not make people honest, they could in the very least close loopholes and restrict opportunities for fraud. The *National Review* dismissed the common objection that a tightening of company law would fetter enterprise, asserting that this "can hardly be urged against bringing rascals to justice."[31] The new attitude toward state intervention was put succinctly by the *Edinburgh Review* in 1886: "It is surely time Parliament interfered to protect people who in financial matters are utterly incapable of protecting themselves."[32]

The classical economic theories of Adam Smith and his brethren were posited in a pre-industrial economy where it was assumed that buyers and sellers had knowledge of each other and that financial information was relatively easy to come by. In such a world good reputations would drive out bad, and persons would do business with those whom they knew and trusted. The Industrial Revolution brought about an increasingly complex economy and an impersonal company investment structure that was national rather than local in its arrangements. With the breakdown of the pre-modern economic system, information was more difficult to come by and investors found it hard to distinguish between fraud, incompetence and bad luck. As the liberal outlook proved increasingly at odds with experience, people turned to the government as the only agency with the resources and authority to protect them from fraud. Many reformers also argued that the common law principle of *caveat emptor* was a relic of the distant past and thus of limited application for many contemporary financial transactions. In 1894 the *Nineteenth Century* contended that "if the Legislature permits the creation of companies, it is indeed time that modern machinery should be provided, and the Courts should not be left to apply the principles of law which were laid down years ago for other purposes to an office of modern growth."[33] A year later the *National Review* reiterated the need for government regulation, arguing: "It is absurd to tell the investor that he must take care of himself, and talk to him about *caveat emptor*. The government might just as well leave off stamping coins, and tell us that if we do not know a piece of fine gold when we see it, we ought to, and that in the future we must accept change at our own risk."[34]

The champions of company law reform emphasized precedents for state regulation of public companies, citing the 1868 Regulation of Railways Act (31/32 Vict. c. 119), the 1870 Life Assurance Companies Act (33/34 Vict. c. 61), the 1871 Gas Works Act (34/35 Vict. c. 41), the banking provisions of the 1879 Companies Act (42/43 Vict. c. 76) and the 1882 Electric Lighting Act (45/46 Vict. c. 56). These earlier exceptions to *laissez-faire* had been justified on the grounds that public interest was at stake in certain types of companies such as railways, banks and utilities. By late century many people felt that joint-stock organization had become such an important part of the British economy that the public interest would better be served by subjecting all companies to the same standards of accounting and auditing which were applied to railways and utilities.

In 1886 the Royal Commission on the Depression of Trade and Industry called for more stringent commercial regulations to combat fraud.[35] In 1888 the Queen's speech at the opening of Parliament also mentioned the problem of financial fraud and asserted the need for sweeping reform of company law.[36] A Company Bill was introduced in 1888 embodying several recommendations that had been rejected in 1877, including a two-stage registration process and a minimum subscription before allotment. The Bill required the publication of audited accounts and further stipulated that directors must hold 20% of allotted shares. To no one's surprise business interests opposed the Bill and it was buried in a committee in the House of Lords where it died a quiet death.[37]

Reformers decided to focus on less ambitious goals and in 1890 succeeded in passing two amendments to the Companies Acts aimed at narrowing the field of company fraud. The Companies Winding-Up Act of 1890 facilitated company liquidation under court supervision.[38] Previous to this Act, promoters and directors usually resorted to voluntary liquidation – where there was no control on the part of the Bankruptcy Court or the Board of Trade and it was thus easier to conceal negative information from shareholders and creditors.[39] Unscrupulous promoters still avoided court interference by registering their companies in Scotland, where the 1890 Act did not apply and where liquidation was unsupervised.[40] Other territories of the British Crown such as Jersey, Guernsey and the Isle of Man still enjoyed significant autonomy from the English judiciary, and some Victorian financiers took advantage of these archaic privileges. A number of Bottomley companies, for example, were registered on Guernsey in order to place them one remove from the English law courts.[41]

The Directors' Liability Act had also been passed in 1890 in an attempt to make company directors responsible for the publication of false statements.[42] The Act allowed shareholders to recover damages if they could prove that directors had issued a prospectus containing untrue statements with an intent to defraud. In practice, however, directors easily shielded themselves from shareholders' claims by arguing that they believed in any inaccurate statements themselves. Incompetence was not prosecutable under this law, which was cynically labeled the "Directors' Immunity

Act."[43] Some directors further shielded themselves from the law by inserting into their Articles of Association stipulations that they should be under no liability to the company for any act of commission or omission unless involving fraud or wilful deceit – in effect, an escape clause for lazy or incompetent directors.[44]

The 1890 Acts were widely criticized as but another feeble patching-up of a hopelessly leaky vessel, and demands for the complete overhaul of the 1862 Act mounted once more during the nineties. John Smith, Inspector General of Company Liquidation, issued yearly reports detailing the shortcomings of company law and urging reform.[45] In 1892 the collapse of the Liberator Building Society pointedly drew public attention to the ease with which fraudulent balance sheets and delusive reports could be manufactured.[46] In the aftermath of the Liberator scandal a Company Law Amendment Committee under the chairmanship of Lord Davey was appointed by the Commons in 1894. The Davey Committee reported the next year, suggesting major revisions in Company Law. The tone of the Report was somewhat cautious and the Committee dismissed suggestions for a permanent state investigating agency, but a growing distrust of *laissez-faire* was also manifested:

. . . it must be generally acknowledged that a person who is invited to subscribe to a new undertaking has practically no opportunity of making any independent inquiry before coming to a decision. Indeed, the time usually allowed between the issue of the prospectus and the making of an application does not permit of any real investigation. The maxim of Caveat Emptor has in the opinion of your Committee but a limited application in such cases.[47]

The Committee's recommendations were embodied in a Bill which was passed by Commons in 1896 and sent to the Lords, where it remained stalled in committee for four years. In the meantime new scandals in the business world, most notably the 1898 bankruptcy of Ernest Hooley, inflamed public opinion against Parliamentary delay. As *The Economist* argued, "while Parliament is leisurely inquiring into the working of the Companies Acts and discussing their amendment, investors are being fleeced, and the worst types of company promoters are flourishing."[48] Some persons questioned the Lords' commitment to reform. After all, seven of the eleven members of the Lords' Committee on the Company Bill were themselves directors of public companies. Of the entire upper house, 162 peers were directors of some 435 companies.[49] Not surprisingly, some of the Davey Bill's most onerous provisions were rejected in the Lords, including the proposal that the liability of directors could be declared unlimited by the courts if it were found that the company was carried on for fraudulent purposes.

The Companies Act was finally passed in 1900, and despite the years of foot dragging, represented the most significant alteration in the law since 1862. The Act specified matters which the prospectus must contain, including the promoter's fee and the number of shares held by each director. There could be no waiver clause as to the listing of contracts in the prospectus and that document had to be signed by the directors and filed with the Registrar before it could be published.[50] The Act aimed at preventing the improper allotment of shares by requiring the prospectus to state the minimum subscription needed to proceed to allotment.[51] Underwriting was legalized so long as the terms were disclosed in the prospectus.[52] The most significant provisions of the Act concerned auditing. For the first time since 1856, all joint-stock companies had to submit to a yearly audit.[53] In their annual report to shareholders, auditors had to affirm that the company's balance sheet was "properly drawn-up so as to exhibit a true and correct view of the state of the company's affairs as shown by the books of the company."[54]

Most criticism directed against the 1900 Companies Act concerned its auditing provisions. Many persons believed that directors still had too much discretion in the drawing up of yearly accounts and that a profit and loss statement would have been more useful to shareholders than the obligatory balance sheet.[55] Others worried that auditors were too much under directors' authority and were unable to exercise independent initiative.[56] The *Nineteenth Century* concluded:

The fact that the appointment of auditors is made compulsory does not mean very much, because in nearly every company of importance an auditor of some kind has usually been appointed; the serious matter having always been the kind of man put into the office, and by whom. More often than not, the nomination of auditor will, as before, fall into the hands of directors and promoters.[57]

Because auditors' statements had to affirm the accuracy of the balance sheet "as shown by the books of the company," the impression was created in some minds that auditors legally had to do no more than check the arithmetical accuracy of the balance sheet according to the books – in which case their certificates would be of little practical value. To remove this impression an Act was passed in 1907 requiring auditors to affirm whether a balance sheet was correct "according to the best of their information and the explanations given to them."[58]

The Companies Acts as amended in 1900 remained essentially unchanged for over twenty years. In 1918 a Parliamentary Committee was appointed to consider revision, but recommended no alterations in the law. A voice of dissent, however, was raised by Committee member A.S.C. Carr, who predicted that the post-war economy would bring "a large crop of new schemes appealing for public support, mostly *bona fide*, but offering unique opportunity to the fraudulent and oversanguine."[59] Events proved Carr right, and the Farrow's Bank debacle of 1920, the Bevan and Bottomley prosecutions of 1922 and the Hatry crash of 1923 gave fresh impetus to company law reform. In 1925 the Board of Trade appointed a Committee under the chairmanship of Wilfred Greene to again consider changes in the Companies Acts. The Greene Committee reported in 1926 and many of its recommendations were embodied in a new and more stringent Companies Act in 1928. Yet by the time this legislation emerged, another company mania was well under way, the dire consequences of which could not be averted.

The 1928 Act strengthened directors' liability by declaring void any escape clauses for directorial negligence.[60] Directors were also liable to pay compensation for prospectuses containing untrue statements, and simply believing in the statements' truth was no longer to be an excuse. The 1900 Companies Act had required prospectuses to list a "minimum subscription" needed to proceed to allotment, but this provision became a dead letter since most companies simply fixed the minimum at seven shares. The 1928 Act demanded greater precision, defining "minimum subscription" as the amount needed for working capital, preliminary expenses and promotional fees, and the purchase price of any property to be acquired by the company.[61] The Act also limited underwriting commissions to 10%, since many companies had been forced to pay as high as 75% to 80% for underwriting, a percentage which Parliament considered illegitimate and deleterious.[62] For the first time companies were required to keep detailed books, directors had to provide shareholders with a profit and loss statement in addition to the usual balance sheet, and balance sheets had to separate fixed from floating assets.[63]

The 1928 Companies Act was generally welcomed as an effective tightening of commercial law, though informed opinion felt that accounting requirements were still too lax.[64] The balance sheets of English companies remained non-uniform. Directors were free to lump assets together, ignore contingent liabilities, and follow whatever practice they desired with regard to depreciation.[65] The Society of Incorporated Accountants and Auditors particularly criticized the Act for not demanding that holding companies publish unified balance sheets for all of their subsidiaries.[66]

Although state intervention in financial matters had increased markedly since the Victorian period, the goal of such intervention seemed principally to ensure that the public had access to accurate financial information. The law was still trying, consciously or unconsciously, to achieve the ideal of the classical economists: a free market where the individual made investment decisions based on an evaluation of information. The fact that most investors lacked the capacity to evaluate financial data had little impact on lawmakers' decisions. Regardless of what the law specified about prospectuses, most people only read the front page. Regardless of what the law specified about Articles of Association, most people never read them at all.[67] The general public was largely incapable of understanding legal contracts and business documents, couched as they were in obscure jargon, and neither the Stock Exchange nor the financial press offered investors effective mediation. Even after the Great Crash of 1929, the British state avoided taking on regulatory responsibilities akin to the United States' Securities and Exchange Commission or system of federal bank inspection. Parliamentary Committees on Finance and Industry in 1931 and Share Pushing in 1937 recommended a more activist role for the government, but the reform effort was delayed by the War.[68] Only in 1948 did Britain adopt a Companies Act with a regulatory vigor comparable to European and American law. That same year Scotland Yard established its Fraud Squad to coordinate investigation and prosecution of City crime.

In many cases of white-collar crime, the nature of company law was almost irrelevant, since the very expense and difficulty of prosecutions favored the criminal rather than the victim. As early as 1844 Parliament recognized that financial frauds were often committed with impunity because victims were too impoverished to litigate, because they were ashamed to publicize their connection with a fraudulent concern, and because of cumbrous legal proceedings – particularly in the Court of Chancery.[69] Then as now it was difficult to prosecute persons of prestige and wealth who had access to the best legal counsel and were in a position to prolong a court battle almost indefinitely. During the 1870s, for example, it took over a year and more than £10,000 to secure the conviction of the Eupion Gas Company directors – in a case where guilt for fraud was palpable.[70] For holders of small or moderate amounts of shares, the expense of legal proceedings was hardly commensurate with the sum that might be recovered.

Company law focused on a rather narrow field of criminal activities, in particular false accounts and fraudulent publicity. The exploitation of positions of trust for personal gain, as in insider trading or the noncompetitive awarding of contracts to friends was not criminally accountable. Neither was the reckless promotion of overcapitalized businesses. Ernest Hooley and Whitaker Wright were never prosecuted for their monstrous paper shuffles and deceitful floatations during the 1890s. Wright was tried for the incidental crime of falsifying books and Hooley was ultimately brought to justice for petty swindles. In light of financiers' seeming impunity to prosecution, *Blackwood's* commented in 1904 "that a coach-and-six can be driven through any of the joint-stock Acts. As safeguards against fraud, or maladministration of any kind on the part of directors, they are mere make-believes."[71]

Criminal proceedings for fraud were difficult to sustain by the necessary evidence. Directors often destroyed records, or else left no "paper trails" linking them to misappropriated funds. In 1908, for example, Horatio Bottomley escaped fraud charges in connection with illegally duplicated shares in the Joint Stock Trust and Finance Company because ledgers had been badly kept and certain account books turned up missing.[72] Ernest Hooley was frank in his acknowledgment of shady bookkeeping: "I suppose I might as well admit that I never made the slightest attempt to keep any proper books. In fact it would have been almost impossible for me to keep any accurate record of the innumerable deals I did, and the payments I made to people for services which it would not have been the least desirable to place on record."[73] Before 1928, the failure to keep detailed accounts was no crime, and in the absence of proper bookkeeping, conspiracy to defraud was almost impossible to prove in a court of law.

White-collar criminals often had the financial means to elude capture and fled abroad with their ill-gotten gains. Before the late nineteenth century, poor transportation and communication hampered the tracking of absconding criminals, and extradition policies were badly defined. Bankrupts and defendants in civil cases had only to move to Jersey or the Isle of Man to put themselves outside the jurisdiction of the English law courts.[74] Victimized shareholders sometimes took the law into their own hands by hiring private detectives to track down absconding embezzlers. During the 1840s, for example, John and Daniel Forrester were well known for pursuing white-collar criminals abroad. In countries without extradition treaties the Forrester brothers would break into the rooms of criminals and steal back the plunder.[75] Even after improvements in extradition law, the government only bothered to invoke these cumbrous proceedings against major frauds such as Jabez Balfour or Whitaker Wright.

Until the 1950s the agencies of law enforcement in England played a minimal role in the prevention, discovery or prosecution of white-collar crime. The machinery of the criminal justice system was overwhelmingly directed against lower-class criminals who were perceived as a threat to the dominant social order. The creation of a Victorian police force contributed to an overall decrease in the English crime rate during the nineteenth century – especially among petty crimes against property. The very presence of policemen patrolling the streets inhibited theft and facilitated the apprehension of thieves.[76] Police activity, however, had little impact on white-collar criminals, who perpetrated crimes in the midst of otherwise legitimate business, and who were assumed to be "respectable" by their very social status. Certain police detectives specialized in fraud cases and as early as the 1840s two policemen were assigned to the Stock Exchange to look after the "stags,"[77] but this represented a token commitment when compared to the vast resources directed against shoplifters, pickpockets and other petty offenders.

In 1877 George Jessel, the Master of Rolls, argued that the chief problem with company fraud was not so much in the leniency of the law, but in the unwillingness of the state to root out and prosecute white-collar criminals. Jessel emphasized:

. . . the law is amply sufficient, but the machinery of the law is defective; and defective in this way, that what is everybody's business is nobody's business. We have no public prosecutor and no one willing to incur the enormous expense and trouble of instituting prosecutions under these Acts [Companies Acts], as a rule, without expecting to derive any pecuniary advantage from it.[78]

In England a system of public prosecution was not developed until late in the nineteenth century. Hitherto, the burden of prosecution rested solely upon the victims, whose decisions to prosecute depended on their level of grievance and their financial resources. In 1855, for example, the Reverend John Griffiths initiated legal proceedings against his bankers Messrs. Strahan, Paul and Bates for embezzlement, at which time he told the Court: "I felt I had a public duty to perform, it was a duty I owed to society to proceed, and that I could not conscientiously pass over so grave an offense."[79] Griffiths was also a wealthy man who could well afford the prosecution, and, as Canon of Rochester Cathedral, could not be seen allowing immorality to go unpunished. Most shareholders, however, were not persons of great wealth and preferred to accept their losses rather than pursuing costly litigation in which there was little chance of recovering their investments.

Despite the creation of the Office of Public Prosecutions in 1879, private prosecution remained the general rule.[80] The state resisted taking on criminal cases, usually doing so only when no private plaintiff was forthcoming or when the case was a *cause célèbre*. In 1903, for example, the Solicitor General declined to prosecute Whitaker Wright, on the dubious grounds that falsification of a balance sheet was no crime if the falsifier did not benefit personally from his deception. Therefore, an aggrieved stockbroker, Mr. Flower, undertook a private prosecution of Wright.[81] In 1917 government tax inspectors uncovered massive fraud at Farrow's Bank, but since the fraud was directed at the bank's depositors and not at the Treasury, the matter was dropped. Farrow thus continued his system of fraud until 1920 when the bank's insolvency was revealed by a private source.[82] Had the government intervened at the earlier date and mounted a prosecution against Farrow, the eventual loss to shareholders and depositors would have been considerably smaller.[83]

Official statistics support the view that the state pursued white-collar criminals with great reluctance. In 1900 only 16 of the 94 total fraud prosecutions for England and Wales were undertaken by the Director of Public Prosecutions.[84] In 1924 the Public Prosecutor only tried 38 fraud cases out of an annual total of 269.[85]

According to the records of the City of London Police, between 1910 and 1936, 177 firms were known or suspected of engaging in securities frauds, though a mere 37 prosecutions were mounted.[86] The City Police were reluctant to pursue fraud cases and seldom turned such cases over to the Department of Public Prosecutions. The police usually told the victim of fraud that "he would receive full police assistance if and when he instituted a prosecution at his own expense."[87] In 1937 Parliament recommended that a special branch be established at Scotland Yard to coordinate fraud cases, though this was not effected until 1948.

As a result of the leniency of commercial law and the practical difficulties of prosecuting privileged persons, white-collar criminals were brought to trial much less frequently than their proletarian brothers in crime. In 1858 the journal *Meliora* commented:

For a long period, and in a very great measure, the practical rule amongst us has been that the great swindlers escape and the small ones are caught and put in prison. The net which poor blind Justice spreads over the robbers' den seems to be constructed on a principle precisely the reverse of that which regulates other nets – the big fishes get through, and the little ones are taken.[88]

The great bulk of criminal prosecutions were for petty thefts, robberies and burglaries. According to the criminal statistics, between 1896 and 1900 there were on average 51,000 trials a year in England and Wales. During that same period embezzlement trials averaged only 1,200 a year and fraud trials a mere 115 a year.[89] This small white-collar share of criminal trials changed little over the next twenty-five years. Between 1915 and 1919, trials averaged out at 58,000 a year, with embezzlement cases averaging 690 and fraud cases 135. Between 1920 and 1924 the annual average for all criminal trials was 59,000, with embezzlement cases averaging 780 and fraud cases 250.[90]

Those white-collar criminals that do appear in the criminal record probably represent only a small fraction of all such malefactors. Such was the opinion of informed observers before the numerous Parliamentary hearings on company law and in the journals of Victorian and Edwardian England. In 1879 the *Nineteenth Century* noted:

Criminal prosecutions in cases of commercial fraud in this country are apt to go by fits and starts; sensation trials take place at the call of an angry public; but it is very seldom that the real authors and inventors of fraudulent schemes find their way into the dock. Some unfortunate dupe or over-sanguine capitalist becomes the scapegoat of the sins of others.[91]

For example, when the government prosecuted the Royal British Bank directors for fraud in 1858, *The Times* alleged that these men had been singled out for harsh treatment because they were not prominent City people, while other bankers, equally guilty, were shielded by their influence and connections. *The Times* warned that:

In consequence of the rapid extension of the joint-stock system there are few persons in prominent life who do not in some way become connected with public companies. If the Attorney General is to have the power of capriciously selecting cases of mismanagement, for the purpose of commencing criminal proceedings against any particular set of individuals, a door is opened to the exercise of political animosity, or of currying favour with certain sections of the community by persecuting those who may be inimical to them, such as has never yet been permitted.[92]

Many persons felt that Ernest Hooley escaped prosecution at the time of his 1898 bankruptcy because he knew too much about the activities of highly placed officials, including a number of peers involved in his promotions. Hooley said as much to an interviewer: "Look here! I have not said one-fiftieth part of what I can say about the British Peerage. I have still got a lot of cards up my sleeve."[93] It was later suggested that the Attorney General declined to prosecute Whitaker Wright because of influential persons mixed up in his concerns, in particular the Marquess of Dufferin and Ava – formerly Viceroy of India and Governor General of Canada.[94] The country seemed satisfied that with a few sensational trials – such as those of Jabez Balfour or Clarence Hatry – justice was done.[95] The public conscience was quieted, but the system which permitted or even encouraged such frauds went unchallenged.

The privileged situation of white-collar criminals was also reflected in the comparatively lenient sentences they received if convicted. Balfour's fourteen years imprisonment or Bottomley's seven stand out in sharp contrast to the usual light sentences for fraud, but considering the vast sums of money involved in white-collar crimes, even seven years could be considered a relatively mild punishment. The law's bias in favor of upper-class persons was noted in 1844, in the Report of the Select Committee on Joint Stock Companies: "At present a trustee may steal £10,000 and be only liable to be called to account by the Court of Chancery; while the robbery of a mere trifle by a clerk, and often under circumstances of less moral aggravation and greater temptation, is transportable."[96] A glance at notable fraud trials corroborates this view. During the 1870s, for example, William Swindlehurst and Baxter Langley embezzled more than £9,000 from a charitable institution they directed, but only received sentences of eighteen months imprisonment.[97] In 1878 the directors of the City of Glasgow Bank received sentences varying from five to eighteen months imprisonment, although their fraud had involved millions of pounds and caused widespread ruin and misery. In 1912 Ernest Hooley defrauded a young man of several thousand pounds for which he received a token sentence of twelve months imprisonment.[98]

The harshest sentences in cases of white-collar crime were reserved for embezzling clerks. During the 1850s Walter Watts, William Robson and Leopold Redpath were all transported for their massive embezzlements, but even petty theft by an employee frequently resulted in transportation. In 1845, for example, a savings bank clerk was transported for seven years as the result of a £3 embezzlement.[99] If clerks attempted restitution or were recommended to mercy by their employers, they usually escaped transportation, but were still sentenced to terms of hard labor.[100] After the abolition of transportation in the 1860s, clerks continued to receive much harsher sentences than directors or trustees who were guilty of similar crimes. During his prison years, Jabez Balfour noted the inequality of sentences; among his fellow inmates was a clerk who had embezzled £72 and received a sentence of ten years and a solicitor who had embezzled £4,000 but was sentenced to only three years.[101] The bond of trust between clerk and employer seemed more acute than that between director and shareholder, and the clerk's betrayal bore the additional stigma of social insubordination.

Since directors' responsibilities were not well defined by law, they were free to pursue all sorts of reckless policies untenable for other persons in fiduciary positions. Directors might justify their frauds as temporary "borrowing" or well-intentioned attempts to further the company's best interests. The courts were most lenient in those cases where directors did not profit personally from their frauds, or where fraud was meant to benefit the company. Lord Kylsant, for example, received such a light sentence (twelve months imprisonment) because he forcefully maintained that his actions were for the good of shareholders.

Another reason frequently given for the lenient sentencing of most white-collar criminals was that the shame and social disgrace attendant on criminal conviction were punishment enough for middle-class persons. Exclusion from polite society was viewed as a more serious penalty than imprisonment. In pronouncing sentence on the bankers Thomas Farrow and William Crotch in 1921, the judge observed: "The disgrace which the defendants had brought on their families was part, and perhaps the greatest part, of their punishment."[102] There may have been an unconscious belief that genteel persons experienced guilt more profoundly than the common man, and were therefore less in need of corporal punishment. Perhaps this is what Mr. Justice Bruce had in mind when he told Jabez Balfour: "I am sure that no small part of your punishment will be the remorse you must feel at having darkened many a humble home. No prison door can shut out from your ears the cry of the widows and orphans you have ruined."[103] For white-collar criminals prison was seen as ancillary to their personal sense of shame and loss of social status. The frequent suicides of bankrupts and business frauds does lend credence to the belief that they were overwhelmed by feelings of shame – that is, once they were caught.

The prison experience of upper-class criminals tended to be less severe than that of their working-class counterparts. In Holloway and Brixton Prisons, where accused were held awaiting trial, affluent prisoners had greater access to creature comforts. While at Holloway, Balfour noted: "I had a decent bed, and was allowed to pay a prisoner, who was detained for debt, sixpence a day, which he was very glad to earn, to clean out my room and make my bed. All prisoners who can afford it are permitted at Holloway to purchase their own food, which comes from some restaurant or eating house nearby."[104] At Brixton in 1911 Hooley had a specially furnished cell and dined apart from the other prisoners.[105] In 1898 a Parliamentary Act provided for the classification of certain prisoners into first and second "divisions" where they would not be subject to hard labor.[106] Thereafter most white-collar criminals were so classified and escaped the worst rigors of prison life. Hooley recalled that the greater part of his 1912 imprisonment at Wormwood Scrubs was spent in the infirmary, "living on special food and being treated as a privileged sort of person who could still command a certain amount of respect."[107] At Maidstone Jail in the 1920s, Bottomley worked in the prison book bindery, repairing old library books. The financier Gerard Lee Bevan was also at Maidstone during the twenties, working as a compositor in the printing department.[108]

Although white-collar criminals were spared the strain of rockbreaking, they nevertheless found Victorian penitentiaries a far cry from Belgravia. For middle-class persons, used to commanding respect and exercising authority in their daily lives, the prison experience was a rude awakening to a world of discipline, regimentation and austerity. Deprived of bourgeois comforts and thrown among their social inferiors, middle-class prisoners found it difficult to recover their equilibrium. In his memoirs, *My Prison Life*, Jabez Balfour wrote movingly about the squalid living conditions in prisons, the mind-numbing routine of prison work, and the humiliating indignity of strip searches. Bottomley and Bevan were also shocked by prison conditions, and, after they were released, told of their experiences in collections of prison verse.[109]

"Respectable" persons found it difficult to think of themselves as "common criminals," and the law courts and prisons of Victorian and Edwardian England shared in their confusion. During the nineteenth century, it was assumed that "crime" was an activity of the lower orders – the criminal "underworld" or *classes dangereuses* of bourgeois discourse. Crime was *bred* in the squalid rookeries of East London or in the slums of Manchester. Economic deprivation engendered moral degeneration, and once criminal tendencies had been expressed, it was believed that they were biologically transferred to offspring. Victorian assumptions about crime had no place for the privileged malefactor, who was by definition exceptional, marginal, unimportant. Little wonder white-collar criminals were treated with relative leniency. Stockbrokers, bankers and solicitors were "us" to the dominant culture; they might stray from the straight and narrow, but they were far removed from the wild, half-human criminal monsters that populated the middle-class imagination.[110]

Anthony Trollope nicely illustrates bourgeois prejudice in *The Three Clerks*, where he compares the novel's villain, Undecimus Scott, the son of a peer, Member of Parliament and white-collar criminal, to Bill Sikes, the cut-throat burglar from Dickens' *Oliver Twist*. Both men are thieves, Trollope contends:

And yet poor Bill Sykes [sic], for whom here I would willingly say a word or two, could I, by so saying, mitigate the wrath against him, is always held as the more detestable scoundrel. Lady, you now know them both. Is it not the fact, that, knowing him as you do, you could spend a pleasant hour enough with Mr. Scott, sitting next to him at dinner; whereas your blood would creep within you, your hair would stand on end, your voice would stick in your throat, if you were suddenly told that Bill Sykes was in your presence?[111]

Trollope challenged his society's assumptions about criminality, and in a later novel, *The Way We Live Now*, he located the source of moral degeneration not in the slums of Whitechapel, but in the boardrooms of the City. Herbert Spencer also pilloried the double-standard in *The Morals of Trade*, where he argued that public morality would remain a sham until "the merchant who over-trades, the bank director who countenances an exaggerated report, and the railway director who repudiates his guarantee, come to be regarded as of the same genus as the pick-pocket, and are treated with like disdain."[112]

White-collar criminals benefited from the class prejudices of their society, but as cases of fraud and embezzlement mounted over the course of the nineteenth century, it became increasingly difficult to assert that crime was the exclusive province of the lower classes. As experience diverged from popular sentiments, new theories arose attributing criminal behavior to complex psychological factors which affected all social classes. This paradigmatic shift in learned discussions of crime became more pronounced in the early twentieth century, at which time empirical data and informed observation further undermined the Victorian notion of a criminal class.

Two English books appeared in 1913 which made important contributions to the criminological debate. Charles Goring's *The English Convict* was an exhaustive statistical study undertaken for the English Prison Commission. Goring, a prison medical officer, examined the physique and the family background of numerous prisoners, concluding that there was no anthropological "criminal type." His study also found that professional people were vastly overrepresented in the criminal statistics for certain crimes such as fraud and forgery.[113] The Reverend J.W. Horsley also drew upon personal experience for his book, *How Criminals are Made and Prevented*. Horsley, the chaplain of Clerkenwell Prison, came into contact with numerous incarcerated businessmen, and he suggested in his book that commercial morality tended to promote criminal behavior.[114] Horsley and Goring were at the forefront of a more nuanced "modern" explanation of crime which took into account family background and personal psychological development, and which rejected biological theories of a lower-class criminal type.

New ideas about crime and a greater awareness of criminals from privileged social milieus helped break down those prejudices which had for so long worked in favor of white-collar criminals. The concurrent erosion of free trade principles and the strengthening of company law from the 1890s through the 1920s made fraud more difficult to accomplish and easier to punish. The free-booting mentality of the mid-Victorian era had been restrained, but contemporary experience in both Britain and America demonstrates the resiliency of the entrepreneurial ideal and the adaptability of those who abuse it.

CHAPTER 8

Business ethics and professionalization

The permissive nature of commercial law put the onus of regulation on businessmen themselves, and yet the very novelty of big business and corporate organization meant that codes of behavior and standards of business ethics were poorly articulated. Furthermore, the high risk, competitive atmosphere of the City and the Victorian ideals of rugged individualism and free trade were not receptive to set rules or restrictions – even those produced by businessmen themselves. Thus the ethical boundaries remained vague and many businessmen who would never have embezzled clients' money saw nothing wrong in insider trading, balance sheet manipulation or paying journalists for favorable reviews. Likewise, many *bona fide* companies – which were honestly managed and which performed legitimate services – might sometimes in the course of business exaggerate their assets or downplay their liabilities for credit purposes. In effect, many persons in the business community developed private patterns of behavior that were at odds with the professed, public morality. Novelists and journalists seized upon these inconsistencies, which they saw as representative of general financial amorality. By late century the City's negative image alarmed a number of businessmen who sought to disassociate themselves from the likes of Albert Grant and Ernest Hooley. In particular, the drives for professionalization among groups such as bankers and accountants included attempts to promote better conduct and to exclude adventurers. Professional organizations helped raise the standards of business ethics, and, by decreasing amateurism, also eliminated many opportunities for fraud.

Numerous examples have already been given of the City's bad press. Businessmen were often portrayed as predatory creatures who exploited public ignorance for personal profit. This view gained considerable ground during the 1840s, when many people looked upon the Railway Mania as a vast conspiracy for cheating them out of money. In 1845 *The Times* editorialized:

There are some men of business, and a vast gaping crowd. There are some important transactions, and a great quantity of nonsense. There is some honesty, and much fraud. There are tradesmen, and there are mountebanks and thimbleriggers . . . Public morality, which has been so flagrantly outraged by a host of sordid speculators, and still more sordid advocates they have found or procured in a degraded member or two of the daily press, positively demands that the matter should be set right, and that very speedily. It is necessary to remind Englishmen and English gentlemen what is legitimate speculation, and what is not. It is necessary both for morals and for sound commercial prosperity.[1]

Typically, *The Times* saw unethical business practices as a threat not only to public morality but also to the nation's economy. The Liberal view emphasized the market's ability to regulate itself, and evidence to the contrary was met with alarm. Even so sanguine an advocate of free competition as Herbert Spencer expressed disgust at the no-holds-barred mentality of Victorian entrepreneurs. For the free market to work, Spencer argued, trust must be maintained through reliance on widely recognized moral precepts. "A system of keen competition carried on, as it is, without adequate moral restraint, is very much a system of commercial cannibalism."[2]

Social Darwinist thought gave ideological underpinning to a business system that was already "red in tooth and claw." Finance and company promotion were uncertain ventures the success of which often depended upon an aggressive, risk-taking posture. In this casino-like atmosphere winning and losing had little to do with merit. As Sidney Checkland argued in an essay on Victorian business mentality, men such as Albert Grant, Jabez Balfour and Whitaker Wright were respected and admired by many in the City as big men who took big chances. In their downfall, they were not looked upon as scoundrels by their fellow businessmen, but as "victims of unpredictability."[3]

Many in the business community actually believed that success was incompatible with strict integrity. Herbert Spencer found this view very widespread during the 1850s.[4] In 1875, the Parliamentary Committee on Loans to Foreign States was appalled by the blasé manner of brokers who seemed unconcerned about the frauds conducted on the Stock Exchange.[5] In 1893 the Reverend J. Carter surveyed businessmen throughout the country on matters of morality, later publishing his findings in the *Economic Review*. One of Carter's respondents admitted: "The tendency to misrepresent, deceive, or take unfair advantage under circumstances that daily offer the opportunity of doing so, is generally too strong to resist where self interest is the motive power of action, the conventional morality the only check."[6] In 1913 the Reverend J.W. Horsley found similar attitudes expressed by business people. Horsley concluded, "dishonesty in business, short of explicit theft, is considered by some to be inevitable."[7]

Businessmen often justified sharp practice by arguing that they were only doing what thousands of others did. Many ceased to believe in the dishonesty or criminality of their acts – which was not difficult when corrupt practices such as "window dressing" were normal behavior. Some entrepreneurs even argued that their businesses would have suffered if they had not had recourse to white-collar crime.[8] In 1893 a businessman bluntly informed Reverend Carter that "business is based on the gladiatorial theory of existence." It was unfortunate that this was not consistent with Christian truth, but this was nature's law.[9]

Capitalists may have taken refuge in "the survival of the fittest," but the notion was attacked by men of letters as a nihilistic philosophy. In his novel *The Three Clerks*, Anthony Trollope has the embezzling clerk Alaric Tudor justify his descent into crime as courageous behavior: "Why should he attempt to be wiser than those around him? Was it not sufficient for him to be wise in his generation? What man had ever become great, who allowed himself to be impeded by small scruples? If the sportsman returned from the field laden with game, who would scrutinize the mud on his gaiters?"[10] Fifty years later the playwright Granville Barker burlesqued this ethic in *The Voysey Inheritance*, where a dishonest trustee dismisses the law and conventional morality as guideposts for little people: "Good lord! . . . of course it's pleasant and comfortable to keep within the law . . . then the law will look after you. Otherwise you have to look pretty sharp after yourself. You have to cultivate your own sense of right and wrong; deal your own justice. But that makes a bigger man of you, let me tell you."[11] John Galsworthy put similar words in the mouth of Hornblower, the vulgar businessman of his 1920 drama *The Skin Game*: "I've got ambitions – I'm a serious man. Suppose I were to consider this and that, and every potty objection – where should I get to? –

nowhere!"[12] Cultural critics like Trollope and Galsworthy believed that the English had so elevated material success that in financial matters people had little trouble believing that the end justified the means.

Many businessmen who broke the law did not think of themselves as criminals. They were honest men "compelled by necessity" to pay dividends out of capital or to "borrow" clients' money. Often they fully expected to repay their defalcations, thinking as Mr. Macawber did of his fortunes, that "something would turn up." So long as they were not stealing outright (like vulgar highwaymen or housebreakers), financiers had little trouble justifying a vast range of misrepresentations and sharp practices. The imprecision of Victorian commercial law and the laxity of enforcement assisted businessmen in their moral evasions. One might violate the dictates of morality yet stay within the letter of the law.[13] Hooley's prospectuses were full of half-truths, but they were not illegal. Aron Salomon cheated his creditors through incorporation, but he broke no law. The paradox of legal but unethical behavior was addressed by the *National Review* in 1898: "The problem of converting moral into legal fraud is, no doubt, a difficult one; and the company-monger, protected as he is by skilled legal advice and draftsmanship, has brought the art of veiled lying in prospectuses, and otherwise sailing as near the wind as possible, to a high pitch of perfection."[14] The entrepreneurial culture of Victorian England created generations of businessmen who never told direct lies, or were never caught in criminal acts, but whose minds were inured to "legal duplicity."

The complex economy which so increased fraud and dishonesty also made it easier to avoid questions of conscience. According to the Reverend A.J. Morris: "The more complicated the social system is, the more numerous its expedients, the more dove-tailed its parts, the more subdivided its labours, and the more extended its credits, the more difficult is the application to it of moral principles, the more easy and plausible their violation or evasion."[15] The rising scale of financial organization, most significantly represented by the corporate form, lent an air of impersonality to business transactions. White-collar criminals often had little or no contact with their victims. "Shareholders," "investors," and "depositors" were abstractions in a way that burglars' or muggers' victims were not. This same dynamic worked within corporations, where employees seldom had contact with owners or directors. During the trial of Leopold Redpath in 1856, Mr. Justice Martin argued that clerical embezzlements were so common because there were no bonds of personal attachment and loyalty between clerks and management in large companies.[16]

The corporate structure also allowed individuals to spread blame or guilt over the whole body of directors or else to transfer personal responsibility to "the company." Herbert Spencer was among the first to recognize this phenomenon, arguing in 1854 that as a body, directors would do unethical things that they would shrink from doing as individuals.[17] In 1870 the *Quarterly Review* observed "it has almost come to be recognized that there is one standard of morality for private persons, and another for Directors of public companies."[18] In 1896 the *National Review* held forth on this same theme: "It is a curious psychological fact that upright people, who would strongly condemn shady conduct in individuals, will often condone the same conduct in men when acting collectively and in their corporate capacity. What would be dishonourable in a private person is, it would seem, to be excused, or at least palliated, in a board of directors."[19] Because of limited liability, directors were not held financially responsible for a company's trading losses or debts beyond their own shareholdings (which might be very small), even when losses were occasioned by directorial neglect or ineptitude. This separation of personal from corporate responsibility was inconsistent with the Victorian ideal of individualism, as critics of the City never tired of pointing out.

In the face of the business community's limitless ability to justify dishonest behavior or to evade moral responsibility for such behavior, a tightening of company law seemed almost irrelevant. It was also believed by many that politicians were so inextricably bound up in business activity that they were incapable of initiating serious reform.[20] Large numbers of both Houses were directors of public companies as were members of the civil service. There were no rules governing politicians' associations with trade and industry, and so lax were standards of conflicting interests that during the 1870s the Chief Railway Inspecting Officer at the Board of Trade was himself the director of a railway company.[21] It was widely believed that high government officials converted privileged information into hard cash on the Stock Exchange. This was the theme of Oscar Wilde's 1895 play, *An Ideal Husband*, and it was given real expression on numerous occasions.

During the 1880s it was widely believed that the Duchess of Manchester made money on the Stock Exchange by means of privileged information she received from her lover Lord Hartington, a member of the Cabinet.[22] Lord Kylsant used classified information he acquired while sitting as a member of the 1906 Royal Commission on Shipping Rings to further his own shipping business. Kylsant had learned which firm in Alfred Jones' shipping empire was most valuable, and he purchased this business immediately upon Jones' death in 1909.[23] In 1928 three civil servants in the Foreign Office were forced to resign because of speculations they had made in foreign currency.[24]

The most notorious abuse of privileged information was the Marconi Affair of 1912. The Attorney General, Rufus Isaacs, the Chancellor of the Exchequer, David Lloyd George, and the Postmaster General, Herbert Samuel, all purchased shares in the American Marconi Company at the time in which Asquith's Liberal government was negotiating a lucrative contract with the subsidiary British Marconi Company to construct wireless stations for the navy. Matters were further complicated since the chairman of British Marconi, Godfrey Isaacs, was the Attorney General's brother. The press exposed the affair in 1912, causing a Parliamentary furor. At first the Ministers involved simply denied having purchased shares in *British* Marconi, but, when the purchase of American shares was discovered, they argued that the American company was technically distinct and would not benefit from the government's contract.

The House appointed a Committee to investigate the matter. During this proceeding it was further revealed that Lord Murray, former Liberal Party Whip, had purchased shares for the Party Fund. Murray was conveniently out of the country during the investigation, but his purchase came to light when the broker involved absconded. Asquith staunchly supported Isaacs and Lloyd George throughout the inquiry, and in June 1913 the Select Committee issued its Report which white-washed the affair and cleared the Ministers of wrongdoing.[25] The general public was incredulous, and even the Liberal press condemned the whole proceeding. Lord Robert Cecil for the Conservatives issued a separate

Minority Report that was highly critical of the Ministers, charging them with "grave impropriety."[26]

The Marconi Affair dramatized the intimate connections between Parliament and the City as well as the ethical vacuum found in both arenas. During the controversy, Asquith recalled that while he was at the Exchequer earlier in the century, it had never occurred to him that it would have been improper to buy government securities.[27] Rufus Isaacs concluded that no Minister should hold a directorship in or own shares in any company having contractual relations with the government, but, as he emphasized, this was a stricter standard than had ever been set before.[28] Clearly politicians had yet to put their own house in order and were unlikely to impress upon the business community higher standards of behavior.

In the quest for ethical principles in business matters few people looked to the churches for guidance, nor were Victorian religious leaders particularly outspoken in the condemnation of financial fraud.[29] Earlier in the century, Evangelicals had been outspoken in their condemnation of business, viewing the frequent failures, frauds and bankruptcies of the 1820s and 1830s as signs of the coming millennium.[30] By the mid-Victorian period, however, specifically religious condemnations of business had all but disappeared. The complacency of the Established Church was particularly noticeable. In a letter to the Dean of Westminster in 1845, Prince Albert urged bishops in the House of Lords to condemn "the recklessness and wickedness of the projectors of Railway schemes, who, having no funds themselves, acquire riches at the expense of others, their dupes. Here the nation is in the greatest danger, as every individual gets corrupted, and every sense of shame is lost."[31] The bishops were apparently unmoved and at no time did they attempt to use their moral authority to stem the flow of speculation or to strengthen commercial law. The Church's neglect did not go unnoticed by some of its own ministers, and in 1853 the Reverend A.J. Morris observed: "There are hosts of books on the evidences of Christianity, its doctrines, its institutions, its general moralities, but, though we are 'a nation of shopkeepers,' though commerce is enlarging its sphere and strengthening its spirit, though its evils are almost universally admitted, it is feared that little attention is given to it by the pulpit."[32] Morris hoped to redress the imbalance with his book *Religion and Business*.

Morris was not alone in his crusade against white-collar crime, though the religious criticism of business fraud remained sporadic and personal – lacking the institutional support of Victorian churches. William Brock, the Baptist minister of Bloomsbury Chapel, was known for his concern with business ethics, at one point lecturing at the YMCA on "Mercantile Morality." In 1866 Brock's church initiated a disciplinary investigation into the business affairs of one of its most distinguished congregants, Sir Morton Peto. A railway contractor, Peto had declared bankruptcy during the financial panic of 1866 at which time his credit was dangerously overextended. Bloomsbury Chapel cleared Peto of fraud and dishonesty, but concluded:

> . . . in some of the transactions brought under our notice Sir Morton did not evince the moderation and prudence becoming a Christian man, and that he suffered his good name to be associated with questionable acts and misleading representations, without due investigation into their real character and probable results. He did not, indeed, avoid the appearance of evil, with the carefulness which should have distinguished a man professing godliness; and on this account, we deem him to be deserving of our faithful, brotherly reproof.[33]

In 1874 the Reverend William Henry Lyttleton unsuccessfully urged the formation of a commercial organization for the suppression of immoral and illegal business practices. Later preaching before a group of Birmingham businessmen, Lyttleton entreated: "Oh, look at the miseries that have been brought upon thousands and tens of thousands, by wild and unprincipled commercial speculation. Look at banks failing and dragging hundreds upon hundreds of innocent families down with them into hopeless ruin – wasting in one dread moment the hard-earned savings of many a life of honest labour!"[34] In 1893 the Reverend J.S. Watts publicly condemned Jabez Balfour's frauds in his pamphlet *The Biggest Crime of the Nineteenth Century and What the Churches Say to It*. Watts was also active in organizing a relief fund for Balfour's victims.[35] In 1913 the Reverend J.W. Horsley published his influential book, *How Criminals are Made and Prevented*, in which he argued that commercial morality promoted crime and that *caveat emptor* was essentially an immoral doctrine.

The religious critics of the City added their voices to those of the novelists and journalists who had long castigated fraud and sharp business practice. These men represented the "professional ideal" in English society, which stood for service, and they attacked businessmen as money-grubbers who worked for personal profit rather than the national good.[36] Some business people attempted to counter their negative image by adopting professional rhetoric themselves and emphasizing their service to the larger community. By the late nineteenth century many entrepreneurs saw the unregulated financial arena as a threat to legitimate business enterprise. Amateurs, incompetents and frauds were given too easy an entrance into the market and their activities were a drag on the economy and an affront to honest businessmen. Professionalization – that is, the establishment of internal regulations and standards governing a given occupation – enabled segments of the business community to improve performance, exclude adventurers and actively promote a positive public image of themselves.

White-collar crime was an important impetus for professional organization. The founding of professional accountancy bodies during the 1870s was partly intended to counter corporate fraud through the enhancement of bookkeeping and auditing skills. The City of Glasgow Bank scandal in 1878 was the catalyst for establishing the Institute of Bankers in 1879.[37] Exposure of the Barton Stock Frauds in 1890 led the provincial stock exchanges to form a joint association in an attempt to clarify laws regarding the transfer of shares.[38] Under the leadership of the Liverpool broker Edward Rae, the new Council of Associated Exchanges lobbied for legislation that would guarantee the "indefeasibility of transfer." In 1891 Parliament responded by passing the Forged Transfers Act, which required companies to compensate purchasers of fraudulently transferred shares. The Council of Associated Exchanges further sought to lessen fraud by establishing in 1895 uniform rules for allowing quotations of new companies, including the stipulations that companies could not use their funds to purchase their own shares and that directors' interests in contracts must be disclosed in the prospectus.[39]

Professional bodies emphasized high standards of competency as a means of combatting slipshod business methods and fraud. To receive the certificate of the Institute of Bankers – which admitted one to membership – candidates had to pass two examinations in the subjects of arithmetic, bookkeeping, commercial law, political economy and banking methods. Reading lists were supplied for the exams and evening lectures were given at colleges in London and other major cities. The Institute of Chartered Accountants required prospective members to pass examinations in bookkeeping, auditing, bankruptcy law, company law and the rights and duties of liquidators and trustees. Professional certification enhanced the credibility of those who achieved it as well as decreasing the careless bookkeeping methods and amateurish company organization which had characterized the mid-Victorian economy.[40]

The professional movement was assisted by the proliferation of business handbooks and other educational literature during the late nineteenth and early twentieth centuries. The Banking Institute's standard text, *Questions on Banking Practice*, was first issued in 1885. That same year George Rae published his famous manual, *The Country Banker: His Clients, Cares and Work*, which remained in print through the 1920s. By the turn of the century, Sir Isaac Pitman's business handbook series included hundreds of titles in accounting, banking, insurance, management and company law. The publishing houses of Effingham Wilson and Gee and Company also offered a vast range of business textbooks and investment literature for both professionals and the general public. In the early twentieth century a number of distinguished accountants published instructional works. Sir Mark Webster Jenkinson's *The Promotion and Accounts of a Public Limited Company* (1912) offered managers and auditors practical advice on bookkeeping. In 1914 Frederic de Paula published *The Principles of Auditing*, which remained the standard textbook on the subject until the 1950s.

A considerable amount of the business literature dealt with questions of fraud and embezzlement. De Paula's *Principles of Auditing*, for example, offered accountants a wealth of information on preventing and discovering fraud. De Paula explained how to set up a continuous internal audit whereby the work of each clerk was checked by others and the books of different departments were kept strictly separate. He also warned auditors against common tricks such as dummy pass books and double receipts.[41] In I.H. Dearnley's *Fraud and Embezzlement*, a whole series of danger signals of embezzlement were cited. In particular, auditors were to be wary of employees who declined to take vacations, employees who were overly anxious that certain sections of their work be checked, and regularly scheduled audits, with no surprise checks.[42]

Business publications touted the latest technical innovations designed to safeguard against fraud. Indelible ink and carbon receipts rendered the alteration of accounts more difficult. By the 1920s ultra-violet light could be used to reveal alterations. During the twenties a whole series of ingenious machines were designed to hinder fraud in accounts. The "Protectograph" guarded against the alteration of checks by cutting the amount of payment into the check and stamping the cut-out edges with acid-proof ink. The "Parata" receipting machine automatically copied all receipts made, mechanically storing the copies in a locked box. The "Campos" accounting machine assigned all transactions a serial number and then stored them in the machine. In this way falsification was impossible without leaving a positive trace.[43] These machines were indicative of a new systematization that professional development had brought to the business world.

The professional emphasis on educational requirements and standardized methods helped create a business environment where there were fewer opportunities for fraud and where the discovery of fraud was ever more likely. The professions also exerted a moral influence in the City, promoting a higher level of ethical standards than that which had characterized earlier business activity. The new emphasis on ethics was not entirely altruistic, as it was yet another means by which professionals asserted their superiority over competitors and countered the traditional image of businessman as Philistine.

The Institute of Chartered Accountants especially stressed the moral responsibilities of auditors to provide shareholders with fair information and to go beyond the requirements of the law which many in the profession saw as inadequate. The legal limits to an auditor's duties were in part spelled out by the Kingston Cotton Mill Case in 1896. Upon winding up the Kingston Mill it was discovered that the manager had grossly overvalued the stock-in-trade in the company's balance sheet so as to conceal insolvency. Since he had not caught this distortion, the auditor was sued for misfeasance. He was acquitted, however, and in delivering the judgment, Lord Justice Lopes stated: "An auditor is not bound to be a detective, or, as was said, to approach his work with suspicion or with a foregone conclusion that there is something wrong. He is a watch-dog, but not a bloodhound."[44] The leading voices in the accounting profession, however, favored the bloodhound.[45] After all, detective work is what set the best auditing practice apart from the mere arithmetical checks of amateurs.

The 1931 prosecution of the accountant Harold Morland in the case of the Royal Mail renewed the debate over legal versus ethical responsibility.[46] Although Morland was acquitted of endorsing a false balance sheet, many accountants believed that he had not done enough to appraise shareholders of the company's true position. In his 1932 address to the Institute of Chartered Accountants, President H.L.H. Hill emphasized auditors' duties "to bring about the adoption of a higher standard based upon a proper sense of ethical obligation and fiduciary responsibility."[47] Hill went on to assert: "The goodwill of our Institute has been created and maintained not by those who have regarded the letter of the law as their ultimate guide but by those who have developed and adopted a code of ethics embracing, but not restricted to legal requirements."[48] The maintenance of high standards of conduct, or at least the articulation of such standards, was an essential ingredient of the professional mystique.

Reform within certain segments of the business community was probably far more effective in countering white-collar crime than was the simultaneous tightening of company law. Businessmen proved more adept at evading the law than the pressure from their own peers to conform to certain professional standards. Professionalization, however, was a two-edged sword. It helped eliminate some gross abuses, but it also lent itself to obfuscation. Professionals could invoke their "expertise" to cover all manner of unorthodox or unethical behavior. Bankers, brokers, solicitors, accountants and company directors continued to operate in a world that was alien and inscrutable to the general public. It was still difficult (and remains so to this day) to distinguish between fraud, incompetence, carelessness and misfortune. The rules of the game can be narrowed, but cheating does not disappear.

CONCLUSION

Final considerations

Victorian England witnessed the birth of a new, industrial economy and a financial structure characterized by individual shareholdings in joint-stock corporations. By the end of the nineteenth century, the British had invested several billion pounds in company shares, or roughly two-fifths of total national wealth. This level of shareholding had no parallel in the world, amounting to more than twice the sum of French and German company investment combined.[1] Corporate organization facilitated British domination of the world economy and enriched many members of the investing public; yet this novel and peculiar form of economic arrangement also proved vulnerable to abuse. White-collar crime was the soft underbelly of the modern British economy, robbing the public of millions of pounds, undermining trust in commercial integrity and depressing the level of investment in new industries.

A number of structural and ideological factors combined to create a climate favorable to corporate fraud in nineteenth-century England. The divorce of ownership from control in large companies increased the distance between shareholders and directors and heightened the impersonality of the relationship. Directors held vast sums of money in trust for investors, and the temptation to misappropriate or misapply that money was at times irresistible. The primitive nature of accountancy and auditing made fraud difficult to discover and the complexity of modern finance blurred the boundaries between crime and misadventure. The entrepreneurial culture of Victorian England bred aggressive businessmen who were impatient with ethical codes and whose preoccupation with material success led them to fear failure more than fraud. A *laissez-faire* mentality and an emphasis on individual responsibility discouraged state intervention to protect shareholders. Victorian class prejudice permeated the criminal justice

G

system, which directed its greatest wrath against the lower classes and treated upper-class criminal capitalists with relative leniency.

White-collar crime actually posed a far greater threat to property than did the thefts of burglars, shoplifters and pickpockets. In 1894 the journalist A.R. Barnett observed: "there seems to be more danger from the trusted officer and the employee than from the burglar . . . now it is the skilled financier or bank clerk who coolly and quietly abstracts or misapplies the funds, falsifies the accounts, and makes away with millions where the burglar got thousands."[2] To give but one example, in *London Labour and the London Poor*, Henry Mayhew recorded that the property stolen by London's thieves amounted to £71,000 for the year 1860.[3] A substantial sum to be sure, but one that pales in comparison to the £260,000 embezzlement of a single London bank clerk, W.G. Pullinger, also in 1860.[4] Unlike the burglars who made off with the family silver, frauds and embezzlers could deprive people of their capital, or of their life's savings. In commenting on the embezzlements of the bankers Strahan, Paul and Bates, the London *Times* listed the levels of crime from pickpocket to highwayman, but awarded the highest criminal "honors" to financiers who scatter "ruin over hundreds of quiet, respectable, and virtuous households, the scene of sacred economy and the sweet charities of domestic life." *The Times* went on to lament:

How many girls will go portionless! how many young ladies become governesses! how many young men go to Australia, or behind counters, instead of to College or the Guards, in consequence of this bankruptcy! How many hearts will be broken! how many constitutions undermined by trudging and drudging, that have hitherto known nothing worse than a headache after an evening party or the shaking of an ill-hung carriage.[5]

Although the financial frauds of middle-class bankers, brokers and company directors dwarfed the thefts of the Victorian under-world, it was Mayhew's rag-tag pickpockets and audacious burglars (or their literary equivalents, the Artful Dodger and Bill Sikes) that dominated popular images of criminality. Contemporary historians have inherited the class prejudices of the last century, and have for the most part accepted uncritically the assumption that "crime" was a working-class phenomenon. This study rejects such an idea through its emphasis on the criminal "upperworld."

Any examination of social problems is by its very nature bound to present a selective and therefore distorted picture. I have focused on those businessmen and business practices that flouted the laws and ethical standards of modern English society and not on those honest capitalists and companies which were surely in the majority. I do not wish to suggest that fraud and chicanery were the rule in finance and business. But the evidence shows that they were widespread in practice and significant in their effects.

Company investment was a risky enterprise, and the notorious frauds and failures of the Victorian era touched numerous investors. In 1879 *The Economist* complained of the great loss of shareholders' capital from company failures, concluding: "If a balance sheet could be drawn up of the losses and gains to Great Britain from the establishment of companies on the limited principle to work industrial undertakings, we have no doubt the balance would be largely on the wrong side."[6] This pessimistic view was later corroborated by the economist H.A. Shannon, who followed the histories of the first five thousand limited companies and found that 36% of them ceased to exist after five years and 54% after ten years.[7] Of course not all of the failures were due to fraud, but fraud was certainly common and dominated public discourse and public perceptions of the City.

Individual losses from fraud or embezzlement could be considerable. After the Financial Crisis of 1866, the Master of Rolls, Lord Romilly, informed Parliament:

Very few days pass without my receiving letters from contributories in the country, who say that they are entirely ruined by being called upon to pay a contribution, and that they had no conception what the company was which they joined. They are persons, perhaps, who have saved after a long life of industry, £200 or £300, to live upon in their old age, and they have been induced to join a company, and they are utterly ruined.[8]

A specific example from the period involved the three thousand shareholders of the Alliance Building Society who lost between £300,000 and £400,000 when that firm failed in 1866. The Alliance had been recklessly managed, though it drew in shareholders from temperance circles by falsely implying a connection between itself and the United Kingdom Alliance, the principal temperance organization in England. Shareholders included many widows and spinsters who had invested all their savings, and the newspapers noted the suicides of several victims.[9]

The City of Glasgow debacle in 1878 resulted in the loss of

almost £6 million of shareholders' and depositors' money. According to the *Contemporary Review*:

In almost every town and hamlet of our land, however far from the centre of the explosion, there stands some home unroofed and torn open to the hard gaze of public curiosity and public compassion. It is true that the sufferers have in public and in private, shown resignation to God and constancy before men, even beyond belief; but how many lives, maimed and all but cut in two, have crept away beyond our ken into a seclusion where hope and energy are slowly ebbing from the wounded spirit.[10]

Nor was this mere rhetoric. Over one thousand shareholders were bankrupted by demands to meet their unlimited liability and an army of small investors lost their all. So profound was the resulting distress that a charitable relief fund was organized to assist the victims.[11]

The crash of the Liberator Building Society in 1892 also resulted in such widespread suffering that a relief fund for its victims was set up under the patronage of Prince Christian. By 1893 the Liberator Relief Fund had 2,600 individual cases on its books representing an aggregate loss of £750,000, and these were only the cases where loss resulted in "total or semi-destitution." Over half the victims were widows or spinsters, and many were more than sixty years old. The Relief Fund hoped to raise enough money to pay the most destitute and aged a sum equivalent to their lost dividend. Appeals for contributions appeared in the press, circulars were sent through the mail, churches took up special collections and a number of benefit concerts and plays were held.[12]

The Relief Fund's appeals highlighted the most desperate cases, dramatizing the vulnerability of investors to corporate fraud. One seventy-year-old woman who lost all her money hung herself rather than face an old age afflicted by poverty.[13] An old man from Newcastle wrote: "I have lost close to £700 in the companies. I was induced to join them from the agent here telling me the directors was all good men and the companies perfectly safe, and now I am left in poverty and no relatives to help me in my sorrow and distress. I may say that I am dreading the winter cumming on, for I am so very bare of warm clothing and no money to buy them with [sic]."[14] A schoolmistress who had invested in the Liberator stated her desperate case:

Every penny of my money was in the Liberator, £1,200. The interest paid my rent and taxes, and with the help of that I was able to get my living in a small private school. I am 55 years of age, and have worked as hard as any woman could since I was 17. I was straining every nerve to save a little more to pull my income to £100 a year, that I might cease from my labours at 60 and live at rest and in peace to the end . . . Unfortunately for me this trouble with its sleepless nights of racking anxiety has so crushed me – some days are dragged through in agony – my future is dark enough, I know not in the least what will become of me. I can only sob out in the night (the only time I can allow myself the luxury of crying). Oh God, I have worked so hard, and looked forward to my little home, with my books, so longingly, save me, oh save me from the workhouse.[15]

Such cases as these were no doubt extreme, but they did illustrate actual risks for many investors.

Those investors most vulnerable to fraud were persons of slender means, such as the elderly, widows, spinsters, clergymen, half-pay officers, small tradesmen and domestic servants. Possessed of relatively small savings, modest investors were unable to diversify, and tended to place all their funds into a single investment, very often a bank, building society or insurance company. As early as 1844, the Parliamentary Committee on Joint-Stock Companies realized that humble investors were the greatest sufferers from company fraud:

The extent of the evil is to be measured rather by the circumstances of the victims than the amount of plunder. They are usually persons of very limited means, who invest their savings in order to obtain the tempting returns which are offered. Annuity Companies have proved the most dangerous in this respect. Old people, governesses, servants, and persons of that description, are tempted to invest their little all, and when the concern stops, they are ruined.[16]

The insurance company frauds and savings bank embezzlements of the 1840s had sent a number of small depositors to the work-house.[17] This particular class of investor continued to be most adversely affected by the frauds and failures of Victorian and Edwardian England.

The more affluent investor, of course, could afford a greater margin of error than his *petit bourgeois* counterpart. Wealthy investors also lessened their risks by diversifying their stock port-folios. Corporations were especially well placed to offset losses from fraud. In 1860, for example, the Union Bank of London was able to cover the £260,000 embezzlement of its chief cashier by transferring £220,000 from its reserve fund along with £40,000 from the yearly profits. Despite the enormity of the loss, the Union Bank was still able to pay a respectable 5% dividend that year.[18] With the growth of investment trusts and institutional shareholdings during the twentieth century, individual losses from white-collar crime have been minimized even further.

Even more profound than shareholders' losses was fraud's impact on the economy as a whole – both in undermining commercial trust and depressing levels of investment. As the *National Review* put the case in 1898: "this is not merely a question as is often urged of a few credulous investors or speculators losing their money. Other and larger issues are involved, such as the lowering of hitherto accepted standards of commercial integrity."[19] The commercial world was bound together by stocks, bonds, contracts, bills of exchange, letters of credit and promissory notes. Fraud was seen as a "canker at the heart of this complicated system"[20] because it threatened the inviolability of contracts and the integrity of financial instruments. According to D.M. Evans: "In a commercial country such as England, no crime can be more heinous against society, as constituted, than a breach of mercantile trust. To tolerate it, or to pass it over with ill-judged sympathy, or equally ill-timed mercy, would be to sap the foundations of mercantile prosperity."[21] By late century, some critics of the City believed that fraud was sapping the vitality of the entire nation:

There is something disagreeably un-English about the new financial methods and the vulgar trickery and chicane which characterize them; and in these days when finance and politics are connected by the closest ties their demoralizing influence is especially to be deplored . . . there are still a few who believe that the national character is one of the main foundations of our greatness both at home and abroad, and that anything which tends to impair it is a source of national weakness. As a commercial people our credit rests on our good name, and as a nation with an imperial mission we can ill afford to play fast and loose with it . . . It is not merely rectitude, unctuous or otherwise, it is plain common sense – "good business," in fact – to recognize that this good name and this national character are things worth preserving, and that the beginnings of pecuniary corruption may also, whatever our new Machiavellians may say, be the seeds of a nation's decadence.[22]

Claims of national decadence are difficult to sustain, but white-collar crime certainly created a wealth of suspicion within the City, impeding the smooth transaction of business. During the 1870s, for example, a group of London merchants who were floating a loan to

Santo Domingo obtained a quotation on the Stock Exchange by falsely claiming that the loan had been fully subscribed. Mihill Slaughter, a member of the Stock Exchange Committee, later told Parliament: "There is no doubt that the committee were deceived; but because they trusted merchants of London. I do not think the committee are to be so much blamed; it was a new thing, we had always been in the habit of trusting the merchants of London."[23] The "habit of trusting" was soon broken. Businessmen were increasingly dubious of one another and many entrepreneurs especially avoided joint-stock proceedings. According to the *National Review*, "when a man of business receives a prospectus nowadays he generally assumes it to be a swindle, and throws it into the waste-paper basket; and too often he is right."[24] The *Journal of Finance* believed that good businessmen frequently refused to join boards of directors because they distrusted promoters. Since it was "so easy to foist absolutely hopeless schemes on the public, . . . any man who values his reputation will hesitate to risk it in a venture of whose success he is not perfectly confident."[25]

The exposure of enormous frauds, particularly at times of speculative disaster, depressed the flow of private capital into company investment. The collapse of the South American boom in 1825 kept the British public away from foreign investments until mid-century.[26] The disastrous outcome of the Railway Mania alienated people from new railway investment for decades. As *Blackwood's* remarked in 1876: "It is only comparatively lately that the most flourishing of our English railways have begun to overcome the prejudice created against railway property by the lavishness, carelessness, and corruption of so many of the original promoters."[27] The Overend and Gurney Crash of 1866 and the subsequent disclosures of promotional fraud and financial irregularities among joint-stock companies significantly depressed the rate of company formation. It took twenty years before the amount of capital raised through company promotion again reached the level of the mid-sixties.[28] The collapse of the mining boom in the early twentieth century created stagnation in the money market, and the Great Crash of 1929 effectively ended speculation for a decade. Contemporaries emphasized that the fraud attendant on these financial crises deterred investment. In 1907, for example, the *Nineteenth Century* argued that "the frequent public exposures of financial swindles tends to make investors

unduly suspicious even of substantial and legitimate undertakings."[29] In 1930 that same journal maintained: "To allow dealings
to take place in worthless shares which are hoisted by pool operations to extreme and ridiculous heights and are then heavily sold, is
to cause grievous losses to fall on the unsuspecting public, with the
result that more people are driven away from the Stock
Exchange."[30] The English investment structure was characterized
by cycles of overspeculation, default and depression. These booms
and busts might affect the entire economy as in 1866 and 1929, or
they might be focused on particular sectors, such as railways in the
1840s, banks in the 1850s and home industrials in the 1890s.

New industries and new technologies were especially vulnerable
to fraudulent promotion. Lacking the business connections and
proven reputations of established industries, they were easy prey
for unscrupulous promoters. The economist William P. Kennedy's
study of new industrial floatations in the late nineteenth century
has led him to describe a pattern whereby disastrous share issues
crippled later development.[31] For example, in the electric company
boom of 1882, £7 million was raised by various floatations, but
most of the money was squandered on promotional fees and
"dubious, fraudulent and useless patents."[32] The public then shied
away from investing further in the electric industry which was hard
pressed to secure capital for expansion. The same pattern characterized the bicycle and automobile industries in the 1890s, where
an early rush of promotions, many of which were neither sound nor
honest, made investors leery of further issues by firms in those
industries.

The ease with which companies could be promoted and the
permissive nature of English company law enabled too many reckless and fraudulent schemes to compete with *bona fide* businesses for
public contributions. In England there was no formal weeding-out
process by the Stock Exchange or the Company Registrar. Neither
did banks nor brokers serve as an informal screen by refusing to act
for dubious promotions. The market eventually separated the
wheat from the chaff, but in the process unscrupulous men were
enriched, many investors lost their capital and negative associations fastened on particular industries. In the long run this process
proved deleterious to the development of the surviving companies
and may well have contributed to Britain's industrial decline.[33]

The accumulated losses from Stock Exchange crises and the

constant fear of fraud led investors to seek out safe places to put their money. Conservative advice had always warned investors against high yield, but high risk, securities. As *Blackwood's* cautioned its readers in 1876, "wary investors should hold more closely than ever by the good old-fashioned maxim that great interest means bad security."[34] Most advice warned investors away from industrial securities as being too risky (with the exception of the established railway lines) and instead recommended Consols and foreign government securities which held out a steady and more or less guaranteed return. In 1885, Messrs. Endean and Company, a firm of London brokers, prepared a "selection of safe investments" for their customers which consisted almost wholly of Consols, municipal bonds, public utilities and the great trunk railway lines.[35] In 1901, C.H. Thorpe's *How to Invest and How to Speculate* advised investors to err on the side of caution by purchasing government securities and railway shares.[36] During the late nineteenth and early twentieth centuries, English investors were turning in greater numbers to foreign government bonds as a more secure alternative to domestic industrial shares.[37] As long as investors avoided Latin American bonds and purchased European and Colonial government stock, they did very well for themselves and avoided most of the risks – including fraud – associated with joint-stock companies.[38] For whatever else people may have thought about the Kaiser, they would rather entrust their savings to him than to the likes of Mr. Hooley.

The inefficiency and fraud associated with English company promotion took a heavy toll on the economy, and yet the nation was painfully slow in responding to the problem. Much of the delay is attributable to the tenets of *laissez-faire* which undermined efforts at company law reform well into the twentieth century. Business interests were well represented by Members of Parliament, many of whom were company directors. The defenders of the liberal view vigorously maintained that government regulation of business would only result in more fraud by instilling in investors a false sense of confidence. The individual investor, free traders argued, must be held responsible for his actions.

Victorian emphasis on individualism led many people to view the problem of white-collar crime in personal rather than structural terms. Novelists and journalists alike personalized evil, castigating individual villains for their frauds and embezzlements and not the system of finance which fostered such crimes. Men such as Hudson, Balfour and Hooley were scapegoats of their age, singled out for opprobrium and therefore deflecting attention from larger issues of corporate accountability and law reform. Insistence on personal integrity substituted for real economic improvements.

Given the risks of the British share market, it seems remarkable that there was never a shortage of investors willing to finance a whole array of new companies. In spite of frequent failures and frauds and in the face of massive negative publicity regarding financiers, the British public seemingly threw caution (and a great deal of money) into the wind. Contemporary cultural critics attributed such behavior to greed and gullibility. According to this view, whenever scheming company promoters dangled the promise of great wealth before the public, prudence and sobriety vanished. In Dickens' novel *Little Dorrit* the protagonist expressed the hope that the downfall of the great fraud, Merdle, and the ruination of his victims would act as a warning to people against such crimes. The hero's more worldly friend, however, was dubious:

"My dear Mr. Clenham," returned Ferdinand, laughing, "have you really such a verdant hope? The next man who has as large a capacity and as genuine a taste for swindling, will succeed as well. Pardon me, but I think you really have no idea how the human bees will swarm to the beating of any old tin kettle; in that fact lies the complete manual of governing them. When they can be got to believe that the kettle is made of the precious metals, in that fact lies the whole power of men like our late lamented."[39]

The struggle between rogues and fools was an uneven contest.

Public gullibility, however, was not an unlimited resource. All who succumbed to the temptations of frauds and schemers cannot have been ignorant of the risks. Nor was the public forced to buy speculative securities. Investors could have put all their money in Consols or in post-office savings banks and never have worried about default or fraud. Obviously many persons were willing to risk their money for a chance at greater prosperity.

Certain members of the middle class were especially prone to taking risks because of their desire to maintain respectable social standing. Single women, the elderly, clergymen and other genteel, but economically marginal, members of the middle class were likely to "gamble" with their money in their constant struggle to keep up appearances. Putting their capital in government securities was safe and sure, but the two and one half percent interest might mean sacrificing the paraphernalia of respectability and consequently losing social status. The desire to maintain a good address, to dress well and to send their children to the right schools (in other words, to remain middle class) led some people into the arms of reckless or dishonest financiers.

There are limits, however, to rationalizing speculation. As one scholar recently pointed out, the very word "speculation" originally referred to divination and fortune telling, especially through astrology.[40] Throughout the nineteenth century, popular behavior with regard to the Stock Market had striking parallels to more traditional games of chance and fortune telling.[41] Victorian capitalists went to great lengths to rationalize economic cycles and fluctuations in the money market and to legitimize stock speculation as opposed to other disreputable forms of gambling. Yet the fact remains that capitalist culture promoted a spirit of acquisitiveness that frequently ignored sober warnings about the low odds of winning or the real dangers of economic loss.

Despite more stringent Companies Acts in the 1920s and 1940s and a new emphasis on professional ethics by some business people, white-collar crime has persisted. The complex structures of the modern, industrial economy which gave birth to white-collar crime continue to foster it. The vast Byzantine networks of international finance and corporate organization shield dishonest businessmen from exposure, making it difficult both to pin down specific crimes and to bring the perpetrators to justice with the necessary evidence. The complexity of high finance makes it almost impossible to distinguish between fraud and misfortune. This was the case with company promoters in Victorian England just as it is the case with directors of Savings and Loan institutions in contemporary America.

Notes

INTRODUCTION WHITE-COLLAR CRIME AND THE
CRIMINAL "UPPERWORLD"

1 Mihir Bose and Cathy Gunn, *Fraud: The Growth Industry of the Eighties* (London: Unwin Hyman, 1989).
2 Charles Dickens, "Very Singular Things in the City," *All the Year Round* 3 (July 1860): 325–26.
3 "Finance, Frauds and Failure," *Temple Bar* 17 (June 1866): 393.
4 Hugh Stutfield, "The Higher Rascality," *National Review* 31 (March 1898): 75.
5 Witness, for example, Margaret Thatcher's repeated calls to return to Victorian values.
6 J.H. Clapham, *An Economic History of Modern Britain*, 3 vols. (Cambridge: Cambridge University Press, 1926–38), vol. 3, 289.
7 Harold Perkin, *Origins of Modern English Society, 1780–1880* (London: Routledge and Kegan Paul, 1969), 442.
8 Edwin Sutherland, *White Collar Crime* (1949; reprint, New Haven: Yale University Press, 1983), 7.
9 For a discussion of the fiduciary nature of professional society, see Harold Perkin, *The Rise of Professional Society: England Since 1880* (London: Routledge and Kegan Paul, 1989), esp. chapter 1.
10 Mercantile fraud has been largely ignored by historians. Some mention of it can be found in W.H. Fraser, *The Coming of the Mass Market, 1850–1914* (Hamden, Conn.: Archon Books, 1981), For Victorian dialogue on the problem, see Reverend W.H. Lyttleton, *The Sins of Trade and Business* (London: Mowbray and Company, 1891), and Reverend J.W. Horsley, *How Criminals are Made and Prevented* (London: T. Fisher Unwin, 1913).
11 Politics probably offered the most lucrative possibilities for corruption, though this type of crime is extraordinarily difficult to document. "Old Corruption" has been explored by W.D. Rubenstein, "The End of Old Corruption in Britain, 1780–1860," *Past and Present* 51 (1983): 55–86, and modern corruption in G.R. Searle, *Corruption in British Politics, 1895–1930* (Oxford: Clarendon Press, 1987), and Alan

Doig, *Corruption and Misconduct in Contemporary British Politics* (New York: Penguin Books, 1984), though Victorian malversations remain largely uncatalogued.

12 For the best early work, see Clapham, *An Economic History of Modern Britain*; B.C. Hunt, *The Development of the Business Corporation in England 1800–67* (Cambridge Mass.: Harvard University Press, 1936), and H.A. Shannon, "The Limited Companies of 1866–83," *Economic History Review* 4 (October 1933): 290–316.

13 Edward Smithies, *The Black Economy in England Since 1914* (London: Gill and Macmillan, 1984).

14 David J. Jeremy, ed., *Dictionary of Business Biography*, 6 vols. (London: Butterworths, 1984–86).

15 R.P.T. Davenport-Hines, ed., *Speculators and Patriots* (London: Frank Cass, 1986); Philip Cottrell, *Industrial Finance, 1830–1914* (London: Methuen, 1980), and William P. Kennedy, *Industrial Structure, Capital Markets and the Origins of British Economic Decline* (Cambridge: Cambridge University Press, 1987).

16 Among the best work is J.J. Tobias, *Crime and Industrial Society in the Nineteenth Century* (New York: Schocken Books, 1967); Kellow Chesney, *The Victorian Underworld* (London: Maurice Temple Smith, 1970); David Philips, *Crime and Authority in Victorian England* (London: Croom Helm, 1977); Michael Ignatieff, *A Just Measure of Pain* (New York: Pantheon Books, 1978); David Jones, *Crime, Protest, Community and Police in Nineteenth-Century Britain* (London: Routledge and Kegan Paul, 1982), and Martin J. Wiener, *Reconstructing the Criminal: Culture, Law and Policy in England, 1830–1914* (Cambridge: Cambridge University Press, 1990).

17 See esp. E.P. Thompson, *Whigs and Hunters* (New York: Pantheon Books, 1975), and George Rude, *Criminal and Victim: Crime and Society in Early Nineteenth-Century England* (New York: Oxford University Press, 1985).

18 See the important review article by Philip Jenkins, "Into the Upperworld? Law, Crime and Punishment in English Society," *Social History* 12 (January 1987): 93–102. The term "upperworld crime" was first used by Albert Morris in his textbook *Criminology* in 1934.

19 For a detailed look at Sutherland's influential work on white-collar crime, see Gilbert Geis and Colin Goff's introduction to the 1983 reprint of *White Collar Crime* or else the historiographical essay by the same authors, "Edwin H. Sutherland's White Collar Crime in America," *Criminal Justice History* (1986).

20 The recent scholarly outpouring on white-collar crime can be measured in J.T. Skip Duncan and Marc Caplan, *White-Collar Crime: A Selected Bibliography* (Washington: U.S. Department of Justice, 1980). Notable work includes Gilbert Geis and Robert Meier, eds.,

White-Collar Crime: Offenses in Business, Politics and the Professions (New York: Free Press, 1977); John M. Johnson and Jack Douglas, eds., *Crime at the Top* (Philadelphia: Lippincott, 1978), and Jack Katz, "The Social Movement Against White-Collar Crime," *Criminology Review Yearbook* (1980). Yale University Press launched a new series on white-collar crime with Susan Shapiro's *Wayward Capitalists* in 1984.

21 Popular accounts include, Aylmer Vallance, *Very Private Enterprise: An Anatomy of Fraud and High Finance* (London: Thames and Hudson, 1955); Judge Gerald Sparrow, *The Great Swindlers* (London: John Long, 1959); R.A. Haldane, *With Intent to Deceive: Frauds Famous and Infamous* (Edinburgh: William Blackwood, 1970), and Edward Stamp et al., eds., *Notable Financial Causes Célèbres* (New York: Arno Press, 1980).

22 Rob Sindall, "Middle-Class Crime in Nineteenth-Century England," *Criminal Justice History* (1983). Sindall's article is based on his unpublished M.Phil. thesis from the University of Leicester, "Aspects of Middle-Class Crime in the Nineteenth Century."

23 Criminal records examined by Sindall were from the Quarter Sessions and Assize Courts of Middlesex 1855–65, 1878–88, Surrey 1855–65, 1878–88, Birmingham 1880–1900 and Manchester 1882–84. Sindall also included samples from the Central Criminal Court in London for 1857–59 and 1881–83.

24 Sindall, "Middle-Class Crime," 31. Because Sindall defines "middle class" according to 1921 census categories, it is to be expected that his percentages for the middle class and middle-class crime would decrease as he goes back in time.

25 Sir Leon Radzinowicz and Roger Hood, *A History of English Criminal Law*, vol. 5, *The Emergence of Penal Policy* (London: Stevens, 1986), 117n.

26 For a summary of the criminological debate, see George B. Vold and Thomas J. Bernard, *Theoretical Criminology*, 2nd ed. (New York: Oxford University Press, 1979). My discussion of the statistical controversy follows heavily Philip Jenkins, "Into the Upperworld?"

27 V.A.C. Gatrell, "The Decline of Theft and Violence in Victorian and Edwardian England," in *Crime and the Law*, eds. V.A.C. Gatrell, Bruce Lenman and Geoffrey Parkers (London: Europa Publications, 1980). See also V.A.C. Gatrell and T.B. Hadden, "Criminal Statistics and Their Interpretation," in *Nineteenth Century Society*, ed. E.A. Wrigley (Cambridge: Cambridge University Press, 1972), and Clive Emsley, *Crime and Society in England, 1750–1900* (London: Longman, 1987), chapter 2.

28 Tobias, *Crime and Industrial Society*, 21. See also Tobias' second chapter and his appendix on the use of statistics.

29 See K.K. Macnab, "Aspects of the History of Crime in England and Wales between 1805–60" (Ph.D. diss., University of Sussex, 1965).

Macnab argued that the police's role was more proactive than reactive, and they tended to pursue only those cases where the victims were highly aggrieved or willing to bear the costs of prosecution.

30 Jenkins, "Into the Upperworld?," 98–99.

31 Figures given are from Sindall, "Middle-Class Crime," 30–31.

32 The most noteworthy use of literary evidence for criminal history can be found in Tobias, *Crime and Industrial Society*. For a criticism of Tobias' approach, see Philips, *Crime and Authority*.

33 J.A. Sharpe, *Crime in Early Modern England, 1550–1750* (London: Longman, 1984), chapter 7.

34 Norman Russell, *The Novelist and Mammon: Literary Responses to the World of Commerce in the Nineteenth Century* (New York: Oxford University Press, 1988), Conclusion.

35 Jenkins, "Into the Upperworld?," 101.

36 Charles Dickens, *Little Dorrit* (1857; reprint, New York: Oxford University Press, 1953), 542.

1 THE NEW ECONOMY: TRANSFORMATION OF FINANCE AND
OPPORTUNITIES FOR CRIME

1 Innovations in public borrowing are the subject of P.G.M. Dickson, *The Financial Revolution in England, 1688–1756* (London: Macmillan, 1967).

2 John Francis, *Chronicles and Characters of the Stock Exchange* (London: Willoughby and Company, 1849), 29.

3 Act to Regulate Stock Jobbing, 1696. 8/9 Wm. III c. 32., preamble.

4 Francis, *Chronicles and Characters*, 44.

5 For examples, see Charles Duguid, *The Story of the Stock Exchange* (London: Grant Richards, 1901), 104–5.

6 Ibid., 27–28.

7 Francis, *Chronicles and Characters*, 45–46.

8 Duguid, *Story of the Stock Exchange*, 98–115.

9 Quoted in Duguid, *Story of the Stock Exchange*, 19. See also pp. 19–33, for general discussion of eighteenth-century attitudes toward the Stock Exchange.

10 Quoted in E.V. Morgan and W.A. Thomas, *The Stock Exchange: Its History and Functions* (London: Elek Books, 1962), 21.

11 Francis, *Chronicles and Characters*, 103–4.

12 Duguid, *Story of the Stock Exchange*, 70–72.

13 This account of the South Sea Bubble is derived from Dickson, *Financial Revolution*, 90–157, and John Carswell, *The South Sea Bubble* (London: Cresset Press, 1961).

14 Carswell, *South Sea Bubble*, 89.

15 Ibid., 240, and Dickson, *Financial Revolution*, 96, 142.

16 Carswell, *South Sea Bubble*, 155–56.

17 Duguid, *Story of the Stock Exchange*, 40–41.
18 Dickson, *Financial Revolution*, 147–49.
19 For discussion of the aftermath of the Bubble, see ibid., 153–97. For a recent evaluation of the Bubble Act, see Margaret Patterson and David Reiffen, "The Effect of the Bubble Act on the Market for Joint Stock Shares," *The Journal of Economic History* 50 (March 1990): 163–71.
20 H.A. Shannon, "The Coming of General Limited Liability," *Economic History* 2 (1930–31): 269–70.
21 See B.C. Hunt, *The Development of the Business Corporation in England 1800–67* (Cambridge, Mass.: Harvard University Press, 1936), 30–55, for discussion of 1825 company boom.
22 Francis, *Chronicles and Characters*, 264.
23 Hunt, *Development of the Business Corporation*, 50–55.
24 Shannon, "Coming of Limited Liability," 276.
25 J.R. McCulloch, "Joint-Stock Banks and Companies," *Edinburgh Review* 63 (July 1836): 423.
26 Francis, *Chronicles and Characters*, 351–56.
27 Charles Dickens, *Martin Chuzzlewit* (1844; reprint, London: Penguin Books, 1968), 515–16.
28 *Hansard* LVII (1841), 842.
29 Select Committee on Joint Stock Companies, *Parliamentary Papers*, 1844, VII, Report, 361–62.
30 Ibid., 357.
31 Act for the Registration, Incorporation and Regulation of Joint Stock Companies, 1844. 7/8 Vict. c. 110.
32 Ibid., sections IV, XIX, XXIII.
33 Ibid., sections VII, XI, XVIII, XXV, XXXVI, XLIII.
34 Rondo Cameron, "England 1750–1844," in *Banking in the Early Stages of Industrialization*, ed. Rondo Cameron (New York: Oxford University Press, 1967), 20. Interestingly, the Scottish banking system, unlike the English, was highly developed in the eighteenth century.
35 Clapham, *Economic History*, vol. 1, 264–66.
36 P.L. Cottrell and B.L. Anderson, eds., *Money and Banking in England: The Development of the Banking System, 1694–1914* (Newton Abbot: David and Charles, 1974), 151.
37 Clapham, *Economic History*, vol. 1, 266.
38 S.E. Thomas, *The Rise and Growth of Joint Stock Banking* (London: Sir Isaac Pitman and Sons, 1934), 53n.
39 David Morier Evans, *Facts, Failures and Frauds* (London: Groombridge and Sons, 1859), 107–8.
40 David Morier Evans, *The City, or the Physiology of London Business* (London: Baily Brothers, 1845), 11.
41 *Hansard* XIV (1826), 640.
42 Joint-Stock Banking Act, 1826. 7 Geo. IV c. 46.

43 Cottrell and Anderson, *Money and Banking*, 249.
44 Clapham, *Economic History*, vol. 1, 511–12. See also Charles W. Munn, "The Emergence of Joint-Stock Banking in the British Isles: A Comparative Approach," *Business History* 30 (January 1988): 69–83.
45 Cottrell and Anderson, *Money and Banking*, 249.
46 James White, "The Murdering Banker," *Blackwood's Edinburgh Magazine* 44 (December 1838): 823. Banking figures are from Clapham, *Economic History*, vol. 1, 512.
47 Thomas Joplin, *An Essay on the General Principles and Present Practice of Banking* (1827), reprinted in Cottrell and Anderson, *Money and Banking*.
48 McCulloch, "Joint-Stock Banks and Companies," *Edinburgh Review* 63 (July 1836): 429.
49 A. Andreades, *History of the Bank of England 1640–1903*, trans. Cristabel Meredith (London: P.S. King and Son, 1909), 269.
50 Report of the Select Committee on Bank Acts, *Parliamentary Papers*, 1837–38, VII, and Report of the Select Committee on Banks of Issue, *Parliamentary Papers*, 1841, V.
51 Bank Notes Act, 1844. 7/8 Vict. c. 32.
52 Joint Stock Bank Act, 1844. 7/8 Vict. c. 113.
53 Shannon, "Coming of Limited Liability," 290.
54 Report of Company Registrar, *Parliamentary Papers*, 1846, XLIII, 1.
55 Evans, *Facts, Failures and Frauds*, 2.
56 *Illustrated London News*, 2 December 1843.
57 David Morier Evans, *Speculative Notes and Notes on Speculation* (London: Groombridge and Sons, 1864), 52.
58 W.E. Aytoun, "The National Debt and the Stock Exchange," *Blackwood's Edinburgh Magazine* 66 (December 1849): 656.
59 F.G. Hilton Price, *Handbook of London Bankers* (London: Leadenhill Press, 1891), 137–42.
60 Charles Dickens, "Very Singular Things in the City," *All the Year Round* 3 (July 1860): 325.
61 For example, of the 211 shareholders of the Northumberland and Durham District Bank during the 1850s, half were lone women: 67 spinsters and 38 widows. "Durham Bank Fraud," *Bankers' Magazine* (March 1858): 316.
62 Peter Laurie, before the Select Committee on Joint Stock Companies, *Parliamentary Papers*, 1844, VII, Minutes, 65.
63 Herbert Spencer, "Railway Morals and Railway Policy," *Edinburgh Review* 100 (October 1854): 442.
64 Company Law Amendment Act, 1847. 10/11 Vict. c. 78, section IV.
65 Select Committee on Assurance Associations, *Parliamentary Papers*, 1853, XXI, Report, 4–5.
66 Shannon, "Coming of Limited Liability," 281–82.

67 For an extended encomium on *laissez faire*, see Robert Lowe's speech in the Commons, *Hansard* CXL (1856), 110–38.

68 Railway companies were an exception to this rule, and the popularity of railway investment during the 1840s helped promote the principle of limited liability.

69 Select Committee on the Savings of the Middle and Working Classes, *Parliamentary Papers*, 1850, XIX, Report.

70 Ibid., Minutes, 174.

71 Ibid., J.M. Ludlow, 181.

72 Select Committee on the Law of Partnership, *Parliamentary Papers*, 1851, XVIII, Report.

73 J.R. McCulloch, *Considerations on Partnerships with Limited Liability* (London: Longman, Brown, Green and Longmans, 1856), 6.

74 Ibid., 10.

75 Select Committee on the Savings of the Middle and Working Classes, Minutes, 174.

76 Limited Liability Act, 1855. 18/19 Vict. c. 133, section I.

77 Joint Stock Company Act, 1856. 19/20 Vict. c. 47, section V.

78 Ibid., sections VIII, XVII, XXXII.

79 *Hansard* CXL (1856), 138.

80 Companies Act, 1862. 25/26 Vict. c. 89.

81 This figure does not include railways which were not governed by the regular Companies Acts.

82 Figures for registrations from Shannon, "Coming of Limited Liability," 290, and Richard Brown, "The Genesis of Company Law in England and Scotland," *Juridical Review* (June 1901): 187.

83 Hunt, *Development of the Business Corporation*, 157.

84 See below, chapter 5, for more details.

85 See Walter Houghton, *The Victorian Frame of Mind* (New Haven: Yale University Press, 1957), 191–95.

86 Thomas Carlyle, *Past and Present* (1843), in *Complete Works of Thomas Carlyle*, 20 vols. (New York: Thomas Y. Crowell and Co., 1902) vol. 12, 142.

87 Matthew Arnold, *Culture and Anarchy* (1869; reprint, Cambridge: Cambridge University Press, 1932), 157.

88 Geoffrey Todd, "Some Aspects of Joint Stock Companies, 1844–1900," *Economic History Review* 4 (1932–33): 59n.

89 For examples, see below, chapter 6.

90 Hunt, *Development of the Business Corporation*, 120.

91 Ibid., 87–89.

92 S.F. Van Oss, "The 'Limited Liability' Craze," *Nineteenth Century* 43 (May 1898): 731.

93 A.C. Clauson, "The Reform of Company Law," *Quarterly Review* 191 (April 1900): 374.

94 P.L. Cottrell, *British Overseas Investment in the Nineteenth Century*

(London: Macmillan, 1975), 13. For the recent debate on the level of British foreign investment, see D.C.M. Platt, *Britain's Investment Overseas on the Eve of the First World War: The Use and Abuse of Numbers* (New York: St. Martin's Press, 1986), and Charles Feinstein, "Britain's Overseas Investment in 1913," *Economic History Review* 2nd series, 43 (May 1990): 288–95.

95 Clapham, *Economic History*, vol. 3, 289.
96 Ibid., 289.
97 L.E. Davis and R.A. Huttenback, *Mammon and the Pursuit of Empire* (New York: Cambridge University Press, 1986).
98 Ibid., chapter 7, tables. The figures I give are not to be found directly in the authors' tables. I have made different use of the data and have rearranged certain categories for the purpose of class analysis.
99 Figures on share denominations from H.A. Shannon, "The First Five Thousand Limited Companies and their Duration," *Economic History* 3 (1932): 407–8.
100 Today institutional shareholdings account for the majority of British company investment.
101 A. Innes Shand, "Speculative Investments," *Blackwood's Edinburgh Magazine* 120 (September 1876): 294–95.
102 "A Detective," *The Ways of Swindlers* (London: T.H. Sheppard, 1879), 37.

2 THE RAILWAY MANIA

1 Harold Perkin, *The Age of the Railway* (Newton Abbot: David and Charles, 1971), 176.
2 Frederick Gale, "The Railway Bubble," *The Cornhill Magazine* 54 (December 1886): 585.
3 Railway statistics from H.G. Lewin, *The Railway Mania and Its Aftermath 1845–52* (London: The Railway Gazette, 1939), 1, 115, and B.R. Mitchell, "The Coming of the Railways and United Kingdom Economic Growth," *Journal of Economic History* 24 (September 1964): 321.
4 See Mitchell, "The Coming of the Railways"; S.A. Broadbridge, "The Sources of Railway Share Capital," in *Railways in the Victorian Economy*, ed. M.C. Reed (New York: Augustus M. Kelly, 1968), and M.C. Reed, "Railways and the Growth of the Capital Market," in ibid.
5 Thomas Tooke, *A History of Prices*, 6 vols. (London: Longman, Orme, Brown, Green and Longmans, 1838–57), vol. 5, 234.
6 Clapham, *Economic History*, vol. 2, 357.
7 The best biography of George Hudson remains R.S. Lambert's classic, *The Railway King, 1800–1871; A Study of George Hudson and the Business Morals of His Time* (London: G. Allen and Unwin, 1934). My discussion of Hudson relies heavily on Lambert's study.

8 Quoted in Lambert, *The Railway King*, 195.

9 Thomas Carlyle, "Hudson's Statue," in *Latter Day Pamphlets* (1850), in *The Complete Works of Thomas Carlyle*, 20 vols. (New York: Thomas Y. Crowell and Co., 1902), vol. 12, 326–27.

10 Robert Bell, *The Ladder of Gold* (New York: F.W. Purgess, 1851), and Anthony Trollope, *Doctor Thorne* (1858; reprint, New York: Oxford University Press, 1980).

11 W.M. Thackeray, "Diary and Letters of C. Jeames de la Pluche," 1845–46, in *The Complete Works of William M. Thackeray*, 30 vols. (New York: The Kelmscott Society, 1904), vol. 15, 114–15.

12 For a discussion of the professional ethos, see Perkin, *Origins of Modern English Society*, chapter 7.

13 Walter Bagehot, *Lombard Street* (1873; reprint, Homewood, Illinois: Richard D. Irwin, 1969), 78. See also Evans, *Facts, Failures and Frauds*, 1.

14 Bell, *The Ladder of Gold*, 63.

15 *The Times* (London), 31 October 1845.

16 *Hansard* LXXXV (1846), 946. See also Duguid, *Story of the Stock Exchange*, 148–49.

17 Lambert, *The Railway King*, 112.

18 Edmund Beckett Denison, "Railways," part 1, *Fraser's Magazine* 39 (June 1849): 615.

19 Lambert, *The Railway King*, 68.

20 Select Committee on Railway Acts, *Parliamentary Papers*, 1846, XIV, Minutes, 103.

21 David Morier Evans, *The Commercial Crisis of 1847–48* (London: Letts, Son and Steer, 1849), 12.

22 Denison, "Railways," part 2, *Fraser's Magazine* 40 (July 1849): 109.

23 *Bradshaw's Railway Gazette*, 11 March 1846.

24 Ibid., 28 February 1846, and 20 June 1846.

25 *The Times* (London), 8 December 1845.

26 See Harold Pollins, "The Marketing of Railway Shares in the First Half of the Nineteenth Century," *Economic History Review* 7 (1954).

27 Gale, "The Railway Bubble," 589.

28 Guinea-pig directors were first prominent in the 1825 company boom. See Hunt, *Development of the Business Corporation*, 36. For information on guinea pig directors during the Railway Mania, see *Hansard* LXXXV (1846), 947–49.

29 Samuel Smiles, *The Life of George Stephenson* (Boston: Ticknor and Fields, 1858), 386–87.

30 *Hansard* LXXXV (1846), 947–49.

31 Gale, "The Railway Bubble," 589.

32 *The Railway Times*, 3 January 1846. See also Lambert, *The Railway King*, 116.

33 *History of* The Times; vol. 2: *The Tradition Established 1841–1884* (London: Times Publishing Company, 1939), 17.

34 *Bradshaw's Railway Gazette*, 25 February 1846.

35 *Hansard* LXXXV (1846), 898–99.

36 The origin of the term "stag" is obscure. For a discussion of possible meanings, see Norman Russell, *The Novelist and Mammon* (New York: Oxford University Press, 1988), 31–33.

37 Gale, "The Railway Bubble," 590. See also Evans, *The Commercial Crisis of 1847–48*, Introduction.

38 Evans, *The City*, 61.

39 Lambert, *The Railway King*, 148–49.

40 See Reed, "Railways and the Growth of the Capital Market." Fraudulent companies welcomed applications from stags, as this helped create the illusion that company shares were in demand.

41 *Hansard* LXXXV (1846), 931.

42 John Francis, *A History of the English Railway: Its Social Relations and Revelations, 1820–1845*. 2 vols. (London: Longman, Brown, Green and Longmans, 1851), vol. 2, 145.

43 Smiles, *Life of George Stephenson*, 384.

44 The Parliamentary deposit was decreased to 5% of proposed capital in 1844, but returned to 10% in 1845.

45 Arthur Smith, *The Bubble of the Age*, 3d ed. (London: Sherwood, Gilbert and Piper, 1848), 30, and Francis, *History of the English Railway*, vol. 2, 1–2.

46 Francis, *History of the English Railway*, vol. 1, 297.

47 Smiles, *Life of George Stephenson*, 384n.

48 *Hansard* LXXXV (1846), 944–50.

49 Regulation of Railways Act, 1840. 3/4 Vict. c. 97. See also, Henry Parris, *Government and the Railways in 19th-Century Britain* (London: Routledge and Kegan Paul, 1965), chapters 1 and 2.

50 Regulation of Railways Act, 1844. 7/8 Vict. c. 85. See also Evans, *Facts, Failures and Frauds*, 24–25, and Lambert, *The Railway King*, chapter 5.

51 See Parris, *Government and the Railways*, chapter 3. See also Lewin, *The Railway Mania and Its Aftermath*, 11–19.

52 Regulation of Railways Act, 1846. 9/10 Vict. c. 105.

53 Railway Department Act, 1851. 14/15 Vict. c. 64.

54 See Parris, *Government and the Railways*, chapter 4.

55 Regulation of Railways Act, 1844. 7/8 Vict. c. 85, section v.

56 Company Clauses Consolidation Act, 1845. 8/9 Vict. c. 16, sections CI, CVII, CXXI.

57 *The Times* (London), 30 September 1850.

58 Select Committee on the Audit of Railway Accounts, *Parliamentary Papers*, 1849, x, Report, x.

59 Harold Pollins, "Aspects of Railway Accounting Before 1868," in *Studies in the History of Accounting*, eds. A.C. Littleton and B.S. Yamey (Homewood, Illinois: Richard D. Irwin, 1956).

60 Ibid.

61 Lewin, *The Railway Mania and Its Aftermath*, 288–90.
62 Geoffrey Alderman, *The Railway Interest* (Leicester: Leicester University Press, 1973), 25–26.
63 Lambert, *The Railway King*, 166–67.
64 Ibid., 186. See also 115–9.
65 Table compiled from Eastern Counties Railway, Shareholders' Committee of Investigation, 1849. PRO, Rail 186/62. See also Lambert, *The Railway King*, 253–55.
66 Smith, *The Bubble of the Age*, 26–29.
67 Ibid., 7, and Parris, *Government and the Railways*, 15.
68 Smith, *The Bubble of the Age*, 14–15.
69 Spencer, "Railway Morals and Railway Policy," 424. See also James Morrison, *Defects of the English System of Railway Legislation* (London: Longman, Brown, Green and Longmans, 1846).
70 Smith, *The Bubble of the Age*, 53, and Evans, *Facts, Failures and Frauds*, 20.
71 Lambert, *The Railway King*, 249.
72 Select Committee on the Audit of Railway Accounts, Report, vi–x.
73 Lambert, *The Railway King*, 239–40.
74 *The Economist*, 11 October 1845.
75 Lambert, *The Railway King*, 164.
76 *The Times* (London), 17 November 1845.
77 *The Economist*, 25 October 1845.
78 *The Times* (London), 17 November 1845.
79 Lewin, *The Railway Mania and Its Aftermath*, chapter 12.
80 *Hansard* LXXXV (1846), 906–7, 945–58.
81 Examples of such cartoons are reprinted in Michael Steig, "*Dombey and Son* and the Railway Panic of 1845," *The Dickensian* 67 (1972): 140–48.
82 Emma Robinson, *The Gold Worshippers, Or the Days We Live In* (New York: Harper and Brothers, 1851).
83 Francis, *A History of the English Railway*, vol. 2, 195.
84 Lambert, *The Railway King*, 170.
85 Dividend averages were figured from Table IX in Lewin, *The Railway Mania and Its Aftermath*, 365. See also *The Economist*, 21 October 1848.
86 York and North Midland Railway, Shareholders' Committee of Investigation, 1849. PRO, Rail 770/13, Rail 770/65.
87 York, Newcastle and Berwick Railway, Shareholders' Committee of Investigation, 1849. PRO, Rail 772/15.
88 See above, for details of dividend inflation.
89 Select Committee on the Audit of Railway Accounts, Appendix.
90 Thomas Carlyle, *Journal* (17 May 1849), quoted in Lambert, *The Railway King*, 275.
91 Evans, *Facts, Failures and Frauds*, 3.
92 Quoted in Lambert, *The Railway King*, 261.

93 Evans, *Facts, Failures and Frauds*, 7.
94 See Harold Pollins, "Railway Contractors and the Finance of Railway Development in Britain," in *Railways in the Victorian Economy*.
95 Thomas Hennell, "Railway Finance," *Quarterly Review* 122 (April 1867): 489–506.
96 See above, for discussion of loan notes.
97 Hennell, "Railway Finance." See also Pollins, "Railway Contractors and the Finance of Railway Development."
98 See below, chapter 3.
99 Eastern Counties Railway, Shareholders' Committee of Investigation, 1855. PRO, Rail 186/62.
100 Ibid., PRO, Rail 186/62, Rail 186/74.
101 Evans, *Facts, Failures and Frauds*, 432–83. See also *The Times* (London), 15 November 1856, and 17 January 1857.
102 Great Northern Railway, Committee of Investigation, 1857. PRO, Rail 236/424: 14, 32; Rail 236/428.
103 Evans, *Facts, Failures and Frauds*, 439.
104 Great Northern Railway, Committee of Investigation, 1857. PRO, Rail 236/424: 2a, 2b, 29; Rail 236/426.
105 Ibid., PRO, Rail 236/424: 15.
106 Ibid., PRO, Rail 236/424: 31.
107 Michael Robbins, *The Railway Age* (London: Routledge and Kegan Paul, 1962), 108.
108 Report of the Select Committee on the Audit of Railway Accounts. See also Lewin, *The Railway Mania and Its Aftermath*, 355.
109 See below, chapter 3.
110 See Regulation of Railways Act 31/32 Vict. c. 119. See also Pollins, "Aspects of Railway Accounting Before 1868," and Parris, *Government and the Railways*, chapter 7.

3 BANKING AND CREDIT FRAUD

1 Quoted in Cottrell and Anderson, eds., *Money and Banking in England*, 224.
2 Thomas, *Rise and Growth of Joint-Stock Banking*, 554–68. Banking statistics from Hunt, *Development of the Business Corporation*, 157; Philip Cottrell, "Railway Finance and the Crisis of 1866: Contractors' Bills of Exchange and the Finance Companies," *Journal of Transport History*, new series 3 (1975): 24, and Cameron, "England 1750–1844," in *Banking*, 33–35.
3 For a discussion of pre-1840s banking, see above, chapter 1.
4 See above, chapter 1.
5 Clapham, *Economic History*, vol. 2, 371.
6 See Houghton, *The Victorian Frame of Mind*, 183–95.

7 Catherine Gore, *The Banker's Wife* (New York: Harper and Brothers, 1846), 68, 78.

8 Dickens, *Little Dorrit*, 710.

9 Dion Boucicault, *The Poor of New York* (New York: Samuel French, 1857).

10 Savings Bank Act, 1817. 57 Geo. III c. 130.

11 Cameron, "England 1750–1844," 30.

12 See Arthur Scratchley, *On Savings Banks* (London: Longman, Brown, Longman and Roberts, 1862), 65–68. See also *The Times* (London), 1 and 11 December 1849.

13 Scratchley, *On Savings Banks*, 55–57.

14 Ibid., 60–63.

15 Ibid., 70. See also *The Times* (London), 2 and 3 May 1853.

16 Scratchley, *On Savings Banks*, 49–52.

17 Post Office Savings Bank Act, 1861. 24/25 Vict. c. 14.

18 *The Economist*, 27 September 1857.

19 Information on bank frauds from Anon., *British Losses by Bank Failures* (1858), in S.E. Thomas, *The Rise and Growth of Joint-Stock Banking*, 669–74.

20 *The Times* (London), 29 October 1855. See also Central Criminal Court, *Minutes of Evidence*, 1854–55, PRO, Crim 10/42; Evans, *Facts, Failures and Frauds*, 106–53, and *The Times* (London), 26 June and 27 October 1855.

21 Russell, *The Novelist and Mammon*, 70–71.

22 Evans, *Facts, Failures and Frauds*, 226–67.

23 *The Times* (London), 21 June 1856.

24 Evans, *Facts, Failures and Frauds*, 272–73. For details of the case, see 268–390.

25 Ibid., 385.

26 "Royal British Bank Fraud," *Bankers' Magazine* (January 1857): 247.

27 *The Times* (London), 1 October 1857.

28 Evans, *Facts, Failures and Frauds*, 596–630. See also *The Times* (London), 26 March, 1 June, 21 July, 8 September and 8 December 1857.

29 Clapham, *Economic History of Modern Britain*, vol. 2, 368–70.

30 Evans, *The History of the Commercial Crisis, 1857–58* (London: Groombridge and Sons, 1859), 37.

31 Select Committee on the Bank Acts and Recent Commercial Distress, *Parliamentary Papers*, 1858, v, Report.

32 Ibid., Minutes, 288–97.

33 Ibid., Minutes, 246–47.

34 Anon., *British Losses by Bank Failures* (1858). Quoted in S.E. Thomas, *The Rise and Growth of Joint-Stock Banking*, 676.

35 Report of Shareholders' Committee of Investigation, Western Bank of Scotland. Quoted in Select Committee on the Bank Acts, 461.

36 W.T.C. King, *History of the London Discount Market* (London: George Routledge and Sons, 1936), xvi–xvii.

37 Ibid., 27. See also Cottrell and Anderson, *Money and Banking in England*, 154–55, and William Holdsworth, *A History of English Law*, 3rd ed., 15 vols. (London: Methuen, 1903–72), vol. 13, 374.

38 Bagehot, *Lombard Street*, 4.

39 Ibid., 11.

40 Herbert Spencer, *The Morals of Trade* (London: Mowbray and Company, 1891), 44–49.

41 "Business of the Present Day," *St. Paul's* 1 (January 1868): 427.

42 Select Committee on Bank Acts, 238–40, 372–73.

43 King, *History of the London Discount Market*, 223–25.

44 Evans, *Facts, Failures and Frauds*, 162.

45 Ibid., 154–225. See also Central Criminal Court, *Minutes of Evidence*, 1855–56, PRO, Crim 10/41.

46 Thomas, *The Rise and Growth of Joint-Stock Banking*, 546.

47 Select Committee on Bank Acts, 112–14.

48 Ibid., 112.

49 Ibid., 133.

50 Ibid., 250.

51 Banking Act, 1857. 20/21 Vict. c. 49.

52 J.E. Wadsworth, *A Hundred Years of Joint-Stock Banking* (London: Hodder and Stroughton, 1936), 31.

53 *The Economist*, 6 February 1858.

54 Clapham, *Economic History of Modern Britain*, vol. 1, 511.

55 Cottrell and Anderson, *Money and Banking*, 247–49.

56 Hunt, *Development of the Business Corporation in England*, 146–47, and King, *History of the London Discount Market*, 217–37.

57 See Cottrell, "Railway Finance and the Crisis of 1866."

58 *The Economist*, 28 April 1866.

59 Stephanos Xenos, *Depredations; or Overend Gurney and Co., and the Greek and Oriental Steam Navigation Co.* (London: the author, 1869), 65.

60 *The Economist*, 1864, 315. Quoted in Cottrell, "Railway Finance and the Crisis of 1866."

61 For *post mortems* of the Finance Company Mania and 1866 Crash, see "John Skeeme, the Promoter," *All the Year Round* 18 (October 1867), and "Finance, Frauds and Failure," *Temple Bar* 17 (June 1866).

62 King, *History of the London Discount Market*, 256–57, and *The Times* (London), 3 February 1869.

63 "Overend, Gurney and Co. Limited," *Bankers' Magazine* (December 1893): 809; *The Times* (London), 11 September 1866, and King, *History of the London Discount Market*, 238–54.

64 Hunt, *Development of the Business Corporation in England*, 157.

65 See below, chapter 8.

66 Bagehot, *Lombard Street*, 128.

67 Edwin Green, *Debtors to Their Profession: A History of the Institute of Bankers 1879–1979* (London: Methuen and Company, 1979), 26–48.
68 Bagehot, *Lombard Street*, 128.
69 Leo Rosenblum, "The Failure of the City of Glasgow Bank," *Accounting Review* 8 (December 1933): 285–91, and Aylmer Vallance, *Very Private Enterprise*, 35–39.
70 Quoted in Rosenblum, "The Failure of the City of Glasgow Bank," 287.
71 Ibid., 285–90.
72 Source of Table 2, ibid., 290.
73 Companies Act, 1879. 42/43 Vict. c. 76. See also, Cottrell and Anderson, *Money and Banking*, 249, and Michael Collins, "The Banking Crisis of 1878," *Economic History Review*, 2nd series 42 (November 1989): 504–27.
74 Green, *Debtors to Their Profession*, Appendix 3. Also, see below, chapter 8.
75 C.A.E. Goodhart, *The Business of Banking 1891–1914* (London: Weidenfeld and Nicolson, 1972), 122–24.
76 Green, *Debtors to Their Profession*, 97.
77 Ibid., 75–97.
78 Philip Ziegler, *The Sixth Great Power: Barings, 1762–1929* (London: Collins, 1988), and L.S. Pressnell, "Gold Reserves, Banking Reserves and the Baring Crisis of 1890," in *Essays in Money and Banking*, eds. C.R. Whittlesey and J.S.E. Wilson (Oxford: Clarendon Press, 1968). For an interesting account of the Baring Crisis by a participant, see Henry O. O'Hagan, *Leaves from My Life* (London: John Lane, 1929), vol. 1, 376–82.
79 Green, *Debtors to Their Profession*, 75.
80 Goodhart, *The Business of Banking*, chapter 2, and Wadsworth, *A Hundred Years of Joint-Stock Banking*, 30–39.
81 Hartley Withers, "The Mysteries of Money Articles," *The Cornhill Magazine* 75 (May 1897): 687–88.
82 Goodhart, *The Business of Banking*, chapter 2.
83 Vallance, *Very Private Enterprise*, 80–82.
84 Ibid., 102–3. See also Haldane, *With Intent to Deceive*, 122–29.
85 Thomas Farrow, *Banks and People* (London: Chapman and Hall, 1911).
86 *The Times* (London), 11 June 1921.
87 Ibid., 11 June 1921.
88 Ibid., 7 June 1921.
89 Ibid., 9 June 1921.
90 Ibid., 11 June 1921.
91 Ibid., 10 June 1921.
92 Ibid., 15 June 1921.
93 Haldane, *With Intent to Deceive*, 128–29, and *The Times* (London), 21

December 1920. Information on shareholder composition from Farrow's Bank Records, PRO, BT 31/18100.
94 Report of the Select Committee on Finance and Industry. *Parliamentary Papers*, 1931, XIII, 156–57.

4 STOCK FRAUD

1 Such was the conclusion of David Kynaston in his doctoral thesis "The London Stock Exchange, 1870–1914: An Institutional History" (Ph.D. diss., University of London, 1983). For a more positive view of the London Stock Exchange, see Ranald Michie, "Different in Name Only? The London Stock Exchange and Foreign Bourses, c. 1850–1914," *Business History* 30 (January 1988): 46–68.
2 For the early history of the Exchange, see above, chapter 1.
3 See above, chapter 2.
4 Statistics from Morgan and Thomas, *The Stock Exchange*; Clapham, *Economic History of Modern Britain*, vol. 2, 325, and W.A. Thomas, *The Provincial Stock Exchange* (London: Frank Cass, 1973), 3–4 and chapter 3.
5 See Francis Chiswell, *Key to the Rules of the Stock Exchange* (London: Effingham Wilson, 1902), 7.
6 Clapham, *Economic History of Modern Britain*, vol. 2, 323. See also Chiswell, *Key to the Rules of the Stock Exchange*, 21–25.
7 Morgan and Thomas, *The Stock Exchange*, 239.
8 Francis, *Chronicles and Characters*, 329.
9 Shand, "Speculative Investments," 310.
10 Select Committee on Loans to Foreign States, *Parliamentary Papers*, 1875, XI, and Royal Commission on the Stock Exchange, *Parliamentary Papers*, 1878, XIX.
11 Select Committee on Loans to Foreign States, Minutes, 18, 59.
12 Ibid., Report, xxviii.
13 A.J. Wilson, "Immorality and Cowardice of Modern Loan-Mongering," *Contemporary Review* 73 (March 1898): 329.
14 Chiswell, *Key to the Rules of the Stock Exchange*, 136–39.
15 Royal Commission on the Stock Exchange, Minutes, 60, 83, 151. See also A Member of the House, "The Stock Exchange and its Morals," *Journal of Finance* (April 1899): 263.
16 Select Committee on Loans to Foreign States, Minutes, 18.
17 Ibid., 474.
18 Royal Commission on the Stock Exchange, Report, 11–12. See also Duguid, *The Story of the Stock Exchange*, 229–31.
19 Royal Commission on the Stock Exchange, Report, 20.
20 Select Committee on Loans to Foreign States, Report, xlvii.
21 Royal Commission on the Stock Exchange, Report, 15. See also Clapham, *Economic History*, vol. 2, 325. Pre-allotment stock fraud had

been a serious problem during the Railway Mania; see above, chapter 2.

22 Royal Commission on the Stock Exchange, Report, 12. See also Duguid, *Story of the Stock Exchange*, 199–200.

23 Duguid, *Story of the Stock Exchange*, 193–98.

24 Royal Commission on the Stock Exchange, Report, 17.

25 Morgan and Thomas, *The Stock Exchange*, 149.

26 Duguid, *Story of the Stock Exchange*, 328–29.

27 A.P. Poley, *The History, Law and Practice of the Stock Exchange* (London: Sir Isaac Pitman and Sons, 1907), 71.

28 *The Economist*, 19 November 1898.

29 Rule 54, Chiswell, *Key to the Rules of the Stock Exchange*, 48.

30 Select Committee on Loans to Foreign States, Minutes. Barnard's Act was a 1733 statute restricting speculative bargains and Leeman's Act an 1867 statute which attempted to prevent speculation in bank shares.

31 Chiswell, *Key to the Rules of the Stock Exchange*, 29–30. The amount of the sureties to be pledged varied somewhat over time. Three £500 sureties was the requirement during the late nineteenth and early twentieth centuries.

32 Kynaston, "The London Stock Exchange," 75.

33 Chiswell, *Key to the Rules of the Stock Exchange*, 29–30.

34 *The Economist*, 5 November 1904.

35 Royal Commission on the Stock Exchange, Report, 23. See also Duguid, *Story of the Stock Exchange*, 228–29, and Poley, *History, Law and Practice of the Stock Exchange*, 150.

36 Interestingly, in 1989, when forty members of the Chicago Commodities Exchange were indicted for fraudulent trading, the governing board of that Exchange argued that tightening regulations would only send business overseas.

37 Thomas, *The Provincial Stock Exchange*, 92, and Morgan and Thomas, *The Stock Exchange*, 141.

38 C.H. Thorpe, *How to Invest and How to Speculate* (London: Grant Richards, 1901), 31–32.

39 Evans, *The City, or the Physiology of London Business*, 62.

40 Board of Trade, Departmental Committee on Share Pushing, *Parliamentary Papers*, 1937, xv, Report.

41 Ibid., 7–15.

42 Ibid., 10–11.

43 Ibid., 9–12.

44 Ibid., 17.

45 Edward Smithies, *The Black Economy*, 55–56.

46 Committee on Share Pushing, Report, 32–33, and Smithies, *The Black Economy*, 57.

47 Committee on Share Pushing, Report, 12.

48 Ibid., 42–47.
49 Ibid., 48–49.
50 For earlier stock frauds involving false information, see above, chapter 1.
51 Duguid, *Story of the Stock Exchange*, 294.
52 See *The Economist*, 5 January 1889.
53 Van Oss, "The 'Limited Liability' Craze," 742.
54 For later scandals, see W.R. Lawson, "A Black Year for Investors," *Blackwood's Edinburgh Magazine* 137 (February 1885): 271.
55 Shand, "Speculative Investments," 301.
56 Anthony Pulbrook, *The Handy Book on the Law and Practice of Joint Stock Companies* (London: Effingham Wilson, 1906). 255.
57 Ibid., 256.
58 *The Times* (London), 28 October, 4, 11, 25, 26 November 1858.
59 Thomas, *The Provincial Stock Exchange*, 193–94.
60 For an example from banking, see the case of Strahan, Paul and Bates, above, chapter 3.
61 *The Times* (London), 30 July 1931. See also entry on Wheeler in the *Dictionary of Business Biography*, vol. 5, 759–62.
62 Anthony Trollope, *The Three Clerks* (1857; reprint, London: Richard Bentley and Son, 1884), 492.
63 Granville Barker, a well-known writer in his own day, is now all but forgotten. Recently, however, the National Theatre in London staged a production of *The Voysey Inheritance* which drew connections between that play and financial fraud in contemporary Britain.
64 Harley Granville Barker, *The Voysey Inheritance* (1905), in *Plays by Harley Granville Barker*, ed. Dennis Kennedy (Cambridge: Cambridge University Press, 1987), 119.

5   COMPANY FRAUD: PROMOTION

1 It is useful to distinguish between those frauds which occur in the formation of companies and those which occur during the actual management of companies after they have been formed. This second type of company fraud will be dealt with in chapter 6: "Company fraud: management."
2 For discussion of company law, see above, chapter 1, and chapter 7 below.
3 Select Committee on the Limited Liability Acts, *Parliamentary Papers*, 1867, x.
4 Ibid., Minutes, 53.
5 Ibid., Minutes, 81.
6 See above, chapter 2.
7 See above, chapter 3.
8 See above, chapter 4.

9 W.R. Lawson, "Company Promoting a la Mode," *National Review* 32 (September 1898): 106. For a more recent explication of fraud's variation with the business cycle, see J.K. Galbraith, *The Great Crash 1929* (London: Penguin Books, 1955), 152–53.

10 "A Detective," *The Ways of Swindlers* (London: T.H. Sheppard, 1879), 73–78. See also, Evans, *Speculative Notes*, 80, and A.D. Tyssen, "Company Law Reform," *Law Magazine and Review* (May 1899): 281–82.

11 Van Oss, "In Hooley Land," *Journal of Finance* (January 1899): 8.

12 Shannon, "The Limited Companies of 1866–83," 295.

13 Clapham, *Economic History*, vol. 3, 202.

14 Select Committee on the Reform of the Joint Stock Companies Acts, *Parliamentary Papers*, 1895, LXXXVIII, Report, and 1898, IX, Report.

15 Shannon, "The Limited Companies of 1866–83," 298.

16 For a discussion of the inadequacy of English investment banking, see Cottrell, *Industrial Finance*, chapter 7.

17 Evans, *The City*, 76.

18 Van Oss, "In Hooley Land," 8.

19 Hugh Stutfield, "The Higher Rascality," 77. For other examples, see Stutfield, "Investors and their Money," *National Review* 26 (November 1895): 509–11, and Lawson, "A Black Year for Investors," *Blackwood's Edinburgh Magazine* 137 (February 1885): 276.

20 King, *History of the London Discount Market*, 251–52.

21 Companies Act, 1867. 30/31 Vict. c. 131, section 38.

22 See for example, "On Life Insurance," *Quarterly Review* 64 (October 1839): 289; Select Committee on Joint-Stock Companies, *Parliamentary Papers*, 1844, VII, Minutes, 236, and "Finance, Frauds and Failure," *Temple Bar* 17 (June 1866): 384.

23 *The Times* (London), 28 September 1843.

24 See above, chapter 4.

25 Royal Commission on the Stock Exchange, *Parliamentary Papers*, 1878, XIX, Minutes, 229–34.

26 P.L. Cottrell, "David Chadwick," *Dictionary of Business Biography*, vol. 1, 625–32.

27 For a brief biography of Grant, see P.L. Cottrell, "Albert Grant," *Dictionary of Business Biography*, vol. 2, 623–29.

28 The company was originally unconnected with the celebrated Credit Mobilier of France, though Grant no doubt profited from an assumed connection in the minds of the public.

29 Royal Commission on the Stock Exchange, Report, 11.

30 *The Economist*, 26 March 1870.

31 Hubert A. Meredith, *The Drama of Money Making* (London: Sampson Low, Marston and Company, 1931), 114.

32 O'Hagan, *Leaves from My Life*, vol. 1, 37.

33 Select Committee on Loans to Foreign States, *Parliamentary Papers*, 1875, XI, Report.

34 Meredith, *Drama of Money Making*, 113.
35 Ibid., 113–15. See also *Dictionary of Business Biography*, vol. 2, 623–26.
36 O'Hagan, *Leaves from My Life*, vol. 1, 32–38.
37 Meredith, *Drama of Money Making*, 115, and Cottrell, "Albert Grant," 626–27.
38 *The Times* (London), 13 February, 9 May, 4 June 1877.
39 For examples, see above, chapter 3 and chapter 4.
40 Anthony Trollope, *The Way We Live Now* (1875; reprint, London: Oxford University Press, 1951), 77–78.
41 Laurence Oliphant, "The Autobiography of a Joint-Stock Company, Limited," *Blackwood's Edinburgh Magazine* 120 (July 1876): 96.
42 Clapham, *Economic History*, vol. 2, 135.
43 Leslie Hannah, *Rise of the Corporate Economy* (Baltimore: Johns Hopkins University Press, 1976), 20. See also Lawson, "Company Promoting a la Mode," 106.
44 See R. Griffith, "Limited Liability," *Edinburgh Review* 163 (January 1886): 73, and Van Oss, "The 'Limited Liability' Craze," 738.
45 In effect the traders (as debenture holders) would loan themselves (as company) money.
46 Select Committee on Company Law, *Parliamentary Papers*, 1895, LXXXVIII, Report, vii. See also Tyssen, "Company Law Reform," 272–73, and Clauson, "The Reform of Company Law," *Quarterly Review* 191 (April 1900): 378–79.
47 "One Man Companies," *Bankers' Magazine* (July 1895): 9–12, and "The Hindrance of Company Frauds," *Bankers' Magazine* (September 1895): 364.
48 Select Committee on Company Law, 1895, LXXXVIII, Appendix. See also, Van Oss, "The 'Limited Liability' Craze."
49 W.S. Gilbert and Arthur Sullivan, *Utopia, Limited; or, the Flowers of Progress* (1893), in *The Complete Plays of Gilbert and Sullivan* (New York: The Modern Library, n.d.).
50 See below, chapter 7.
51 *The Economist*, 2 October 1897. See also A.E. Harrison, "Joint-Stock Company Floatations in the Cycle, Motor Vehicle and Related Industries, 1882–1914," *Business History* 23 (July 1981): 165–90, and Richard Storey, "Henry John Lawson," *Dictionary of Business Biography*, vol. 3, 685–87.
52 Clapham, *Economic History*, vol. 3, 237–38.
53 See Kenneth and Margaret Richardson, "Ernest Terah Hooley," *Dictionary of Business Biography*, vol. 3, 329–32.
54 Meredith, *Drama of Money Making*, 163–69.
55 Lawson, "Company Promoting a la Mode," 108.
56 Anon., *The Hooley Book* (London: John Dicks, 1904), 21.
57 *The Economist*, 20 August 1898, and Annual Report of Bankruptcy, *Parliamentary Papers*, 1899, LXXXVIII.

58 E.T. Hooley, *Hooley's Confessions* (London: Simpkin, Marshall, Hamilton, Kent and Company, 1925), 12.

59 Lawson, "Company Promoting a la Mode," 108–9.

60 *The Economist*, 11 June 1898.

61 John Armstrong, "Hooley and the Bovril Company," in *Speculators and Patriots*, ed. R.P.T. Davenport-Hines (London: Frank Cass, 1986), 30–31.

62 See John Armstrong, "J.L. Johnston" and "G.L. Johnston," *Dictionary of Business Biography*, vol. 3, 510–21.

63 *Hooley Book*, 141–45.

64 Lawson, "Company Promoting a la Mode," 108–110.

65 Hooley, *Confessions*, 212–18, 232–37.

66 Central Criminal Court, *Minutes of Evidence*, 1904–5. Trial of E.T. Hooley and H.J. Lawson. PRO, Crim 10/95, and *The Times* (London), 17, 19 December 1904.

67 Central Criminal Court, *Minutes of Evidence*, 1911–12. Trial of E.T. Hooley. PRO, Crim 10/102.

68 *The Times* (London), 7 April 1922.

69 Van Oss, "Whitaker Wright Finance," *Blackwood's Edinburgh Magazine* 175 (March 1904): 400.

70 R.P.T. Davenport-Hines, "Whitaker Wright," *Dictionary of Business Biography*, vol. 5, 901–4.

71 *The Times* (London), 27 January 1904.

72 *The Times* (London), 23 January 1904, and Van Oss, "Whitaker Wright Finance," 400–402.

73 O'Hagan, *Leaves from My Life*, vol. 2, 187–88, and Meredith, *Drama of Money Making*, 194–96.

74 For a short biographical sketch, see Christine Shaw, "Horatio Bottomley," *Dictionary of Business Biography*, vol. 1, 391–96. Shaw's portrait is derived largely from Julian Symons' highly readable *Horatio Bottomley* (London: Cresset Press, 1955).

75 Symons, *Horatio Bottomley*, 48–58.

76 Ibid., 112–13.

77 Ibid., 122–60.

78 *The Times* (London), 30 May 1922, and Symons, *Horatio Bottomley*, 206–21.

79 Reuben Bigland, *The Downfall of Horatio Bottomley, M.P.* (Birmingham: R. Bigland, 1921).

80 Symons, *Horatio Bottomley*, 232–55.

81 Morgan and Thomas, *The Stock Exchange*, 138.

82 "Finance, Frauds and Failure," *Temple Bar* 17 (June 1866): 385.

83 Sir Mark Webster Jenkinson, *The Promotion and Accounts of a Public Limited Company* (London: Gee and Company, 1912), 94–95.

84 Board of Trade, Departmental Committee on Share Pushing, *Parliamentary Papers*, 1937, xv, Report, 9–10.

85 *The Times* (London), 16 August 1898.

86 Ibid., 26 July 1899.

87 A. Still, "The Unpopularity of the Stock Exchange," *Journal of Finance* (June 1898): 545.

88 O'Hagan, *Leaves from My Life*, vol. 1, 154.

89 David Finnie, *Capital Underwriting* (London: Sir Isaac Pitman and Sons, 1934), 1–8.

90 Jenkinson, *Promotion and Accounts*, 52–55.

91 Withers, "How to Scan a Prospectus," *The Cornhill Magazine* 76 (July 1897): 105. See also "Hindrance of Company Frauds," *Bankers' Magazine* (September 1895): 364, and parody of prospectus in Pulbrook, *The Handy Book on the Law*, Appendix.

92 *The Economist*, 31 July 1897.

93 A. Still, "Front Sheet Reflections," *Journal of Finance* (November 1898): 988–92.

94 "Starting the Rio Grande Railway," *All the Year Round* 14 (November 1865): 369.

95 Still, "Front Sheet Reflections," *Journal of Finance* (November 1898): 994.

96 Ibid., 992. See also Harrison, "Joint-Stock Company Floatation," 174–76.

97 Davenport-Hines, "Whitaker Wright," vol. 5, 905. A popular joke of the day asked "When was Whitaker Wright?" – the answer being, "When he took a Dufferin."

98 For examples of such cartoons, see *Hooley Book*.

99 Hugh Stutfield, "The Company Scandal: A City View," *National Review* 32 (December 1898): 577–78.

100 *Hooley Book*, 146.

101 Meredith, *Drama of Money Making*, 117, and R.P.T. Davenport-Hines, "Edgar Vincent and the Eastern Investment Company," in *Speculators and Patriots*, ed. Davenport-Hines, 46.

102 *The Times* (London), 12 July 1899.

103 Symons, *Horatio Bottomley*, 60–86.

104 Dilwyn Porter, " 'A Trusted Guide to the Investing Public': Harry Marks and the *Financial News* 1884–1916," in *Speculators and Patriots*, ed. Davenport-Hines, 1.

105 Ibid., 2–5, and *The Economist*, 1 November 1913.

106 See Dilwyn Porter, "Harry Hananel Marks," *Dictionary of Business Biography*, vol. 4, 133–35.

107 Quoted in Porter, "A Trusted Guide," 3.

108 David Kynaston, The Financial Times: *A Centennial History* (London: Viking, 1988), 30.

109 Van Oss, "The 'Limited Liability' Craze," 742. See also, *The Economist*, 11 June 1898.

110 Charles Duguid, *How to Read the Money Article* (London: Wilson, 1901),

99. Duguid was variously editor of *The Economist* and financial editor of *The Times*.

111 Ibid., 100.

112 *The Economist*, 11 June 1898.

113 Symons, *Horatio Bottomley*, 83–86. See also Duguid, *How to Read the Money Article*, 101.

114 *The Economist*, 1 November 1913.

115 Duguid, *How to Read the Money Article*, 96. See also case of Hooley and Lawson, Central Criminal Court, *Minutes of Evidence*, 1904–5, PRO, Crim 10/95, 233–34.

116 *The Economist*, 1 November 1913.

117 See for example, above, case of Rubery vs. Grant, and in chapter 2 the case of William Delane.

118 Joseph Conrad, *Chance* (1913; reprint, London: Hogarth Press, 1984), 73.

119 *Hooley Book*, 52.

120 Gilbert and Sullivan, *Utopia Limited*, 620–21.

121 The phrase is Baldwin's, referring to the Conservative industrialists and businessmen in the post-war Parliament.

122 Hannah, *Rise of Corporate Economy*, chapter 2.

123 E.H. Davenport, "After Hatry," *Nineteenth Century and After* 107 (March 1930): 354.

124 P.S. Manley, "Clarence Hatry," *Abacus* 12 (1976): 51.

125 David Fanning, "Clarence Charles Hatry," *Dictionary of Business Biography*, vol. 3, 110–13.

126 Manley, "Clarence Hatry," 51.

127 Davenport, "After Hatry," 355.

128 Select Committee on Finance and Industry, *Parliamentary Papers*, 1931, XIII, 166.

129 Finnie, *Capital Underwriting*, 132–33, and W.A. Thomas, *Provincial Stock Exchange*, 252–53.

130 *The Economist*, 17 August 1929. See also *Financial News*, 14 December 1929, and *The Financial Times*, 22 January 1930.

131 *Financial News*, 6 December 1929.

132 Economicus, "Hatry Scandal," *Review of Reviews* (February 1930): 113–14.

133 See below, chapter 6.

134 Davenport, "After Hatry," 355–56.

135 Manley, "Clarence Hatry," 51–55.

136 Ibid., 54–60.

137 *The Times* (London), 21, 22, 23, 24 January 1930.

138 *The Financial Times*, 22 September 1979.

139 *The Times* (London), 25 January 1930.

140 Select Committee on Finance and Industry, 1931, XIII, 166.

6 COMPANY FRAUD: MANAGEMENT

1 This chapter focuses primarily on crimes committed by directors, managers and other employees of public companies against shareholders and the investing public. An area of criminality somewhat outside the scope of this study, but deserving of historians' attention, includes those crimes committed by companies themselves: unfair labor practices, unsafe working conditions, patent and trademark infringements, secret pricing agreements, etc.

2 See above, chapter 3.

3 *Westminster Popular* No. 5, "The Story of the Liberator Crash," 6 March 1893, 39. For more details about this case, see below.

4 For more details on Bevan, see below.

5 For a discussion of the financial press, see above, chapter 5.

6 Spencer, "Railway Morals and Railway Policy," *Edinburgh Review* 100 (October 1854): 441–42.

7 See Pulbrook, *Handy Book on the Law*, 6.

8 Duguid, *How to Read the Money Article*, 95–98.

9 See H.B. Samuel, *Shareholders' Money* (London: Sir Isaac Pitman and Sons, 1933), 270.

10 Hartley Withers, *The Quicksands of the City and a Way Through for Investors* (London: Jonathan Cape, 1930), 52.

11 Sir Mark Webster Jenkinson, *The Value of a Balance Sheet* (London: Gee and Company, 1928), and Report of the Select Committee on Company Law Reform, 1928, VI.

12 For account of Farrow's fraud, see above, chapter 3. For the Docker case, see R.P.T. Davenport-Hines, *Dudley Docker* (Cambridge: Cambridge University Press, 1984), chapter 8, and J.D. Scott, *Vickers: A History* (London: Weidenfeld and Nicolson, 1962).

13 James Hutton, *Suggestions as to the Appointment by the Legislature of Public Accountants* (London: Letts, Son and Company, 1861), 18.

14 See case of Lord Kylsant, below.

15 Quoted in Samuel, *Shareholders' Money*, 313.

16 See Select Committee on the Limited Liability Acts, *Parliamentary Papers*, 1867, x, 113, and Evans, *Facts, Failures and Frauds* (London: Groombridge and Sons, 1859), 19.

17 Select Committee on the Audit of Railway Accounts, *Parliamentary Papers*, 1849, x.

18 Charles Dickens, "Convict Capitalists," *All the Year Round* 3 (June 1860): 202.

19 Dickens, "Very Singular Things in the City," 326.

20 "Bank Audits," *Bankers' Magazine* (November 1893): 677.

21 Pulbrook, *Handy Book*, 105.

22 For numerous examples, see above, chapter 3.

23 Central Criminal Court, *Minutes of Evidence*, 1876–77. Trial of W. Swindlehurst and B. Langley. PRO, Crim 10/66.

24 Such was the case of Whitaker Wright. See Samuel, *Shareholders' Money*, 164–66.

25 Note, however, that railways were adept at evading restrictions on their borrowing. See *The Economist*, 2 May 1863, 26 August 1865, 8 September 1866 and 13 October 1866.

26 See A. Emden, "The Crying Need for Reforms in Our Company Law," *Nineteenth Century* 35 (June 1894): 1041–42.

27 "A Detective," *The Ways of Swindlers*, 83–86. See also, Tyssen, "Company Law Reform," 274–75.

28 Select Committee on the Companies Acts, *Parliamentary Papers*, 1877, VIII, 154.

29 Sparrow, *The Great Swindlers*, 17–18.

30 P.S. Manley, "Gerard Lee Bevan and the City Equitable Companies," *Abacus* 9 (December 1973).

31 *The Economist*, 18 January 1930.

32 Samuel, *Shareholders' Money*, 168. Hooley was known to have profited from insider trading. In 1896, for example, he bought shares in Bovril when he learned of the company's plans to go public, but before that information was officially announced. *The Economist*, 17 October 1896.

33 *The Times* (London), 8 and 10 November 1847.

34 For more details on the Redpath frauds, see above, chapter 2.

35 Frederic de Paula, *The Principles of Auditing* (London: Sir Isaac Pitman and Sons, 1914), 48–49.

36 *Accountant*, 26 February 1898.

37 Royal Commission on Forged Exchequer Bills, *Parliamentary Papers*, 1842, XVIII, Report.

38 Anon., *Fraud in Accounts*, vol. 30 of Accountant's Library Series (London: Gee and Company, 1904), 57–59.

39 *The Times* (London), 28 February 1843.

40 For more details, see below, chapter 7.

41 Such was the assessment of Gregory Anderson, *Victorian Clerks* (Manchester: Manchester University Press, 1976), 37. Victorian agreement can be found in Scratchley, *On Savings Banks*, 58.

42 Central Criminal Court, *Minutes of Evidence*, 1849–50. Trial of Walter Watts. PRO, Crim 10/32; *The Times* (London), 11 May 1850, and Evans, *Facts, Failures and Frauds*, 74–105.

43 Evans, *Facts, Failures and Frauds*, 391–431.

44 Central Criminal Court, *Minutes of Evidence*, 1855–56. Trial of W.J. Robson. PRO, Crim 10/44.

45 *The Times* (London), 11 October 1856, 3 November 1856.

46 See above, chapter 2.

47 Central Criminal Court, *Minutes of Evidence*, 1859–60. Trial of W.G.

Pullinger. PRO, Crim 10/49; *Minute Books* of the Union Bank, vol. 13, 155–61, National Westminster Bank Archives, London, and *Bankers' Magazine* 20 (May 1860). Further examples of clerical fraud can be found in Edgar Jones, ed., *The Memoirs of Edwin Waterhouse* (London: B.T. Batsford, Ltd., 1988).

48 Sindall, "Middle-Class Crime in Nineteenth-Century England," 31.
49 My own sampling of embezzlement cases reported in *The Times* between 1845 and 1905 found the vast majority of clerical thefts to be for sums of under £100.
50 Green, *Debtors to Their Profession*, 7.
51 See Anderson, *Victorian Clerks*, 39.
52 Francis, *Chronicles and Characters*, 101–2.
53 *The Times* (London), 19 September 1846.
54 See, for example, the case of Edmund Webber, *The Times* (London), 21 December 1846, 8 January 1847.
55 Chiswell, *Key to the Rules of the Stock Exchange*, 51.
56 "Frauds on the Union Bank, London," *Bankers' Magazine* (May 1860): 283.
57 Anderson, *Victorian Clerks*, 37–38.
58 Dickens, "Convict Capitalists," 202.
59 Horsley, *How Criminals are Made*, 78–79.
60 Green, *Debtors to Their Profession*, 9–10.
61 Ibid., Appendix 2.
62 *Fraud in Accounts*, 16.
63 For greater details, see below, chapter 8.
64 *Accountant*, 26 February 1898.
65 I.H. Dearnley, *Fraud and Embezzlement* (London: Sir Isaac Pitman and Sons, 1933), chapter 11.
66 *Accountant*, 26 February 1898.
67 Dearnley, *Fraud and Embezzlement*, 99.
68 *Accountant*, 15 May 1909.
69 Samuel, *Shareholders' Money*, 233–34.
70 Ibid., 233–35.
71 Balfour's father, James, was a founding director of the Temperance Permanent Building Society and his mother, Clara, was a popular religious author whose book *Moral Heroism* is said to have inspired Smiles' *Self Help*.
72 O'Hagan, *Leaves from My Life*, vol. 1, 142.
73 *Westminster Popular* No. 5, 9–14.
74 Ibid., 16–19.
75 Ibid., 24.
76 O'Hagan, *Leaves from My Life*, vol. 1, 143–44.
77 *Westminster Popular* No. 5, 17–19.
78 Ibid., 22–27.
79 *The Economist*, 1 April 1893.

80 *Accountant*, 26 February 1898.
81 Reverend J. Stockwell Watts, *The Biggest Crime of the Nineteenth Century and What the Churches Say to It* (London: Liberator Relief Fund, 1893), and Esmond J. Cleary, "Jabez Spencer Balfour," *Dictionary of Business Biography*, vol. 1, 133–34.
82 *Frauds in Accounts*, 70.
83 See above, chapter 5.
84 Economicus, "Scandals of the Company World," 31–32.
85 See above, chapter 3.
86 For biographical details, see R.P.T. Davenport-Hines, "Gerard Lee Bevan," *Dictionary of Business Biography*, vol. 1, 321–24.
87 See above, chapter 5.
88 O'Hagan, *Leaves from My Life*, vol. 2, 335–39; Meredith, *Drama of Money Making*, 263–75, and Manley, "Gerard Lee Bevan," 111–12.
89 Quoted in Manley, "Gerard Lee Bevan," 112.
90 Royal Commission on the Depression of Trade and Industry, *Parliamentary Papers*, 1886, VIII, 378–79.
91 *Fraud in Accounts*, 68–69.
92 "The Royal Mail Steam Packet Company," *The Canadian Chartered Accountant* (November 1931): 181–94.
93 Sir Patrick Hastings, "The Case of the Royal Mail," in *Studies in Accounting*, eds., W.T. Baxter and Sidney Davidson (London: Institute of Chartered Accountants, 1977): 345, and *Accountant*, 8 August 1931.
94 *Accountant*, 8 August 1931.
95 *Accountant*, 15 May 1909.
96 *The Times* (London), 29 October 1931.
97 *The Times* (London), 30 October 1931.
98 See below, chapter 7.

7   COMPANY LAW AND THE COURTS

1 See above, chapter 1.
2 *The Times* (London), 12 September 1856.
3 See for examples, *The Economist*, 11 June 1898, and Lawson, "Company Promoting a la Mode," 114.
4 Quoted in Hunt, *The Development of the Business Corporation*, 101.
5 *Hansard*, LXXXV (1846), 904.
6 Select Committee on the Limited Liability Acts, *Parliamentary Papers*, 1867, x, Report, 16–17.
7 Ibid., Minutes, 53.
8 Companies Act, 1867. 30/31 Vict. c. 131, section 4.
9 P.L. Cottrell, *Industrial Finance 1830–1914* (London: Methuen, 1980), 54.
10 Companies Act, 1867. 30/31 Vict. c. 131, section 38.

11 See above, chapter 3.

12 Emden, "The Crying Need for Reforms in Our Company Law," *Nineteenth Century* 35 (June 1894): 1037, and Tyssen, "Company Law Reform," 287.

13 *Parliamentary Papers*, 1877, VIII. The other inquiries were the Select Committee on Loans to Foreign States, *Parliamentary Papers*, 1875, XI, and the Royal Commission on the Stock Exchange, *Parliamentary Papers*, 1878, XIX, for a discussion of which, see above, chapter 4.

14 Select Committee on the Companies Acts, *Parliamentary Papers*, 1877, VIII, Report.

15 Companies Act, 1877. 40/41 Vict. c. 26.

16 Companies Act, 1879. 42/43 Vict. c. 76.

17 Select Committee on Loans to Foreign States, Report, 50.

18 For statistics, see above, chapter 2, and below.

19 Cottrell, *Industrial Finance*, 61.

20 Select Committee on Limited Liability, 1867. The merchants were George Goschen, David Salomons (former Lord Mayor), John Vance, Kirkman Hodgson (also director Bank of England) and Walter Morrison. Bankers were Stephen Cave, John Hubbard and George Glyn. Samuel Graves was the shipowner and W.E. Forster the industrialist.

21 See for example, the notorious case of Overend and Gurney, "Overend, Gurney and Co. Limited," *Bankers' Magazine* (December 1893): 809.

22 Shannon, "The First Five Thousand Limited Companies," 418n. See also *The Economist*, 24 November 1888.

23 Martin Wiener, *English Culture and the Decline of the Industrial Spirit 1850–1980* (Cambridge: Cambridge University Press, 1981), 14.

24 See Lambert, *The Railway King*, and T.C. Barker, "Lord Salisbury, Chairman of the Great Eastern Railway, 1868–72," in *Business and Businessmen*, ed. Sheila Marriner (Liverpool: Liverpool University Press, 1978).

25 Wiener argues that industrialists were the principal recipients of negative press, while the City (banking, insurance, the Stock Exchange) was looked upon as a comparatively clean and respectable avenue to success. My findings suggest exactly the opposite. Anti-business sentiment was directed overwhelmingly at the City. Industrialists were seen as the embodiment of sobriety and good sense who made money from manufacturing useful articles. Financiers, on the other hand, manipulated securities and gambled away the public's savings.

26 H.C. Edey and Prot Panitpakdi, "British Company Accounting and the Law 1844–1900," in *Studies in the History of Accounting*, eds. A.C. Littleton and B.S. Yamey (Homewood, Illinois: Richard D. Irwin, 1956), 369–70.

27 Griffith, "Limited Liability," *Edinburgh Review* 163 (January 1886): 71–87.
28 Lawson, "A Black Year for Investors," *Blackwood's Edinburgh Magazine* 137 (February 1885): 281–82.
29 Ibid., 276–77.
30 See for example, *The Economist*, 20 December 1879 and 22 March 1884.
31 Stutfield, "The Higher Rascality," 78.
32 Griffith, "Limited Liability," 85.
33 Emden, "Crying Need for Reforms in Our Company Law," 1038.
34 Hartley Withers, "The Investor's Last Hope," *National Review* 26 (September 1895): 137.
35 Royal Commission on the Depression of Trade and Industry, *Parliamentary Papers*, 1886, XXIII, Report.
36 *Hansard*, 1888, CCCXXII, 8, 14.
37 *Hansard*, 1888, CCCXXVII, 1514, CCCXXVIII, 1502.
38 Companies Winding-Up Act, 1890. 53/54 Vict. c. 63.
39 Emden, "Crying Need for Reforms in Our Company Law," 1037–38.
40 See case of Edward Beall and the London and Scottish Bank, *The Times* (London), 22 July 1899.
41 Symons, *Horatio Bottomley*, 116.
42 Directors' Liability Act, 1890. 53/54 Vict. c. 64.
43 Samuel, *Shareholders' Money*, 23–25. See case of London and Universal Bank directors, *The Economist*, 19 November 1898.
44 See case of City Equitable directors, Manley, "Gerard Lee Bevan," 107.
45 Stutfield, "The Higher Rascality," 78–79.
46 See above, chapter 6.
47 Select Committee on the Reform of the Joint Stock Company Acts, *Parliamentary Papers*, 1895, LXXXVIII, Report, vi.
48 *The Economist*, 31 July 1897.
49 Stutfield, "The Company Scandal: A City View," 578–79. See also Van Oss, "In Hooley Land," 10. In percentages, over one quarter of the Lords were company directors.
50 Companies Act, 1900. 63/64 Vict. c. 48, sections 3, 9, 10.
51 Ibid., section 4.
52 Ibid., section 8.
53 Ibid., section 21.
54 Ibid., section 23.
55 Thorpe, *How to Invest and How to Speculate* (London: Grant Richards, 1901), 70–71.
56 See discussion of Davey Bill in *Accountant*, 21 December 1895.
57 Emden, "Defective Additions to Our Company Law," *Nineteenth Century* 48 (December 1900): 967.
58 Companies Act, 1907. 7 Edw. VII c. 50, section 19.

59 Select Committee on the Companies Acts, *Parliamentary Papers*, 1918, VII, Minority Report.
60 Companies Act, 1928. 18/19 Geo. V c. 45, section 78.
61 Ibid., section 35. Also see, *The Economist*, 11 August 1928.
62 Companies Act, 1928. 18/19 Geo. V c. 45, section 38. See also B.C. Hunt, "Recent English Company Law Reform," *Harvard Business Review* 8 (January 1930): 174.
63 Companies Act, 1928. 18/19 Geo. V. c. 45, sections 39, 40, 74.
64 See *The Economist*, 18 August 1928.
65 Norman Grieser, "Sources of Information for Investors" (M.Sc. thesis, University of London, 1940), 15.
66 Dearnley, *Fraud and Embezzlement*, 101–2.
67 See Select Committee on Companies Acts, 1877, 148.
68 Select Committee on Finance and Industry, *Parliamentary Papers*, 1931, XIII, Report, and Board of Trade, Departmental Committee on Share Pushing, *Parliamentary Papers*, 1937, XV, Report.
69 Select Committee on Joint Stock Companies, *Parliamentary Papers*, 1844, VII, Report, 363.
70 Select Committee on Companies Acts, 1877, 142.
71 Van Oss, "Whitaker Wright Finance," *Blackwood's Edinburgh Magazine* 175 (March 1904): 407.
72 Symons, *Horatio Bottomley*, 87–108.
73 Hooley, *Confessions*, 274–75.
74 See *The Times* (London), 8 September, 8 December 1857.
75 *The Times* (London), 2 December 1844.
76 See K.K. Macnab, "Aspects of the History of Crime in England and Wales."
77 See *The Times* (London), 13 October 1845.
78 Select Committee on Companies Acts, 1877, 125.
79 Central Criminal Court, *Minutes of Evidence*, 1854–55, PRO, Crim 10/42.
80 See Philips, *Crime and Authority*, chapter 4.
81 *Hansard*, CXXIX (1903), 162. See also Haldane, *With Intent to Deceive*, 93.
82 See above, chapter 3.
83 Secret Report of the Board of Inland Revenue, 1921, PRO, T172/1209. The Director of Public Prosecutions had known of Farrow's crime since 1918 – having been apprised of the situation by his brother-in-law, a tax commissioner. At the time of Farrow's trial in 1921, the government became alarmed that its prior knowledge of the crime and policy of inaction would be discovered, but this aspect of the story stayed hidden. The relevant documents remained classified until 1972, and, to the best of my knowledge, have never before been divulged.
84 Criminal Statistics for 1900, *Parliamentary Papers*, 1902, CXVII, 31, 79.

85 Criminal Statistics for 1924, *Parliamentary Papers*, 1926, XXIX, 463, 539.
86 Board of Trade, Departmental Committee on Share Pushing, 29.
87 Ibid., 27–28.
88 "The Morals of Business," *Meliora* 1 (1858): 51.
89 Criminal Statistics for 1900, 31.
90 Criminal Statistics for 1924, 463.
91 Henry R. Grenfell, "Banking and Commercial Legislation," *Nineteenth Century* 5 (March 1879): 535.
92 *The Times* (London), 3 May 1858. See also *The Times* (London), 8 December 1857.
93 *Hooley Book*, 47.
94 *Hansard*, CXVIII, 347.
95 It was frequently suggested that Balfour was a scapegoat for countless other directors, equally guilty. See, for example, "The Effect of the Liberator Sentences on Public Morals," *Investors' Review* (January 1896): 8–13, and Lawson, "Company Promoting a la Mode," *National Review* 32 (September 1898): 579.
96 Select Committee on Joint Stock Companies, 1844, 195.
97 Central Criminal Court, *Minutes of Evidence*, 1876–77, PRO, Crim 10/66.
98 Central Criminal Court, *Minutes of Evidence*, 1911–12, PRO, Crim 10/102.
99 Case of John Paul, *The Times* (London), 6 March 1845.
100 See cases of Thomas Vincent, *The Times* (London), 11 March, 5 April 1843, and Thomas Bell Jones, *The Times* (London), 28 November 1844.
101 Jabez Balfour, *My Prison Life* (London: Chapman and Hall, 1907), 286–87.
102 *The Times* (London), 22 June 1921. Both men received two years imprisonment.
103 Quoted in Meredith, *Drama of Money Making*, 161.
104 Balfour, *My Prison Life*, 17.
105 Hooley, *Confessions*, 77.
106 Prison Act of 1898, 61/62 Vict. c. 41.
107 Hooley, *Confessions*, 290.
108 Symons, *Horatio Bottomley*, 260.
109 Horatio Bottomley, *Convict "13": A Ballad of Maidstone Gaol* (London: Stanley Paul and Company, 1927), and *Songs of the Cell* (London: William Southern, 1928). Gerard Lee Bevan, *Russet and Asp* (London: Duckworth, 1929).
110 A fine study of middle-class attitudes toward criminals in nineteenth-century France can be found in Louis Chevalier, *Laboring Classes and Dangerous Classes*, trans. Frank Jellinek (New York: H. Fertig, 1973). See also Kellow Chesney, *The Victorian Underworld* (London: Maurice Temple Smith, 1970).

111 Trollope, *The Three Clerks*, 518.
112 Spencer, *The Morals of Trade*, 62.
113 Charles Goring, *The English Convict: A Statistical Study* (London: His Majesty's Stationery Office, 1913), see esp. 101–2, 212–13.
114 Horsley, *How Criminals are Made*. It should be pointed out that Horsley had other views about criminality that were quite reactionary. See Olive Anderson, *Suicide in Victorian and Edwardian England* (Oxford: Clarendon Press, 1987), 219–27.

8 BUSINESS ETHICS AND PROFESSIONALIZATION

1 *The Times* (London), 18 November 1845.
2 Spencer, *The Morals of Trade*, 50.
3 Sidney Checkland, "The Mind of the City, 1870–1914," *Oxford Economic Papers*, new series 9 (October 1957): 266.
4 Spencer, *Morals of Trade*, 49–50.
5 Select Committee on Loans to Foreign States, *Parliamentary Papers*, 1875, xi, Report, xlvii.
6 Reverend J. Carter, "Commercial Morality," *Economic Review* (July 1893): 327.
7 Horsley, *How Criminals are Made*, 67.
8 See Horsley, "Commercial Morality Tending to Crime," in *How Criminals are Made*, and Carter, "Commercial Morality."
9 Carter, "Commercial Morality," 326.
10 Anthony Trollope, *The Three Clerks*, 170.
11 Granville Barker, *The Voysey Inheritance*, in Kennedy, *Plays by Harley Granville Barker*, 94.
12 John Galsworthy, *The Skin Game* (New York: Charles Scribner's Sons, 1920), 17.
13 The problem is discussed by Evans, *Facts, Failures and Frauds*, 2.
14 Stutfield, "The Higher Rascality," 78.
15 Reverend A.J. Morris, *Religion and Business* (London: Ward and Company, 1853), 10.
16 *The Times* (London), 15 November 1856.
17 Spencer, "Railway Morals and Railway Policy," 426–27.
18 "Life Assurance Companies," *Quarterly Review* 128 (January 1870): 21.
19 Stutfield, "The Company-Monger's Elysium," 844.
20 See above, chapter 7. See also G.R. Searle, "Company Promoting a la Mode: The Stock Exchange and Political Life in Late Victorian and Edwardian Britain," Paper presented at the Institute of Commonwealth Studies seminar "The City and the Empire," June, 1985.
21 Parris, *Government and the Railways*, 130–31.
22 See John Vincent, ed. *The Later Derby Diaries* (Bristol, the author, 1981), 112n.

23 P.N. Davies, "Group Enterprise: Strengths and Hazards. Business History and the Teaching of Business Management," in *Business and Businessmen*, ed. Marriner.

24 The 1928 Report of Enquiry found that privileged information had not been used in the speculation, but that such behavior by civil servants was clearly improper. See Ann Bridge, *Permission to Resign: Goings-on in the Corridors of Power* (London: Sidgwick and Jackson, 1971).

25 Select Committee on the Marconi Affair, *Parliamentary Papers*, 1913, VII.

26 Ibid., Minority Report. See also *Quarterly Review* 219 (July 1913), and Denis Judd, *Lord Reading* (London: Weidenfeld and Nicolson, 1982), chapter 8.

27 Judd, *Lord Reading*, 100.

28 Lucy Masterman, *C.F.G. Masterman* (London: Nicholson and Watson, 1939), 255.

29 For a recent look at religious attitudes toward business, see David Jeremy, ed., *Business and Religion in Britain* (London: Gower, 1988).

30 See Boyd Hilton, *The Age of Atonement: The Influence of Evangelicalism on Social and Economic Thought, 1795–1865* (Oxford: Clarendon Press, 1988), esp. chapter 4.

31 A.R. Ashwell, *Life of Bishop Wilberforce* (New York: E.P. Dutton and Company, 1883), 277.

32 Morris, *Religion and Business*, preface.

33 Brian and Faith Bowers, "Bloomsbury Chapel and Mercantile Morality," Paper presented at seminar on "Christianity and Business," at Business History Unit, London School of Economics, March 1982.

34 Lyttleton, *The Sins of Trade and Business*.

35 See my concluding chapter below.

36 See Perkin, *Origins of Modern English Society*, chapter 7.

37 See above, chapter 3.

38 The Barton frauds are discussed above in chapter 4.

39 W.A. Thomas, *Provincial Stock Exchange*, chapter 9.

40 See Green, *Debtors to Their Profession*, 56–65, and *The History of the Institute of Chartered Accountants in England and Wales 1880–1965* (London: Heinemann, 1966), 26–40, 198.

41 De Paula, *The Principles of Auditing*, 7–10, 33, 76–77.

42 Dearnley, *Fraud and Embezzlement*, 15–16.

43 Ibid., chapter 15.

44 Quoted in de Paula, *Principles of Auditing*, 185.

45 See for example, *Accountant*, 23 May 1896, and de Paula, *Principles of Auditing*, 183–86.

46 For details of the case, see above, chapter 6. The accounting aspects of the case are discussed in J.R. Edwards, "The Accounting Pro-

fession and Disclosure in Published Reports 1925–35," *Accounting and Business Research* 24 (1976): 289–303, and J.R. Edwards, *A History of Financial Accounting* (London: Routledge, 1989).

47 *Accountant,* 7 May 1932.
48 Ibid.

CONCLUSION   FINAL CONSIDERATIONS

1 See above, chapter 1.
2 A.R. Barnett, "Era of Fraud and Embezzlement: Its Causes and Remedies," *Arena* 14 (October 1894): 196.
3 Henry Mayhew, *London Labour and the London Poor*, 4 vols. (1861; reprint, New York: Dover Publications, 1968), vol. 4, 276.
4 See above, chapter 6.
5 *The Times* (London), 22 June 1855.
6 *The Economist,* 1 November 1879.
7 Shannon, "The First Five Thousand Limited Companies," 418–19.
8 Select Committee on Limited Liability Acts, *Parliamentary Papers,* 1867, x, Minutes, 81.
9 *Westminster Popular* No. 5, 3–7.
10 Alexander Taylor Innes, "The Personal Responsibility of Bank Directors," *Contemporary Review* 34 (January 1879): 322.
11 Clapham, *Economic History,* vol. 2, 384.
12 Watts, *The Biggest Crime*; Liberator Relief Fund, *Interim Report and Financial Statement of the Executive Committee,* December 1893, and Liberator Relief Fund, *A Final Appeal,* December 1895.
13 *Westminster Popular* No. 5, 32.
14 Ibid., 32.
15 Watts, *Biggest Crime,* 4.
16 Select Committee Report on Joint Stock Companies, *Parliamentary Papers,* 1844, VII, 363.
17 See Scratchley, *On Savings Banks,* 54–55, and Francis, *Chronicles and Characters of the Stock Exchange,* 355–56.
18 Union Bank, *Minute Books,* vol. 13, 157–61, National Westminster Bank Archives, London.
19 Stutfield, "The Higher Rascality," 77.
20 "Commercial Frauds," *Irish Quarterly Review* 9 (April 1859): 193.
21 Evans, *Facts, Failures and Frauds,* 123.
22 Stutfield, "The Higher Rascality," 84–85. See also Stutfield, "The Company Scandal: A City View," 575–83.
23 Royal Commission on the Stock Exchange, *Parliamentary Papers,* 1878, XIX, Minutes, 41.
24 Stutfield, "Company-Monger's Elysium," 842.
25 Still, "Front Sheet Reflections," 991.
26 Cottrell, *British Overseas Investment,* 19–21.

27 Shand, "Speculative Investments," 299.
28 Clapham, *Economic History*, vol. 2, 358.
29 A.H. Leigh, "Stock Exchange Reform in London," *Nineteenth Century* 62 (July 1907): 85.
30 Davenport, "After Hatry," 362–63.
31 See William P. Kennedy, "Institutional Response to Economic Growth: Capital Markets in Britain to 1914," in *Management Strategy and Business Development*, ed. Leslie Hannah (London: Macmillan, 1976), and Kennedy, *Industrial Structure*.
32 Kennedy, *Industrial Structure*, 135.
33 Ibid., chapter 5.
34 Shand, "Speculative Investments," 316.
35 Messrs. Endean and Company, "Selection of Safe Investments," 1885, Goldsmith Library, University of London.
36 Thorpe, *How to Invest*, 126–35.
37 See Kennedy, *Industrial Structure*, chapter 6, and A.K. Cairncross, *Home and Foreign Investment 1870–1913* (Cambridge: Cambridge University Press, 1953), 170–86.
38 Cairncross, *Home and Foreign Investment*, 222–35.
39 Dickens, *Little Dorrit*, 738.
40 Tatiana M. Holway, "The Game of Speculation: Economics and Representation," paper delivered at Nineteenth-Century Interdisciplinary Studies Conference, Yale Center for British Art, April 1991.
41 See Ann Fabian, *Card Sharps, Dream Books and Bucket Shops: Gambling in 19th-Century America* (Ithaca and London: Cornell University Press, 1990).

Bibliography

PRIMARY SOURCES

GOVERNMENT DOCUMENTS

Parliamentary Select Committees and Special Commissions, listed in date order

Select Committee on the Bank Acts. *Parliamentary Papers*, 1837–38, VII, Report

Select Committee on Banks of Issue. *Parliamentary Papers*, 1841, V, Report

Royal Commission on Forged Exchequer Bills. *Parliamentary Papers*, 1842, XVIII, Report

Select Committee on Joint-Stock Companies. *Parliamentary Papers*, 1844, VII, Minutes and Report

Select Committee on Railway Acts. *Parliamentary Papers*, 1846, XIV, Minutes and Report

Select Committee on the Audit of Railway Accounts, *Parliamentary Papers*, 1849, X, Report

Select Committee on the Savings of the Middle and Working Classes. *Parliamentary Papers*, 1850, XIX, Minutes and Report

Select Committee on the Law of Partnership. *Parliamentary Papers*, 1851, XVIII, Report

Select Committee on Assurance Associations. *Parliamentary Papers*, 1853, XXI, Report

Select Committee on the Bank Acts and Recent Commercial Distress. *Parliamentary Papers*, 1858, V, Minutes and Report

Select Committee on the Limited Liability Acts. *Parliamentary Papers*, 1867, X, Minutes and Report

Select Committee on Loans to Foreign States. *Parliamentary Papers*, 1875, XI, Minutes and Report

Select Committee on the Companies Acts. *Parliamentary Papers*, 1877, VIII, Minutes and Report

Royal Commission on the Stock Exchange. *Parliamentary Papers*, 1878, XIX, Minutes and Report

Royal Commission on the Depression of Trade and Industry. *Parliamentary Papers*, 1886, VIII, Report

Select Committee on the Reform of the Joint Stock Company Acts. *Parliamentary Papers*, 1895, LXXXVIII, Report; and 1898, IX, Report

Select Committee on the Companies Acts. *Parliamentary Papers*, 1906, XCVII, Report

Select Committee on the Marconi Affair. *Parliamentary Papers*, 1913, VII, Report

Select Committee on the Companies Acts. *Parliamentary Papers*, 1918, VII, Report

Select Committee on Company Law Reform. *Parliamentary Papers*, 1926, IX, Report

Select Committee on Company Law Reform. *Parliamentary Papers*, 1928, VI, Report

Select Committee on Finance and Industry. *Parliamentary Papers*, 1931, XIII, Report

Board of Trade. Departmental Committee on Share Pushing. *Parliamentary Papers*, 1937, XV, Report

Parliamentary Returns, listed in date order

Report of Company Registrar. *Parliamentary Papers*, 1846, XLIII
Report of Company Registrar. *Parliamentary Papers*, 1849, L
Annual Report of Bankruptcy. *Parliamentary Papers*, 1899, LXXXVIII
Criminal Statistics for 1900. *Parliamentary Papers*, 1902, CXVII
Criminal Statistics for 1924. *Parliamentary Papers*, 1926, XXIX

Government Papers

Secret Report of the Board of Inland Revenue, 1921. PRO, T172/1209

Statutes, listed in date order

Act to Regulate Stock Jobbing, 1696. 8/9 Wm. III c. 32
Savings Bank Act, 1817. 57 Geo. III c. 130
Joint Stock Banking Act, 1826. 7 Geo. IV c. 46
Regulation of Railways Act, 1840. 3/4 Vict. c. 97
Bank Notes Act, 1844. 7/8 Vict. c. 32
Regulation of Railways Act, 1844. 7/8 Vict. c. 85
Act for the Registration, Incorporation and Regulation of Joint Stock Companies, 1844. 7/8 Vict. c. 110
Joint Stock Bank Act, 1844. 7/8 Vict. c. 113
Company Clauses Consolidation Act, 1845. 8/9 Vict. c. 16
Regulation of Railways Act, 1846. 9/10 Vict. c. 105
Company Law Amendment Act, 1847. 10/11 Vict. c. 78

Railway Department Act, 1851. 14/15 Vict. c. 64
Limited Liability Act, 1855. 18/19 Vict. c. 133
Joint Stock Company Act, 1856. 19/20 Vict. c. 47
Banking Act, 1857. 20/21 Vict. c. 49
Post Office Savings Bank Act, 1861. 24/25 Vict. c. 14
Company Act, 1862. 25/26 Vict. c. 89
Company Act, 1867. 30/31 Vict. c. 131
Regulation of Railways Act, 1868. 31/32 Vict. c. 119
Life Assurance Companies Act, 1870. 33/34 Vict. c. 61
Companies Arrangement Act, 1870. 33/34 Vict. c. 104
Gas Works Act, 1871. 34/35 Vict. c. 41
Companies Act, 1877. 40/41 Vict. c. 26
Companies Act, 1879. 42/43 Vict. c. 76
Companies Act, 1880. 43/44 Vict. c. 19
Electric Lighting Act, 1882. 45/46 Vict. c. 56
Companies Act, 1883. 46/47 Vict. c. 28
Memorandum of Association Act, 1890. 53/54 Vict. c. 62
Companies Winding-Up Act, 1890. 53/54 Vict. c. 63
Directors' Liability Act, 1890. 53/54 Vict. c. 64
Companies Winding-Up Act, 1893. 56/57 Vict. c. 58
Prison Act, 1898. 61/62 Vict. c. 41
Companies Act, 1900. 63/64 Vict. c. 48
Companies Act, 1907. 7 Edw. VII c. 50
Companies Act, 1908. 8 Edw. VII c. 69
Companies Act, 1928. 18/19 Geo. V c. 45
Companies Act, 1929. 19/20 Geo. V c. 23

Criminal Court Documents, listed in date order

Central Criminal Court. *Minutes of Evidence*, 1849–50. Trial of Walter
    Watts. PRO, Crim 10/32
Central Criminal Court. *Minutes of Evidence*, 1854–55. Trial of W. Strahan,
    Sir J.D. Paul and R. Bates. PRO, Crim 10/42
Central Criminal Court. *Minutes of Evidence*, 1855–56. Trial of J.W. Cole.
    PRO, Crim 10/41
Central Criminal Court. *Minutes of Evidence*, 1855–56. Trial of W.J. Rob-
    son. PRO, Crim 10/44
Central Criminal Court. *Minutes of Evidence*, 1859–60. Trial of W.G. Pul-
    linger. PRO, Crim 10/49
Central Criminal Court. *Minutes of Evidence*, 1876–77. Trial of W. Swindle-
    hurst and B. Langley. PRO, Crim 10/66
Central Criminal Court. *Minutes of Evidence*, 1904–5. Trial of E.T. Hooley
    and H.J. Lawson. PRO, Crim 10/95
Central Criminal Court. *Minutes of Evidence*, 1911–12. Trial of E.T.
    Hooley. PRO, Crim 10/102

COMPANY RECORDS

Eastern Counties Railway. Shareholders' Committee of Investigation, Minutes and Report, 1849. PRO, Rail 186/62, Rail 186/74, Rail 186/101

Shareholders' Committee of Investigation, Minutes and Report, 1855. PRO, Rail 186/62, Rail 186/74

Messrs. Endean and Company. "Selection of Safe Investments." 1885. Goldsmith Library, University of London

Farrow's Bank Records. PRO, BT 31/18100

Great Northern Railway. Committee of Investigation, Minutes and Report, 1857. PRO, Rail 236/424–429

Liberator Relief Fund. *Interim Report and Financial Statement of the Executive Committee*, December 1893. British Museum, London

A Final Appeal, December 1895. British Museum, London

Union Bank of London. *Minute Books*. National Westminster Bank Archives, London

York, Newcastle and Berwick Railway. Shareholders' Committee of Investigation, Minutes and Report, 1849. PRO, Rail 772/15

York and North Midland Railway. Shareholders' Committee of Investigation, Minutes and Report, 1849. PRO, Rail 770/13, Rail 770/65

BOOKS

Arnold, Matthew. *Culture and Anarchy*. 1869; reprint, Cambridge: Cambridge University Press, 1932

Bagehot, Walter. *Lombard Street*. 1873; reprint, Homewood, Illinois: Richard D. Irwin, 1969

Balfour, Jabez. *My Prison Life*. London: Chapman and Hall, 1907

Bigland, Reuben. *The Downfall of Horatio Bottomley, M.P.* Birmingham: R. Bigland, 1921

Carlyle, Thomas. *Past and Present*, 1843. In *The Complete Works of Thomas Carlyle*. 20 vols. New York: Thomas Y. Crowell and Co., 1902, vol. 12

"Hudson's Statue." In *Latter Day Pamphlets*, 1850. In *The Complete Works of Thomas Carlyle*. 20 vols. New York: Thomas Y. Crowell and Co., 1902, vol. 12

Chiswell, Francis. *Key to the Rules of the Stock Exchange*. London: Effingham Wilson, 1902

Collet, John K. *Bottomley Frauds*. Cardiff: M.E. and Company, 1922

Dearnley, I.H. *Fraud and Embezzlement*. London: Sir Isaac Pitman and Sons, 1933

de Paula, Frederic. *The Principles of Auditing*. London: Sir Isaac Pitman and Sons, 1914

"A Detective." *The Ways of Swindlers*. London: T.H. Sheppard, 1879

Duguid, Charles. *How to Read the Money Article*. London: Wilson, 1901

The Story of the Stock Exchange. London: Grant Richards, 1901

Evans, David Morier. *The City, or the Physiology of London Business*. London: Baily Brothers, 1845

The Commercial Crisis of 1847–48. London: Letts, Son and Steer, 1849

Facts, Failures and Frauds. London: Groombridge and Sons, 1859

The History of the Commercial Crisis, 1857–58. London: Groombridge and Sons, 1859

Speculative Notes and Notes on Speculation. London: Groombridge and Sons, 1864

Farrow, Thomas. *Banks and People*. London: Chapman and Hall, 1911

Finnie, David. *Capital Underwriting*. London: Sir Isaac Pitman and Sons, 1934

Fox Bourne, H.R. *Romance of Trade*. London: Cassell, Petter and Galpin, 1871

Francis, John. *Chronicles and Characters of the Stock Exchange*. London: Willoughby and Company, 1849

A History of the English Railway: Its Social Relations and Revelations, 1820–1845. 2 vols. London: Longman, Brown, Green and Longmans, 1851

Fraud in Accounts. Vol. 30 of Accountant's Library Series. London: Gee and Company, 1904

Gilbart, James Wilson. *The History and Principle of Banking*. 3rd edition. London: Longman, Rees, Orme, Brown, Green and Longmans, 1837

Goring, Charles. *The English Convict: A Statistical Survey*. London: H.M.S.O., 1913

Hilton Price, F.G. *Handbook of London Bankers*. London: Leadenhill Press, 1891

The Hooley Book. London: John Dicks, 1904

Hooley, E.T. *Hooley's Confessions*. London: Simpkin, Marshall, Hamilton, Kent and Company, 1925

Horsley, Reverend J.W. *How Criminals are Made and Prevented*. London: T. Fisher Unwin, 1913

Hutton, James. *Suggestions as to the Appointment by the Legislature of Public Accountants*. London: Letts, Son and Company, 1861

Jenkinson, Mark Webster, Sir. *The Promotion and Accounts of a Public Limited Company*. London: Gee and Company, 1912

The Value of a Balance Sheet. London: Gee and Company, 1928

Joplin, Thomas. *An Essay on the General Principles and Present Practice of Banking, 1827*. Reprinted in *Money and Banking in England: The Development of the Banking System, 1694–1914*, eds. P.L. Cottrell and B.L. Anderson. Newton Abbot: David and Charles, 1974

Lalor, John. *Money and Morals: A Book for the Times*. London: John Chapman, 1852

Lyttleton, Reverend W.H. *The Sins of Trade and Business*. London: Mowbray and Company, 1891

McCulloch, J.R. *Considerations on Partnerships with Limited Liability*. London: Longman, Brown, Green and Longmans, 1856

Mayhew, Henry. *London Labour and the London Poor*. 4 vols. 1861; reprint. New York: Dover Publications, 1968. Vol. 4

Meredith, Hubert A. *The Drama of Money Making*. London: Sampson, Low, Marston and Company, 1931

Morris, Reverend A.J. *Religion and Business*. London: Ward and Company, 1853

Morrison, James. *Defects of the English System of Railway Legislation*. London: Longman, Brown, Green and Longmans, 1846

O'Hagan, Henry Osborne. *Leaves from My Life*. 2 vols. London: John Lane, 1929

Poley, A.P. *The History, Law and Practice of the Stock Exchange*. London: Sir Isaac Pitman and Sons, 1907

Pulbrook, Anthony. *The Handy Book on the Law and Practice of Joint Stock Companies*. London: Effingham Wilson, 1906

Samuel, H.B. *Shareholders' Money*. London: Sir Isaac Pitman and Sons, 1933

Scratchley, Arthur. *On Savings Banks*. London: Longman, Brown, Longman and Roberts, 1862

Smiles, Samuel. *The Life of George Stephenson*. Boston: Ticknor and Fields, 1858

Smith, Arthur. *Railways as They Really Are*. London: Sherwood, Gilbert and Piper, 1847–48

The Bubble of the Age. 3rd edition. London: Sherwood, Gilbert and Piper, 1848

Spencer, Herbert. *The Morals of Trade*. London: Mowbray and Company, 1891

Thorpe, C.H. *How to Invest and How to Speculate*. London: Grant Richards, 1901

Tooke, Thomas. *A History of Prices*. 6 vols. London: Longman, Orme, Brown, Green and Longmans, 1838–57

Watts, Reverend J. Stockwell. *The Biggest Crime of the Nineteenth Century and What the Churches Say to It*. London: Liberator Relief Fund, 1893

Withers, Hartley. *The Quicksands of the City and a Way Through for Investors*. London: Jonathan Cape, 1930

Xenos, Stephanos. *Depredations; or Overend Gurney and Co., and the Greek and Oriental Steam Navigation Co.*. London: the author, 1869

PERIODICALS AND NEWSPAPERS

Articles written anonymously are listed below alphabetically according to the first significant word in the title.

"Auditing Aspects of the Royal Mail Case." *Accountant*, 8 August 1931

Aytoun, W.E. "The National Debt and the Stock Exchange." *Blackwood's Edinburgh Magazine* 66 (December 1849): 655–78

Baker, George. "The Crisis of the Stock Exchange." *Contemporary Review* 58 (November 1890): 680–92

Barnett, A.R. "Era of Fraud and Embezzlement: Its Causes and Remedies." *Arena* 14 (October 1894): 196–210

Brown, Richard. "The Genesis of Company Law in England and Scotland." *Juridical Review* (June 1901): 185–91

Bundy, Harvey B. "Inside Information." *Atlantic Monthly* 143 (March 1929): 321–25

Carter, Reverend J. "Commercial Morality." *Economic Review* (July 1893): 327–41

Clauson, A.C. "The Reform of Company Law." *Quarterly Review* 191 (April 1900): 373–92

"Commercial Morality in 1898." *Bankers' Magazine* (January 1900): 12–16

"Company Law and the Royal Mail Case." *Accountant*, 15 August 1931

Craig, A.T. "Frauds in Connection with Bookkeeping and Methods to be Used for Their Detection." *Accountant*, 26 February 1898

Davenport, E.H. "After Hatry." *Nineteenth Century and After* 107 (March 1930): 353–64

Denison, Edmund Beckett. "Railways." *Fraser's Magazine* 39 (June 1849): 607–18, and 40 (July 1849): 106–20

Dickens, Charles. "Convict Capitalists." *All the Year Round* 3 (June 1860): 201–4

"Very Singular Things in the City." *All the Year Round* 3 (July 1860): 325–26

Dodd, A.F. "Some Suggestions as to the Discovery and Prevention of Defalcations from the Auditor's Point of View." *Accountant*, 30 May 1903

Economicus. "Scandals of the Company World." *Review of Reviews* (January 1930): 30–32

"Hatry Scandal." *Review of Reviews* (February 1930): 112–15

"The Effect of the Liberator Sentences on Public Morals." *Investors' Review* (January 1896): 8–13

Emden, Alfred. "The Crying Need for Reforms in Our Company Law." *Nineteenth Century* 35 (June 1894): 1033–50

"Defective Additions to Our Company Law." *Nineteenth Century* 48 (December 1900): 955–71

"Finance, Frauds and Failure." *Temple Bar* 17 (June 1866): 384–93

Gale, Frederick. "The Railway Bubble." *The Cornhill Magazine* 54 (December 1886): 585–95

Graves, Ralph H. "Why it is Easy to Steal Half a Million Dollars." *Harper's Weekly* 51 (June 1907): 802–10

Grenfell, Henry R. "Banking and Commercial Legislation." *Nineteenth Century* 5 (March 1879): 534–46

Griffith, R. "Limited Liability." *Edinburgh Review* 163 (January 1886): 71–87

Hennell, Thomas. "Railway Finance." *Quarterly Review* 122 (April 1867): 489–506

"The Hindrance of Company Frauds." *Bankers' Magazine* (September 1895): 363–65

Hunt, B.C. "Recent English Company Law Reform." *Harvard Business Review* 8 (January 1930): 170–83

Innes, Alexander Taylor. "The Personal Responsibility of Bank Directors." *Contemporary Review* 34 (January 1879): 322–40

"John Skeeme, the Promoter." *All the Year Round* 18 (October 1867): 342–46, 376–81

"The Lawson Group of Companies." *The Economist*, 2 October 1897

Lawson, W.R. "A Black Year for Investors." *Blackwood's Edinburgh Magazine* 137 (February 1885): 269–84

  "Company Promoting a la Mode." *National Review* 32 (September 1898): 103–15

  "Stock Jobbing Companies." *National Review* 36 (February 1901): 869–81

Leigh, A.H. "Stock Exchange Reform in London." *Nineteenth Century* 62 (July 1907): 82–87

McCulloch, J.R. "Joint-Stock Banks and Companies." *Edinburgh Review* 63 (July 1836): 419–41

Manson, Edward. "Tinkering Company Law." *Law Quarterly Magazine* (October 1890): 428–35

"The Marconi Affair." *Quarterly Review* 219 (July 1913): 256–69

A Member of the House. "The Stock Exchange and its Morals." *Journal of Finance* (April 1899)

"The Morals of Business." *Meliora* 1 (1858): 45–56

"Mr. Hooley's Bankruptcy." *The Economist*, 11 June 1898

Nixon, H.H. "Methods Employed by Defalcating Bookkeepers and Some Suggestions for the Prevention and Detection of Them." *Accountant*, 26 December 1903

Oliphant, Laurence. "The Autobiography of a Joint-Stock Company, Limited." *Blackwood's Edinburgh Magazine* 120 (July 1876): 96–122

"One Man Companies." *Bankers' Magazine* (July 1895): 9–11

"Overend, Gurney and Co. Limited," *Bankers' Magazine* (December 1893): 807–9

Pegler, Ernest C. "Some Notable Frauds in Accounts." *Accountant*, 15 May 1909

"Results of the Hooley System of Finance." *The Economist*, 20 August 1898

"Royal Mail Steam Packet Company Case." *The Canadian Chartered Accountant* (November 1931): 181–94

"Royal Mail Steam Packet Trial." *Accountant*, 25 July, 1, 8, 15 August 1931

"The Sham Financial Press." *The Statist*, 9 April 1887

Shand, A. Innes. "Speculative Investments." *Blackwood's Edinburgh Magazine* 120 (September 1876): 293–316

Spencer, Herbert. "Railway Morals and Railway Policy." *Edinburgh Review* 100 (October 1854): 216–37

"Starting the Rio Grande Railway." *All the Year Round* 14 (November 1865): 368–93

Still, A. "The Unpopularity of the Stock Exchange." *Journal of Finance* (June 1898): 545–51

"Front Sheet Reflections." *Journal of Finance* (November 1898): 988–94

Stutfield, Hugh. "Investors and Their Money." *National Review* 26 (December 1895): 501–11

"The Company-Monger's Elysium." *National Review* 26 (February 1896): 836–48

"The Higher Rascality." *National Review* 31 (March 1898): 75–86

"The Company Scandal: A City View." *National Review* 32 (December 1898): 574–84

Tyssen, A.D. "Company Law Reform." *Law Magazine and Review* (May 1899): 274–87

Van Oss, S.F. "The 'Limited Liability' Craze." *Nineteenth Century* 43 (May 1898): 731–44

"In Hooley Land." *Journal of Finance* (January 1899): 7–12

"Whitaker Wright Finance." *Blackwood's Edinburgh Magazine* 175 (March 1904): 397–407

Westminster Popular No. 5, "The Story of the Liberator Crash." 6 March 1893

White, James. "The Murdering Banker." *Blackwood's Edinburgh Magazine* 44 (December 1838): 823–32

Wilson, A.J. "Immorality and Cowardice of Modern Loan-Mongering." *Contemporary Review* 73 (March 1898): 326–34

Withers, Hartley. "The Investor's Last Hope." *National Review* 26 (September 1895): 129–39

"The Mysteries of Money Articles." *The Cornhill Magazine* 75 (May 1897): 684–91

"How to Scan a Prospectus." *The Cornhill Magazine* 76 (July 1897): 105–113

NOVELS, PLAYS AND POETRY

Bell, Robert. *The Ladder of Gold.* New York: F.W. Purgess, 1851

Bevan, Gerard Lee. *Russet and Asp.* London: Duckworth, 1929

Bottomley, Horatio. *Convict "13": A Ballad of Maidstone Gaol.* London: Stanley Paul and Company, 1927

Songs of the Cell. London: William Southern, 1928

Boucicault, Dion. *The Poor of New York.* New York: Samuel French, 1857

Conrad, Joseph. *Chance.* 1913; reprint, London: Hogarth Press, 1984

Dickens, Charles. *Martin Chuzzlewit.* 1844; reprint, London: Penguin Books, 1968

Little Dorrit. 1857; reprint, New York: Oxford University Press, 1953

Galsworthy, John. *The Skin Game.* New York: Charles Scribner's Sons, 1920

Gilbert, W.S. and Arthur Sullivan. *Utopia Limited; or, the Flowers of Progress,* 1893. In *The Complete Plays of Gilbert and Sullivan.* New York: The Modern Library, n.d.

Gissing, George. *The Whirlpool.* 1897; reprint, London: Hogarth Press, 1984

Gore, Catherine. *The Banker's Wife.* New York: Harper and Brothers, 1846

Granville Barker, Harley. *The Voysey Inheritance,* 1905. In *Plays by Harley Granville Barker,* ed. Dennis Kennedy. Cambridge: Cambridge University Press, 1987

Robinson, Emma. *The Gold Worshippers, Or the Days We Live In.* New York: Harper and Brothers, 1851

Thackeray, W.M. "Diary and Letters of C. Jeames de la Pluche," 1845–46. In *The Complete Works of William M. Thackeray.* 30 vols. New York: The Kelmscott Society, 1904. Vol. 15

Trollope, Anthony. *The Three Clerks.* 1857; reprint, London: Richard Bentley and Son, 1884

    Doctor Thorne. 1858; reprint, New York: Oxford University Press, 1980

    The Way We Live Now. 1875; reprint, London: Oxford University Press, 1951

Wells, H.G. *Tono-Bungay.* 1908; reprint, New York: The Modern Library, 1935

SECONDARY SOURCES

Adie, D.K. "English Bank Deposits before 1844." *Economic History Review* 23 (1970): 285–97

Alderman, Geoffrey. *The Railway Interest.* Leicester: Leicester University Press, 1973

Anderson, Gregory. *Victorian Clerks.* Manchester: Manchester University Press, 1976

Anderson, Olive. *Suicide in Victorian and Edwardian England.* Oxford: Clarendon Press, 1987

Andreades, A. *History of the Bank of England, 1640–1903.* Trans. Cristabel Meredith. London: P.S. King and Son, 1909

Aranya, N. "Auditors in Britain: Patterns of Role Continuity and Change." Ph.D. diss., University of London, 1970

Armstrong, John. "Hooley and the Bovril Company." In *Speculators and Patriots,* ed. R.P.T. Davenport-Hines. London: Frank Cass, 1986

    "J.L. Johnston" and "G.L. Johnston." *Dictionary of Business Biography.* Vol. 3, 510–21

Ashwell, A.R. *Life of Bishop Wilberforce.* New York: E.P. Dutton and Company, 1883

Barker, T.C. "Lord Salisbury, Chairman of the Great Eastern Railway, 1868–72." In *Business and Businessmen*, ed. Sheila Marriner. Liverpool: Liverpool University Press, 1978

Bose, Mihir and Cathy Gunn. *Fraud: The Growth Industry of the Eighties.* London: Unwin Hyman, 1989

Bowers, Brian and Faith. "Bloomsbury Chapel and Mercantile Morality." Paper presented at seminar on "Christianity and Business," at Business History Unit, London School of Economics, March 1982

Bridge, Ann. *Permission to Resign: Goings-on in the Corridors of Power.* London: Sidgwick and Jackson, 1971

Broadbridge, S.A. "The Sources of Railway Share Capital." In *Railways in the Victorian Economy*, ed. M.C. Reed. New York: Augustus M. Kelly, 1968

Cairncross, A.K. *Home and Foreign Investment 1870–1913.* Cambridge: Cambridge University Press, 1953

Cameron, Rondo. "England 1750–1844." In *Banking in the Early Stages of Industrialization*, ed. Rondo Cameron. New York: Oxford University Press, 1967

Cameron, Rondo, ed. *Banking in the Early Stages of Industrialization.* New York: Oxford University Press, 1967

Carswell, John. *The South Sea Bubble.* London: Cresset Press, 1961

Checkland, Sidney. "The Mind of the City, 1870–1914." *Oxford Economic Papers*, new series 9 (October 1957): 261–78

Chesney, Kellow. *The Victorian Underworld.* London: Maurice Temple Smith, 1970

Chevalier, Louis. *Laboring Classes and Dangerous Classes.* Trans. Frank Jellinek. New York: H. Fertig, 1973

Clapham, J.H. *An Economic History of Modern Britain.* 3 vols. Cambridge: Cambridge University Press, 1926–38

Cleary, Esmond J. "Jabez Spencer Balfour." *Dictionary of Business Biography.* Vol. 1, 129–34

Collins, Michael. "The Banking Crisis of 1878." *Economic History Review*, 2nd series 42 (November 1989): 504–27

Cottrell, P.L. *British Overseas Investment in the Nineteenth Century.* London: Macmillan, 1975

"Railway Finance and the Crisis of 1866: Contractors' Bills of Exchange and the Finance Companies." *Journal of Transport History*, new series 3 (1975): 20–39

Industrial Finance, 1830–1914. London: Methuen, 1980

"David Chadwick." *Dictionary of Business Biography.* Vol. 1, 625–32

"Albert Grant." *Dictionary of Business Biography.* Vol. 2, 623–29

Cottrell, P.L. and B.L. Anderson, eds. *Money and Banking in England: The Development of the Banking System, 1694–1914.* Newton Abbot: David and Charles, 1974

Davenport-Hines, R.P.T. "Gerard Lee Bevan." *Dictionary of Business Biography*. Vol. 1, 321–24

"Whitaker Wright." *Dictionary of Business Biography*. Vol. 5, 901–4

"Edgar Vincent and the Eastern Investment Company." In *Speculators and Patriots*, ed. Davenport-Hines

Dudley Docker. Cambridge: Cambridge University Press, 1984

Davenport-Hines, R.P.T., ed. *Speculators and Patriots*. London: Frank Cass, 1986

Davies, P.N. "Group Enterprise: Strengths and Hazards. Business History and the Teaching of Business Management." In *Business and Businessmen*, ed. Sheila Marriner. Liverpool: Liverpool University Press, 1978

Davis, L.E. and R.A. Huttenback. *Mammon and the Pursuit of Empire*. New York: Cambridge University Press, 1986

Dickson, P.G.M. *The Financial Revolution in England, 1688–1756*. London: Macmillan, 1967

Doig, Alan. *Corruption and Misconduct in Contemporary British Politics*. New York: Penguin Books, 1984

Duncan, J.T. Skip and Marc Caplan. *White-Collar Crime: A Selected Bibliography*. Washington: Department of Justice, 1980

Edey, H.C. and Prot Panitpakdi. "British Company Accounting and the Law 1844–1900." In *Studies in the History of Accounting*, eds. A.C. Littleton and B.S. Yamey. Homewood, Illinois: Richard D. Irwin, 1956

Edwards, J.R. "The Accounting Profession and Disclosure in Published Reports 1925–35." *Accounting and Business Research* 24 (1976): 289–303

A History of Financial Accounting. London: Routledge, 1989

Emsley, Clive. *Crime and Society in England, 1750–1900*. London: Longman, 1987

Fabian, Ann. *Card Sharps, Dream Books and Bucket Shops: Gambling in 19th-Century America*. Ithaca and London: Cornell University Press, 1990

Fanning, David. "Clarence Charles Hatry." *Dictionary of Business Biography*. Vol. 3, 110–13

Feinstein, Charles. "Britain's Overseas Investment in 1913." *Economic History Review*, 2nd series 43 (May 1990): 288–95

Fraser, W.H. *The Coming of the Mass Market, 1850–1914*. Hamden, Conn.: Archon Books, 1981

Galbraith, J.K. *The Great Crash 1929*. London: Penguin Books, 1955

Gatrell, V.A.C. "The Decline of Theft and Violence in Victorian and Edwardian England." In *Crime and the Law*, eds. V.A.C. Gatrell, Bruce Lenman and Geoffrey Parkers. London: Europa Publications, 1980

Gatrell, V.A.C. and T.B. Hadden. "Criminal Statistics and Their Interpretation." In *Nineteenth Century Society*, ed. E.A. Wrigley. Cambridge: Cambridge University Press, 1972

Geis, Gilbert and Colin Goff. "Edwin H. Sutherland's White Collar Crime in America." *Criminal Justice History* (1986)

Geis, Gilbert and Robert Meier, eds. *White-Collar Crime: Offenses in Business, Politics and the Professions.* New York: Free Press, 1977

Goodhart, C.A.E. *The Business of Banking 1891–1914.* London: Weidenfeld and Nicolson, 1972

Green, Edwin. *Debtors to Their Profession: A History of the Institute of Bankers, 1879–1979.* London: Methuen, 1979

Grieser, Norman. "Sources of Information for Investors." M.Sc. thesis, University of London, 1940

Haldane, R.A. *With Intent to Deceive: Frauds Famous and Infamous.* Edinburgh: William Blackwood, 1970

Hannah, Leslie. *The Rise of the Corporate Economy.* Baltimore: Johns Hopkins University Press, 1976

Harrison, A.E. "Joint-Stock Company Flotations in the Cycle, Motor Vehicle and Related Industries, 1882–1914." *Business History* 23 (July 1981): 165–90

Hastings, Sir Patrick. "The Case of the Royal Mail." In *Studies in Accounting*, eds. W.T. Baxter and Sidney Davidson. London: Institute of Chartered Accountants, 1977

Higonnet, R.P. "Bank Deposits in the U.K. 1870–1914." *Quarterly Journal of Economics* 71 (August 1957): 329–67

Hilton, Boyd. *The Age of Atonement: The Influence of Evangelicalism on Social and Economic Thought, 1795–1865.* Oxford: Clarendon Press, 1988

History of The Times. Vol. 2: *The Tradition Established 1841–1884.* London: Times Publishing Company, 1939

Holdsworth, William. *A History of English Law.* 3rd edition. 15 vols. London: Methuen, 1903–72. Vols. 13 and 15

Holway, Tatiana. "The Game of Speculation: Economics and Representation." Paper delivered at Nineteenth-Century Interdisciplinary Studies Conference. Yale Center for British Art, April 1991

Hornby, J.A. *An Introduction to Company Law.* London: Hutchinson University Library, 1959

Houghton, Walter. *The Victorian Frame of Mind.* New Haven: Yale University Press, 1957

Hunt, B.C. *The Development of the Business Corporation in England 1800–67.* Cambridge, Mass.: Harvard University Press, 1936

Ignatieff, Michael. *A Just Measure of Pain.* New York: Pantheon Books, 1978

Institute of Chartered Accountants. *The History of the Institute of Chartered Accountants in England and Wales 1880–1965.* London: Heinemann, 1966

Jenkins, Philip. "Into the Upperworld? Law, Crime and Punishment in English Society." *Social History* 12 (January 1987): 93–102

Jeremy, David J., ed. *Dictionary of Business Biography.* 6 vols. London: Butterworths, 1984–86

Business and Religion in Britain. London: Gower, 1988

Johnson, John M. and Jack Douglas, eds. *Crime at the Top*. Philadelphia: Lippincott, 1978

Jones, David. *Crime, Protest, Community and Police in Nineteenth-Century Britain*. London: Routledge and Kegan Paul, 1982

Jones, Edgar, ed. *The Memoirs of Edwin Waterhouse*. London: B.T. Batsford, Ltd., 1988

Judd, Denis. *Lord Reading*. London: Weidenfeld and Nicolson, 1982

Katz, Jack. "The Social Movement Against White-Collar Crime." *Criminology Review Yearbook* (1980)

Kennedy, William P. "Institutional Response to Economic Growth: Capital Markets in Britain to 1914." In *Management Strategy and Business Development*, ed. Leslie Hannah. London: Macmillan, 1976

Industrial Structures, Capital Markets and the Origins of British Economic Decline. Cambridge: Cambridge University Press, 1987

Keyworth, J. Max. "Sir Arthur Wheeler." *Dictionary of Business Biography*. Vol. 5, 759–62

King, W.T.C. *History of the London Discount Market*. London: George Routledge and Sons, 1936

Kynaston, David. "The London Stock Exchange, 1870–1914: An Institutional History." Ph.D. diss., University of London, 1983

The Financial Times: A Centennial History. London: Viking, 1988

Lambert, R.S. *The Railway King, 1800–1871; A Study of George Hudson and the Business Morals of His Time*. London: G. Allen and Unwin, 1934

Lewin, H.G. *The Railway Mania and Its Aftermath 1845–52*. London: The Railway Gazette, 1939

Littleton, A.C. and B.S. Yamey, eds. *Studies in the History of Accounting*. Homewood, Illinois: Richard D. Irwin, 1956

Macnab, K.K. "Aspects of the History of Crime in England and Wales between 1805–60." Ph.D. diss., University of Sussex, 1965

Manley, P.S. "Gerard Lee Bevan and the City Equitable Companies." *Abacus* 9 (1973): 107–15

"Clarence Hatry." *Abacus* 12 (1976): 49–60

Marriner, Sheila, ed. *Business and Businessmen*. Liverpool: Liverpool University Press, 1978

Masterman, Lucy. *C.F.G. Masterman*. London: Nicholson and Watson, 1939

Michie, Ranald. "Different in Name Only? The London Stock Exchange and Foreign Bourses, c. 1850–1914." *Business History* 30 (January 1988): 46–68

Mitchell, B.R. "The Coming of the Railways and United Kingdom Economic Growth." *Journal of Economic History* 24 (September 1964): 315–36

Morgan, E.V. and W.A. Thomas. *The Stock Exchange: Its History and Functions*. London: Elek Books, 1962

Morris, Albert. *Criminology*. New York: Longmans, Green and Co., 1934

Munn, Charles W. "The Emergence of Joint-Stock Banking in the British Isles: A Comparative Approach." *Business History* 30 (January 1988): 69–83

Parris, Henry. *Government and the Railways in 19th-Century Britain*. London: Routledge and Kegan Paul, 1965

Patterson, Margaret and David Reiffen. "The Effect of the Bubble Act on the Market for Joint Stock Shares." *The Journal of Economic History* 50 (March 1990): 163–71

Payne, P.L. "Emergence of the Large-scale Company in Great Britain." *Economic History Review* 20 (1967): 519–42

Perkin, Harold. *Origins of Modern English Society 1780–1880*. London: Routledge and Kegan Paul, 1969

The Age of the Railway. Newton Abbot: David and Charles, 1971

The Rise of Professional Society: England Since 1880. London: Routledge and Kegan Paul, 1989

Philips, David. *Crime and Authority in Victorian England*. London: Croom Helm, 1977

Platt, D.C.M. *Britain's Investment Overseas on the Eve of the First World War: The Use and Abuse of Numbers*. New York: St. Martin's Press, 1986

Pollins, Harold. "The Marketing of Railway Shares in the First Half of the Nineteenth Century." *Economic History Review* 7 (1954): 230–39

"Aspects of Railway Accounting Before 1868." In *Studies in the History of Accounting*, eds. A.C. Littleton and B.S. Yamey. Homewood, Illinois: Richard D. Irwin, 1956

"Railway Contractors and the Finance of Railway Development in Britain." In *Railways in the Victorian Economy*, ed. M.C. Reed. New York: Augustus M. Kelly, 1968

Porter, Dilwyn. "Harry Hananel Marks." *Dictionary of Business Biography*. Vol. 4, 133–35

" 'A Trusted Guide to the Investing Public': Harry Marks and the *Financial News* 1884–1916." In *Speculators and Patriots*, ed. R.P.T. Davenport-Hines. London: Frank Cass, 1986

Pressnell, L.S. "Gold Reserves, Banking Reserves and the Baring Crisis of 1890." In *Essays in Money and Banking*, eds. C.R. Whittlesey and J.S.E. Wilson. Oxford: Clarendon Press, 1968

Radzinowicz, Sir Leon and Roger Hood. *A History of English Criminal Law*. Vol. 5, *The Emergence of Penal Policy*. London: Stevens, 1986

Reed, M.C. "Railways and the Growth of the Capital Market." In *Railways in the Victorian Economy*, ed. M.C. Reed. New York: Augustus M. Kelly, 1968

Richardson, Kenneth and Margaret. "Ernest Terah Hooley." *Dictionary of Business Biography*. Vol. 3, 329–32

Robbins, Michael. *The Railway Age*. London: Routledge and Kegan Paul, 1962

Rosenblum, Leo. "The Failure of the City of Glasgow Bank." *Accounting Review* 8 (December 1933): 285–91

Rubenstein, W.D. "The End of Old Corruption in Britain, 1780–1860." *Past and Present* 51 (1983): 55–86

Rude, George. *Criminal and Victim: Crime and Society in Early Nineteenth-Century England.* New York: Oxford University Press, 1985

Russell, Norman. *The Novelist and Mammon: Literary Responses to the World of Commerce in the Nineteenth Century.* New York: Oxford University Press, 1988

Scott, J.D. *Vickers: A History.* London: Weidenfeld and Nicolson, 1962

Searle, G.R. "Company Promoting a la Mode: The Stock Exchange and Political Life in Late Victorian and Edwardian Britain." Paper presented at the Institute of Commonwealth Studies seminar "The City and the Empire." June, 1985

Corruption in British Politics, 1895–1930. Oxford: Clarendon Press, 1987

Shannon, H.A. "The Coming of General Limited Liability." *Economic History* 2 (1930–31): 267–91

"The First Five Thousand Limited Companies and their Duration." *Economic History* 3 (1932): 396–419

"The Limited Companies of 1866–83." *Economic History Review* 4 (October 1933): 290–316

Shapiro, Susan. *Wayward Capitalists.* New Haven: Yale University Press, 1984

Sharpe, J.A. *Crime in Early Modern England, 1550–1750.* London: Longman, 1984

Shaw, Christine. "Horatio Bottomley." *Dictionary of Business Biography.* Vol. 1, 391–96

Sindall, Rob. "Aspects of Middle-Class Crime in the Nineteenth Century." M.Phil. thesis, University of Leicester, 1974

"Middle-Class Crime in Nineteenth-Century England." *Criminal Justice History* (1983): 23–40

Smithies, Edward. *The Black Economy in England since 1914.* London: Gill and Macmillan, 1984

Sparrow, Gerald. *The Great Swindlers.* London: John Long, 1959

Stamp, Edward, et al., eds. *Notable Financial Causes Célèbres.* New York: Arno Press, 1980

Steig, Michael. "*Dombey and Son* and the Railway Panic of 1845." *Dickensian* 67 (September 1971): 140–48

Storey, Richard. "Henry John Lawson." *Dictionary of Business Biography.* Vol. 3, 685–87

Sutherland, Edwin. *White Collar Crime.* 1949; reprint, New Haven: Yale University Press, 1983

Symons, Julian. *Horatio Bottomley.* London: Cresset Press, 1955

Thomas, S.E. *The Rise and Growth of Joint-Stock Banking.* London: Sir Isaac Pitman and Sons, 1934

Thomas, W.A. *The Provincial Stock Exchange*. London: Frank Cass, 1973

Thompson, E.P. *Whigs and Hunters*. New York: Pantheon Books, 1975

Tobias, J.J. *Crime and Industrial Society in the Nineteenth Century*. New York: Schocken Books, 1967

Todd, Geoffrey. "Some Aspects of Joint Stock Companies, 1844–1900." *Economic History Review* 4 (1932–33): 46–71

Vallance, Aylmer. *Very Private Enterprise: An Anatomy of Fraud and High Finance*. London: Thames and Hudson, 1955

Vincent, John, ed. *The Later Derby Diaries*. Bristol: the author, 1981

Vold, George B. and Thomas J. Bernard. *Theoretical Criminology*. 2nd ed. New York: Oxford University Press, 1979

Wadsworth, J.E. *A Hundred Years of Joint-Stock Banking*. London: Hodder and Stoughton, 1936.

Whittlesey, C.R. and J.S.E. Wilson, eds. *Essays in Money and Banking*. Oxford: Clarendon Press, 1968

Wiener, Martin J. *English Culture and the Decline of the Industrial Spirit 1850–1980*. Cambridge: Cambridge University Press, 1981

   Reconstructing the Criminal: Culture, Law and Policy in England, 1830–1914. Cambridge: Cambridge University Press, 1990

Wrigley, E.A., ed. *Nineteenth Century Society*. Cambridge: Cambridge University Press, 1972

Ziegler, Philip. *The Sixth Great Power: Barings 1762–1929*. London: Collins, 1988

Index